This "workshop in a book" is a practical guide that helps you improve every moment of your life by teaching you how to build:

- **Confidence:** Remove what's stopping you.

- **Strength:** Move from your wounded ego into your sacred self.

- **Courage:** Make smarter choices by embracing the Four Dimensions of Consciousness.

- **Success:** Rise to your next level of happiness, clarity, and transformation.

"A truly thought-provoking book based on rock solid psychological and spiritual foundations. **Your Ultimate Life Plan** takes the reader on a transformational journey from the dark crevices of the shadow to the heights of subtle transcendence. It's an amazing adventure in self-discovery!"

—Dr. Joe Vitale, author of *Attract Money Now*

"In her book **Your Ultimate Life Plan**, Dr. Jennifer Howard begins where psychology meets spirituality, and ends where passion meets purpose. A workshop within a book, this guide will leave you more conscious and clear about where you're going, and how you'll get there."

—Sherry Gaba, LCSW, author of *The Law of Sobriety*, CBS Radio host, and go-to expert on VH1's *Celebrity Rehab*

"Dr. Jennifer Howard answers one of the most dangerous questions you can ask: Are you ready to live the life you've always dreamed of? If your answer is *yes*, read this book, take responsibility for your life, and see what happens. If the answer is *no*, forget you ever saw this book and go on blissfully blaming others for your misery."

—Rabbi Rami Shapiro, author of *Recovery: The Sacred Art*

"Few books live up to grand titles, but **Your Ultimate Life Plan** delivers on its promise. Dr. Jennifer Howard covers every element of creating and living a conscious life: physical, emotional, mental, and spiritual. She has drawn on her own extensive background as a world-renowned psychotherapist, healer, and coach to help you live more fully "awake, aware, and alive." Here is wisdom drawn from a rich soup of traditions: nondual kabbalistic healing, traditional psychotherapy, meditation, and other healing arts. I don't think any other book

I've read does such an excellent job of weaving these practices together in such an accessible and helpful way."

—Donna Baier Stein, author and publisher of *Tiferet: A Journal of Spiritual Literature*

"Do you long to live in a way that is aligned with your heart? Through meditations and exercises, and clear, deep teachings, Dr. Jennifer Howard offers a luminated pathway to living from our innate wholeness, awareness, and love. This book nourishes the soul!"

—Tara Brach, PhD, author of *Radical Acceptance* and *True Refuge*

"Dr. Howard's interspiritual guide illuminates the path to authentic wholeness and offers practical guidance for overcoming the many obstacles that we all encounter on the journey. Written with clarity and compassion, this book reflects the depth of a true and seasoned spiritual teacher and healer."

—Estelle Frankel, author of *Sacred Therapy: Jewish Spiritual Teachings on Emotional Healing and Inner Wholeness*

"Dr. Jennifer draws from a variety of traditions and practices, giving the reader many choices and methods to work with. This book is compassionate, helpful, and insightful."

—Sharon Salzberg, author of *Real Happiness: The Power of Meditation,* and cofounder of The Insight Meditation Society

"A transformational read that will inspire your natural greatness as well as a practical map to wholeness. Reading these pages will allow you to rest in who you truly are: divine love."

—Jennifer Louden, author of *The Woman's Comfort Book* and *The Life Organizer*

"What a book! **Your Ultimate Life Plan** is a deep river, fast and flowing, filled with fresh wisdom. Any reader can float on the insights Dr. Howard provides. You can trust the buoyancy of the language and let it take you to the life you have always wanted. Immerse yourself in this book and it will help you be the person you have always known you were meant to be."

—John Lee, author of *The Flying Boy* and *The Half-Lived Life: Overcoming Passivity and Rediscovering Your Authentic Self*

"In her new book, **Your Ultimate Life Plan**, Jennifer Howard does the unthinkable, or rather the transthinkable. She leads us beyond the confines of the usual, rational mind to our hidden inner resources wherein lie ultimate life patterns. Once we discover the deep inner self, so mentors Dr. Howard, we find that, like a nested Russian doll, our essence reflects the Whole, including the vast intelligence that shapes the Universe. Such an assertion finds its roots in the holographic science of Einstein's protégé, David Bohm, and assists us in discovering that 'in every moment we have access to everything.' Everything? It appears so. Our ultimate life plan lies in conversation with the Mother of Ubiquity."

—Will Taegel, PhD, Dean of the Graduate School, Ubiquity University, and author of *The Mother Tongue: Intimacy in the Eco-field*

"Dr. Jennifer teaches from experience. A practical and effective approach to living a more meaningful life!"

—Elisha Goldstein, PhD, author of *The Now Effect* and coauthor of *A Mindfulness-Based Stress Reduction Workbook.*

"**Your Ultimate Life Plan** is not your run-of-the-mill self-help book. It's a wonderfully valuable resource for seekers adventurous enough and daring enough to go after what others might consider impossible: living the life of your dreams."

—Steve Farrell, Humanity's Team Worldwide Coordinating Director

"It has become increasingly obvious that neither the psychotherapeutic nor the spiritual path is complete in and of itself. In today's world of pressured self-promotion and materialistic demands and desires, we need to become a friendly presence to ourselves and a compassionate witness to our humanity. Friendliness and compassion must become a way of life within and between ourselves. Dr. Jennifer Howard is an ideal guide in blending the psychological and the spiritual as a wise guide and able teacher in the Four Dimensions of Consciousness."

—Polly Young-Eisendrath, PhD, Jungian Analyst and author of *The Resilient Spirit*

"This is the kind of wise integration of good psychology and good spirituality that so many people need today—instead of just one or the other, which makes both of them weak."

—[Fr.] Richard Rohr, OFM, Center for Action and Contemplation, Albuquerque, New Mexico

"Take this life-altering transformational journey with Dr. Jennifer Howard and your world will never look the same again. Drawing upon years of professional training, wisdom from the ages, and a darn good sense of humor, Dr. Howard will teach you how to uncover forgotten dreams, take bold action as you move towards those dreams, and finally, once and for all, live the life you have always hoped for. This book is a gem!"

—Kristen Moeller, MS, best-selling author of *Waiting for Jack*

"Congratulations to Dr. Howard for her powerful and comprehensive book with an actual step-by-step life plan to help us become more aware and awake. In **Your Ultimate Life Plan** Howard encourages us to love more consciously, and better yet, guides us how to do it with grace and simple practices to live a fully integrated life. What a breath of fresh air. Thank you, Dr. Howard, for your compassion, your incredible experience, and your integrity. I look forward to sharing this book with friends, colleagues, and clients!"

—Carol Look, author of *Attracting Abundance with EFT*, and international speaker

YOUR ULTIMATE LIFE PLAN

How to Deeply Transform
Your Everyday Experience
and Create Changes That Last

DR. JENNIFER HOWARD

New Page Books
A division of The Career Press, Inc.
Pompton Plains, N.J.

YOUR ULTIMATE LIFE PLAN
EDITED AND TYPESET BY KARA KUMPEL
Cover design by Lucia Rossman/Digi Dog Design
Printed in the U.S.A.

To order this title, please call toll-free 1-800-CAREER-1 (NJ and Canada: 201-848-0310) to order using VISA or MasterCard, or for further information on books from Career Press.

The Career Press, Inc.
220 West Parkway, Unit 12
Pompton Plains, NJ 07444
www.careerpress.com
www.newpagebooks.com

Library of Congress Cataloging-in-Publication Data

CIP Data Available Upon Request.

Acknowledgments

It's been an honor and privilege to write this book, and I am grateful to the many people who made it possible. With my deepest, heartfelt appreciation, I say to all of you, thank you...thank you...thank you!

Thanks to my many teachers and colleagues, both in physical form and from the other side. You've helped me grow and develop, and have enriched my life and this book. Thanks especially to Jason Shulman, Alexis Johnson, Judith Schmidt, Barbara Miller, Julie Winter, Joan Poelvoorde, Marjorie Frazier, and Dani Antman.

To my literary agent, John Willig; my publisher, Career Press/New Page Books; my caring, patient editors, Julie Isaac, Kristina Hall, and Kirsten Dalley; my wonderful assistant, Rachael Henning: thank you for all your warm hand-holding.

To the motivated listeners and amazing guests on my radio show, *A Conscious Life*, your generosity and enthusiasm is affirming.

Thanks to the wonderful clients and students I've had the honor of guiding, who allowed me to witness and be inspired by their journeys.

To my incredible family and friends, whose love and support has lifted me up and meant so much.

Special gratitude to Mother and Daddy who in their own unique and sweet ways helped give birth to this book.

And to my husband, my love, my companion, Toby Tobias...your patience, understanding, support, and encouragement added laughter and ease to this project.

Contents

Awakening Together: Awareness Is Curative

Everyone says that they want to change, but who is ready, willing, and able to actually do so? We'd like to get out of our ruts and our stuck places, or so we claim; but are we ready to give up the comfy, secure little nest cozily settled at the bottom of those ruts, those psychological habits, patterns, and entrenched bunker-like mentalities? Who is willing to face the insecurity of the unknown and unfamiliar, and break, recondition, and decondition their habits? And who knows how to effectively pursue new goals and purposes, suffer the inevitable setbacks and mistakes, get up when we fall flat and just keep on going no matter what? Changing ourselves is easier said then done, not to mention the challenges and travails inherent in positively changing the world. And yet we must and do aspire to be able to do so, and *now*. We do need genuine change and transformation, each and all of us. And our broken social systems also need transformation, not to mention our endangered environment. Yet we can't just ask what needs changing without sincerely striving to know and transform ourselves.

Like me, Dr. Jennifer is passionately dedicated to helping people experience deep and lasting transformation for greater ease, freedom, wholeness, well being, enlightenment, and joy. Acceptance too is an important part of the puzzle. When we accept and love ourselves, the whole world will accept and love us. Acceptance has its own transformative magic. Humor is crucial: keeping an eye on the cosmic absurdity of whatever predicament we may currently think or feel we are in. Life ain't much fun if we take ourselves too seriously! I myself am a jolly lama.

People today commonly say that they don't have enough time, are crazy busy and stressed out, and inevitably experience time-crunch in these speeded-up times. However, I find that it's not time we lack, but priorities, focus, and awareness. We actually have all the time in the world, should we choose to use it intelligently. Life is long enough for those who know how to use it. Our longer life spans and many labor-saving devices can contribute to the possibility of us having more time to spend wisely on the things that really matter to us—like quality time, for example—and to choose more skillfully how we spend and use our time rather than foolishly thinking of our time as being taken up by others while giving in to inchoate feelings of time-famine and scarcity.

Life is time, and time is life. Squander it at your peril. Time is an endangered natural resource today. Killing time is just deadening ourselves; you snooze, you lose. And how we live our lives makes all the difference. We need to wake up right now within this gritty existence and not in some later idealized place or state. It's now or never, as always. This is our greatest challenge and our opportunity.

Nowness-awareness is the ultimate therapy, freedom, and cosmic consciousness. In the wholly here and now one is free from past, present, and future, which are all relational, in the radiant and immaculate fourth time or fourth fraction of time, unconditioned by the three times—past, present, and future. Let's tune into the timeless and eternal moment right here, right now, through the potent power of focused nowness-awareness, and transcend time and place, death and change. Every moment of sequential horizontal, linear, ordinary, and conventional relative time is bisected at a vertical right angle (ascending, deepening) by the changeless time, divine time, nirvanic time. We live at that intersection of time and eternity, yet are for the most part unaware of it. This is heaven on earth, nirvana within samsara, the light within the darkness where we can ourselves understand and intuit that shadows are nothing but light in the great Yin-Yang of all things.

May I share with you the secret of time that I've discovered: divine time, changeless heavenly time, nirvanic time? It's *being* there while getting there, every single step of the way. Being *here* while getting there, every step, every moment. Being completely and lucidly here and now, fully present and counted for. Not waiting for any illusory pot of gold at the end of the rainbow, nor procrastinating till later in any way material, spiritual, or cosmological. If you're not here now, you won't be there then; this I can promise you. This is the very nature of karma, of conditioning, habit, and character. Every step of the way *is* the great Way; every step of the way to heaven is heaven, as the mystics sing. It's now or never, as always. You can take this to the bank.

For those of us consciously on the spiritual path, we are extraordinarily interested in personal development, in contributing to a better world and improved relationships at home and abroad through being better people, and longing to live a genuinely meaningful and productive life. Moreover, we certainly don't just wish to carry on "the sins of the fathers," as the Old Testament calls it, which persist for seven generations according to Biblical tradition. Modern psychotherapy—Virginia Satir, for example—has broken that mold, showing how to end this cycle of dysfunctional behavior within family systems, within one generation. I am all for it!

Awareness is curative. Wise awareness is the opposable thumb of consciousness development and evolution, which enables and empowers all the other fingers on the hand of the heart and mind, including knowledge and intelligence, memory, critical thinking, creativity, introspection, self-understanding, and so forth. Nowness-awareness helps me live in a state of awe and amazement. Emaho!

As a longtime practicing psychotherapist and experienced spiritual teacher, Jennifer Howard sees the missing piece for most people on the spiritual path is doing their psychological work, having taken too many spiritual bypasses. We too often sidestep deep traumas as well as more ordinary emotional, familial, energy, and psychic issues which condition, limit, inhibit, and even afflict us throughout every day of our lives, whether we know it or not.

Until we deal effectively with such matters and conflicts, outer and inner, individual and collective, including fear and anxiety, anger and insecurity—and make substantial headway in unfreezing those frozen places and hang-ups in order to clear away the stubbornly persistent problems—we will struggle mightily to be able to fully embrace and embody our authentic spiritual nature, our radiant true self and best nature—what Buddhists call innate Buddha-nature.

Self-deception is a terrible thing, and the river of denial runs deep throughout our culture. If we are truth-seekers and people of character and integrity, I believe that we have to be very honest and candid with ourselves and each other, well beyond subjectivity and mere partisanship, not to mention spin, flimflam, false advertising, and self-deception. I can scarcely stomach reading most news items about things I actually know and am well-informed about, such as certain Buddhist groups, Asian religions, yoga centers, and spiritual gurus. It seems incredibly difficult simply to get it right, without exaggeration or misunderstanding.

Dr. Jennifer's *Conscious Living 2.0* brings principles and practices together, combining psychological work with spiritual practice, honoring our humanity as deeply as our spiritual nature for they are actually one and inseparable. *Your Ultimate Life Plan* will help readers journey from their wounded ego to their sacred self; recognize and begin to unwind the personal programming that keeps them stuck in feelings, thoughts, beliefs, or behaviors that don't serve them; discern and connect to their own wise inner voice; and dive deeply into the Four Dimensions of Consciousness, seeing life through the unique mindset of each of the four worlds we inhabit—physical, emotional, mental, and spiritual—which leads to profound self-understanding and healing.

Just as Christians follow their Golden Rule, or aspire to at least, Vajrayana (Diamond Path) Buddhists too have an adamantine *Diamond* Rule which fairly crackles with energy and blessings. This wish-fulfilling jewel of a Rule reminds and exhorts us to see the light in everyone and everything, the innate clear light which is technically known as Buddha-nature—our innate divinity—but by any other name is still as sweet, for this is our Original Goodness.

Do you want to know the secret? Everything we seek lies within. You are far more Buddha-like than you think. The natural state of things *as they are*—or Reality—is the path from which one can never stray. Awareness is curative, healing, and the most powerful force in the world. Without awareness, what are we? Like sticks and stones. Awakefulness is the active ingredient in each and all of us. One moment of total awareness is one moment of freedom and enlightenment, or so the Dzogchen meditation masters of Tibet tell us. Nowness-awareness is the authentic Buddha, innate in each of us. Check it out.

We are all Buddhas, also known as divine by nature. All we have to do is awaken to and realize who and what we truly are. Let's exploit our inner natural resources for a change. Turn the spotlight, the searchlight, inwards. Wisdom gives life, and is the pearl beyond price.

Meditate as fast as you can.

Lama Surya Das
Concord, Mass. 2012

Introduction

Are You Ready to Live the Life You've Always Dreamed Of?

Are you living the life you've always dreamed of? I mean, really? Are you the person you want to be? Or is there a persistent issue in your life you've yet to change or improve? If any of these questions leaves you longing for something more out of life, then this book is for you!

Whether you're a teacher or CEO, are frustrated with your job, have a challenging relationship with your spouse or partner, are longing to live your passion and purpose more fully in the world, or feel that life wasn't meant to be such a struggle, it's often your desire for greater peace and happiness that sets you on the path of living a more conscious life.

In your search for change and growth, you may have begun your transformational journey with self-help books, workshops, or some kind of counseling or coaching. Maybe you've been looking at certain problems for a while, yet they still persist. You might have seen some positive changes at first, only to notice they didn't seem to last. Maybe it's been a while since you sat down and thought about what *you* want. Perhaps your already full life keeps you so busy that you aren't able to spend as much time as you'd like on what you're learning, or old habits and *issues* get in the way.

No matter where you're starting from, you can go to your next level of happiness, wholeness, transformation, and success. Using *Your Ultimate Life Plan* and the *Conscious Living 2.0* principles and practices on a daily basis will take you there. You'll feel more deeply, experience life more profoundly, and enjoy a more intimate connection with yourself, your soul, and others.

So how do you do it? How do you stay on course to reach your ultimate life and create real, lasting change? By diving deeper. Going deeper means getting to know your internal dialogue and emotional connections by paying attention to your thoughts and feelings, which allows you to be more conscious of what's initiating the vibratory quality that actually creates your life experiences. This is the fuel that ignites your co-creation with God in every moment.

If you're willing to stay on your cutting edge, increasing insight and consciousness, and becoming more awake and aware, then you'll be happier, and have more freedom and aliveness. Diving deeper helps you achieve authentic and lasting happiness. It's your path to freedom and it's worth every bit of effort. You go deeper because you want to understand, and create real and lasting change. You go deeper because you want to experience the core of your being. You go deeper because, really, what could be more important?

As you live more consciously, moment by moment, you continue growing in ways that allow you to experience and embody more wholeness and freedom. This path leads you to uncover, grieve, and work through historical difficulties, opening the door to the emergence of your real self. Consider the possibility of living a fully integrated life—physically, emotionally, mentally, and spiritually.

With this book, you'll learn that your ego isn't your enemy. Instead, you'll discover that you can integrate and refine the ego, which encourages the unveiling of your inner mystic and inner guidance, answering your deepest longing to know the True Self.

When you're living a conscious life, your job is to be with whatever arises, and to address any difficult or painful thoughts and feelings that block you from experiencing yourself as Wholeness, or nondual consciousness. As you identify and heal these obstacles, you naturally return to being present in the *now*. Out of frustration you might say, "I've been through this before and I don't want to feel it again." Yet here it is, right in front of you. If you deny what arises, you just create a stronger energetic charge that holds on to that difficulty. When you live in, "I don't wanna," the tension and resistance just magnifies what's there.

Persistent problems, however unpleasant they may seem, contain the unprocessed and unexamined thoughts and feelings that, if left alone, keep you from your greatness. That's why the pain, emptiness, and longing you feel can be your greatest gift—it can motivate you to examine parts of yourself that have been overlooked, forgotten, or hidden. It's the irritant of sand in the oyster, which is the impetus for the pearl. In walking the conscious life path, you reveal your deepest Reality, layer by layer. From here you can let yourself *be*. You come home.

In addition to navigating all the aspects of your inner life, you also have to contend with the environment around you. Our planet is changing at a dizzying rate. Globally, there is intensifying unrest, escalating conflict, financial instability, unemployment, alarming climate change, and environmental destruction. We grieve with those experiencing the devastation of earthquakes, tsunamis, and other natural disasters. Our old way of living and relating has been fundamentally disturbed, and it's easy to be frightened by the unknown.

Most of the world's problems affect us, while leaving us without any sense of what we can do to change them. This book is an inward look at the things you *can* affect. Living a conscious life is empowering. It facilitates change and helps you live a life of integrity, passion, and contentment.

Along with the signs of an outward shift in our world, we're also experiencing an emerging shift in consciousness. These shifts can potentially mire us in confusion or raise us to our next level, our next evolution of consciousness, which is different for each individual. *Your Ultimate Life Plan* doesn't shy away from the complexities of life, but instead addresses them head-on, and contains the ideas, practices, and tools that will assist you in successfully navigating these shifts.

Based upon solid psychological principles and profound spiritual practices, this book provides material proven successful in more than 20 years of working with clients and students, and seeing people's lives change.

Working with these principles and processes, you'll realize greater joy, wholeness, transformation, and success. Your potential for bliss lies in the consciousness in which you hold life, with all of its burdens and pleasures. If you've read this far, you likely feel moved to create positive change in yourself and the world around you, and you can. You *can* make a difference! This new paradigm is about embracing responsibility for your life and developing a deeper, richer awareness of yourself and the world around you.

This book will guide you to achieve change on all levels: physical, emotional, mental, and spiritual. By diving into these multiple layers of existence you'll recognize the abundance that you already embody, as well as all that's available to you. You'll learn to live from a deeper sense of self. You'll know how to slow down, recognize your gut feelings or intuition, and determine what's truly best for you. You'll have the opportunity to connect within, distinguish your wise internal voice from the voice of your childhood programming, and make your inner wisdom the rudder for your life.

The material in this book was derived from seminars and workshops I've created and presented, so please use this book as your own transformational workshop. Write in the margins, take notes, dog-ear the pages. I've included meditations, exercises, and self-awareness questions that will deepen and enrich your work and experience. This book is intended to support you in embodying your own wisdom.

You now have the opportunity to live a rich, profound, and intimate life, connected to yourself, others, and God. You'll find that deep change isn't derived from a fantasy, but is grounded in an expanded awareness that takes rewarding effort to grow and cultivate. Your true nature will shine!

My Story

One day when I was 8 years old, while shopping with my mother, I was asked to do a local department store commercial. I agreed, and I loved it! I also loved dancing, starting classes at age 5, and learning to sing as a teenager. When I was 16, I landed a job at a large country music theme park. But then, doesn't everyone in Nashville, Tennessee, sing?

With my undergraduate degree in education from George Peabody College for Teachers of Vanderbilt University, I moved to New York City to pursue an MFA in dance at New York University's Tisch School of the Arts. I was beyond excited! It was nearly impossible to get into this program, but I auditioned and was accepted. Nine weeks later, I ripped the ligaments in my hip and had to give up the performance program with its rigorous dance schedule. Not to be deterred from my dreams, I turned my attention to acting, singing, and television, and still danced a little.

I threw myself into my craft. I thought, "If I'm going to do this, I want to be great at it." So I studied acting with highly respected teachers, and many of my fellow students are now well-known actors. Looking back, I see how much I was driven by the desire to connect deeply with others and to have a profound understanding of human nature. And I really wanted to make a difference. Even when I was singing, acting, doing TV, and dancing, I wanted to move people, and help them somehow.

Just like every actor in New York, I took various gigs to pay the bills. I did a fair amount of commercials and print advertising. I posed for a beer ad that ran in magazines for years. I was told just recently that there is still a picture of me at Wendy's headquarters playing Wendy on the floor of the New York Stock Exchange the day the restaurant chain went public. Of course, I also spent a lot of time waiting tables and spraying perfume at Bloomingdales. After a while I began to wonder, "Is this it? Is this really the right path for me? Am I making a difference?"

I remember sitting in a chair one day, getting made up for a photography shoot. I tried to participate in an interesting conversation between the director and photographer, and I was completely ignored, as though I wasn't even there. I suddenly realized they didn't see me as a person. I was just a face, an object for a picture. I could have been the toothpaste I was supposed to hold up. In that moment, I saw how much I wanted my thoughts, ideas, and expression to extend far beyond my appearance. I thought, "What am I, just cheekbones?"

Another time, I was filming a commercial for insecticide. There I was, in a red dress, singing a sexy song and dancing around a can of roach spray. It was loads of fun, everyone on the set laughed a lot, and it turned out to be a good commercial. But how was I making a difference with my work? Sure, if you had roaches you needed the spray, but there had to be something bigger, a way for me to make a significant difference in the world. Dancing around a can of bug spray wasn't it.

I found myself feeling anxious at auditions. So much so that I was trembling and it was hard to read the scripts. When the stakes were high, such as for a lead in a movie or soap opera, I found myself feeling a lot of fear and anxiety. Because I wasn't as grounded and present as I was in acting class, I didn't perform as well, and that felt very disappointing. The entertainment business is fraught with a fantasy of perfection, so I often felt that *I* wasn't good enough, as well. That, combined with all my unfulfilling jobs, prompted me to start looking for ways to transform my life.

I began studying meditation and developing a regular meditation practice. I attended weekly classes with guided meditations and personal growth exercises for 13 years. I became deeply immersed in studying healing modalities, including attending the Barbara Brennan School of Healing, studying with Rosalyn Bruyere, and learning Shamanic methods, Health Kinesiology, and Nondual Kabbalistic Healing. I took numerous other classes and transformational workshops, as well, from weekend seminars to a variety of multi-year and decade-long, or longer trainings.

A few years into my spiritual studies I added my personal psychotherapy to the mix. That's when I began seeing more significant change in my life. I could feel big shifts happening, and the journey was absolutely thrilling! My heart and mind began to open, and I thought, "This is a way I could help people, too." I felt as though I'd come home. I'd found my true path, and it connected me with my deepest intentions, enabling me to experience a greater sense of alignment and resonance with my life. Becoming a psychotherapist, while continuing to deepen spiritually, would allow me to work at the interface of psychology and spirituality, which was clearly right for me.

I chose to dive just as deeply into studying the mind and its mysteries as I had with spirituality. I went back to graduate school, where my studies included British Object-Relations, Analytic Approaches, Attachment, and Trauma Psychotherapies, as well as Self-Psychology, Hypno-Behavioral Therapy, Core Energetics, Mind-Body modalities, Family Systems, Energy Psychology,

Transpersonal Psychology, and Buddhist Psychology—all while doing my own emotional healing work.

It excited me to study and grow. Along the way much of my training included personal process work, accelerating my growth and change both professionally and personally. I began giving seminars, running meditation groups, and offering energy healings, all while building a thriving psychotherapy practice. All of the work on myself and my studies helped me be a better teacher and psychotherapist with the clients and students I worked with.

Years later, while attending a seminar, I had lunch with a fellow participant, a successful author of several books. She said to me, "Jennifer, would you stop going deep, now? Deep books don't sell. Nobody cares, so stop studying already. Write your book, get out there, and teach what you know." I was floored. I didn't feel as if I'd learned enough or was fully prepared to start teaching other people the work I was developing. I knew I wasn't clear enough, yet, about what I was here to bring forth. Other friends and students urged me for years to begin sharing my methods because of the great results they experienced. I wasn't sure what it all meant; I just didn't feel ready. I thought, "I'll know when the time is right, and I'll know it from the deepest part of myself. I have to wait until then."

After many years of working as a psychotherapist and teacher, as well as extensive meditation and spiritual study, I had an experience while at a retreat that showed me I had finally crossed the threshold and walked through that door. It happened while I was sitting in meditation, which I'd done hundreds or perhaps thousands of times before. What I thought had been a 20-minute meditation turned out to be four hours of sitting in *no thought*.

When I started the meditation, I played at the edge where thought begins. Then there was silence. The deep, velvety black silence I'd longed for. When I came out of the meditation practice I felt renewed and blessed; my soul felt nourished. Father Thomas Keating says, "When we do not notice the passage of time or when it seems very short, we must have been in a deep place."[1] This was the rite of passage I needed, and it brought me to an epiphany—I knew it was time.

This experience, along with the personal work I'd done, and my ability to process, contain, and communicate my feelings and thoughts with others, showed me clearly I had matured enough psychologically and spiritually to teach. Of course, I'm not perfect, and I will always have more to learn, but I felt the internal connection and unified consciousness so deeply, I knew I could now point the way for others. And I keep learning and growing. I do my best to stay on my own razor's edge. Life always shows us where to look next.

❧

At the end of this *workshop in a book*, you'll do more than understand wholeness, you will experience it. By reading and allowing yourself to absorb this material, and by incorporating the tools and practices into your daily life, you'll grow and integrate physically, emotionally, mentally, and spiritually. You'll have access to a new vitality, peace of mind, clarity, and freedom in living. When pain arises, you'll be able to move with it in a new way. You'll have a newfound ability to trace the pain to its source, and allow new levels of profound healing.

You'll also feel an alignment with your purpose, and you'll naturally share your joy and unique gifts with the world around you. You'll peel back the layers to uncover your true, authentic self. With practice, you'll continue to reach new levels of awareness and compassion for yourself and others.

Are you ready?

Your Ultimate Life Plan is based on a philosophy that has evolved and grown throughout many years of working with clients and speaking to groups. It answers questions I've been asked repeatedly, in lectures and private sessions, by men and women longing to create real and lasting change in their lives. It's designed to guide you to a deeper inner landscape—to your own razor's edge—in order to support you in finding your own answers to these questions, as well. After reading the myriad of popular self-help books available, many students and clients have asked me, in their frustration due to a lack of progress or results, "How do I do this? How do I actually change?" This book examines the *how* on a much deeper level, moving you toward the wholeness you long for.

While reading and doing the exercises in this book, I encourage you to stay open to and aware of whatever's going on within you physically, emotionally, mentally, and spiritually. Pay attention to any physical sensations that may arise, as well as your thoughts and feelings. Please move at your own pace and pause when the need arises. As best you can, work with and embody the information. This is so that you move more fully toward the *experience* of living from Wholeness, rather than just gaining an intellectual understanding of the concepts presented.

There are many meditations throughout this book. You can read them, make a recording you can listen to with your eyes closed, or go to the Website YourUltimateLifePlan.com where you'll find recordings of numerous meditations from this book that you can either download or get on CDs. If you read the meditations, take your time and connect with each line physically, emotionally, mentally, and spiritually. If you find yourself closing your eyes to feel a line more deeply, when you open your eyes and start reading again, be easy about finding where you left off. Slow yourself down. You might even be drawn to reread a line and go deeper with it. Trust that your inner wisdom is drawing your attention to what will benefit you most. You can revisit these meditations as often as you'd like.

This book is divided into three sections, each with exercises, self-awareness questions, and meditations. Writing down your answers to the questions, as well as any insights or experiences you have in response to this material, will help reinforce your learning, growth, and change.

In the first section, you'll dive into this work and discover what it means to live a conscious life, identifying and exploring your current viewpoint of reality. You'll see where your unhappiness originates and what the components of real and lasting change are. You'll learn the ego isn't your enemy, but your sense of self, and you'll naturally begin to sink into the sacred ego—the sense of yourself as sacred. You'll access the potential to live from an integrated state of being in which you experience both your individuality and oneness with the world. You'll develop and refine discernment, so you know when you're living from your highest self—your essence—and when you're not.

In the second section, you'll learn about and experience the Four Dimensions of Consciousness, based upon the Four Universes of the Kabbalah. These include the Action-Physical Dimension, the Formation-Emotional Dimension, the Creation-Mental Dimension, and the Emanation-Spiritual Dimension. You'll learn their mindsets, understand their nested and holographic nature, and see how working with them can help you embody greater awareness. Whereas you may be familiar with the concept of *body, mind, and spirit*, many other teachings barely skim the surface of the self-understanding, transformation, and enlightenment to which this multidimensional reality of your being holds the key. Resources for creating your **Dimension Profiles** can be downloaded at *www. YourUltimateLifePlan.com.*

In the third section of this book, you'll discover more about Your Ultimate Life Plan, and yourself, by diving deeply into the unique and innovative *Multidimensional Awareness Practice* (or *M.A.P.*), which not only asks you to be aware of the Four Dimensions of Consciousness, but also the motivations, historical connections, and unconscious programming that affect your experience of life. You'll learn three *M.A.P.s*, and how each one moves you toward greater healing, freedom, and spaciousness. You'll expand on your *Conscious Living 2.0* skill-set including breathing exercises, grounding practices, and self-inquiry and meditation techniques designed to help you create the life you want. You'll come to see the longer you walk this path, the more energy, clarity, and insight you'll gain from connecting with deeper, more powerful, and more peaceful levels of your own being. This is your path to Wholeness, to becoming a spiritual warrior.

Your Ultimate Life Plan uses an interspiritual approach inclusive of many traditions, including Jewish, Christian, Islamic, and Hindu mystical paths, as well as Native American and Buddhist traditions. I'll also be drawing upon psychological and scientific perspectives, from developmental psychology to quantum physics. Life and change will be fully embraced from both the psychological and spiritual realms, from the perspective of Self *and* Soul.

With this multi-perspective viewpoint, I use a variety of terms to define the universal essence, including God, Universe, the Absolute, Presence, Reality, Spirit, Source, and Wholeness, as well as others. I use *God* more often as a shorthand, unless another name is specific to what I'm writing, but please translate to what works for you. I choose to honor the sacredness and truth in all traditions, and I invite you to include any word that resonates with you, and dismiss those that do not. Also, when a word is capitalized, I'm intending it to be viewed as Divine.

The examples and names used in the book are crafted to protect the wonderful people who have given me the opportunity to be a guide and help for them in my years of practice and teaching.

The meditations and exercises woven throughout the book provide an experience similar to a workshop. They'll deepen and anchor the transformation available here. Some of the meditations, exercises, journaling prompts, and worksheets from the book, along with additional material, can be downloaded for free on my Website, *www.YourUltimateLifePlan.com*, and will enhance your experience of this book. So, let's begin.

This is it.

This work can transform you. If you apply yourself seriously to what you learn in this book, you can have the life you've always dreamed of. It won't always be easy, and it's not going to be quick, but moment by moment and day by day this work will help you get clearer about what you want and who you are. It will help you feel better, get stronger, and be happier, no matter what's arising for you to face, and will help your life flow more easily and smoothly in every way.

Life will always be full of ups and downs, but how you deal with them and feel about them depends on how much work you've done to clean up the fears, negative beliefs, and unconscious programming that get in the way of living your life from a place of inner clarity and peace.

I'm not asking you to make a commitment to me. I'm asking you to make a commitment to yourself, to your dreams, to your happiness—to your life.

I'm asking you to say YES to YOU!

You *can* do it.

You *must* do it.

Your heart and soul are calling you to live the life you came here to live.

PART I

THE FOUNDATION OF A CONSCIOUS LIFE

CHAPTER 1

Why Aren't We Happier?

*Happiness is your nature. It is not wrong to desire it. What
is wrong is seeking it outside when it is inside.*

—Sri Ramana Maharshi

Welcome!

Take a moment to become present. Breathe in and out a few times.

Begin when you feel ready.

If happiness is our nature, why aren't we happier?

Maybe it's because we're conditioned to think happiness is somewhere other than already within us. Maybe we equate particular kinds of lives, moods, relationships, or cars with happiness.

Maybe it's because we're too busy to be fully present to our lives. We're overwhelmed with tasks, decisions, and copious amounts of information to digest, barely taking time to breathe, much less connect within. It could also be that anxiety, caused by global chaos, war, and environmental and financial concerns, keeps happiness at bay. Surely, we experience greater stress in our lives than ever before.

For most of us, happiness depends upon whatever's happening around us. It's relative to the moment, our circumstances, our relationships, our culture, our jobs, and our understanding of ourselves. Of course we're affected by our circumstances, and there will certainly be times of confusion, anger, and sadness, but as we continue to grow we learn to embrace our difficulties and suffering. We become fulfilled. Like a great river, we become stronger, wider, and deeper.

I'd like you to learn that happiness is a mindset, underlying everything you think and feel. It's a deeper level of contentment and peace, a greater connection to life, God, and the world. Even if you feel happy much of the time, you're always capable of being happier.

Creating the life you long for is a navigated journey. Embodying all of you is a dance. It's a movement toward receiving personal fulfillment, where hidden parts of yourself are discovered. In the midst of this dance something happens, and you swing back into the relative humanness of pain, disappointment, and setback. Mired in suffering, you'll call forth Grace and tenderness, revealing the sweetness and beauty of your soul. You'll learn to weave the fragments of yourself together; come to know meaning, value. Your vision opens up to new possibilities. As you continue through life, clearing the brush out of the way, you will find the *Self* you long for. You'll discover the happiness you seek has been there all along!

Maybe you never knew, you've forgotten, or no one told you that you have the inner strength necessary to develop your innate potential. You might not feel sure of all that's possible; what you've tried didn't work as you'd hoped and so you assume this is all there is. You feel stuck or just can't see your greatness. You don't know how amazing you really are!

So how do you accomplish what you know deep down is possible? What will it take to live a deeply satisfying life and achieve lasting change? What steps will get you from A to Z, or at least to D?

This book provides a plan. Most life plans are about action and accomplishment, and take you step by step toward achieving your goals. *Your Ultimate Life Plan* is very different, and much simpler. There's only one step—to meet every moment as consciously as you can; there's only one goal—to live the fullness of who you truly are.

As you may have already learned, simple isn't always easy. Distractions and inner blocks stop you from being fully present and conscious in the moment. This book will teach you how to clear away those blocks. It will show you how to connect deeply with your essential self, living the amazing life you were born to live, on every level of being—physical, emotional, mental, and spiritual. Self-discovery is life's greatest adventure.

As you apply the principles and practices in this book, you'll be better able to accept yourself, move through fear, and recognize and heal your limiting belief systems. They will help you reach important goals, create healthy relationships, improve your physical health, and enable you to access your creativity. You can fulfill your birthright of happiness, clarity, joy, and peace!

It doesn't matter where you are in life. Whether you're teaching yoga, being a mompreneur, running a company, juggling work and family, or experiencing a major life transition, it's often your pain, unhappiness, or a sense that *There's got to be more* calling you to live more consciously. Some begin the process of transformation from an emptiness or longing, ranging from a vague feeling that something isn't quite right to deep distress. A single event, such as the death of a loved one or loss of a job, can leave you wanting more. I've often seen discomforts such as these be the motivation needed for us to recognize hidden or forgotten parts of ourselves.

We often see ways we'd like to improve our lives to make ourselves happier. Perhaps you want better relationships, more time for yourself, or greater prosperity. Maybe you've been plugging away at the same desires and blocks for a while, but every time you reach for deeper meaning or satisfaction, those lifelong issues get in the way. Or maybe your progress is so slow, your hope and vision fades. Or perhaps one area of your life has become amazing while others don't work as well.

This book will help you achieve lasting change on physical, emotional, mental, and spiritual levels. By diving into these multiple layers of existence, you'll grow aware of who you are now and everything available to you. It answers the question, *How do I change?* The answer isn't something that manifests with magical thinking, but is grounded in awareness that takes effort and attention to cultivate. You're worth it. Through growth and development, your ego will relax and your true nature will shine through. When you learn the fundamental aspects of change, you'll awaken to your unique God-given personality, your Divine spiritual essence.

How Do We Change?

Perhaps you've begun your journey toward greater happiness and transformation with self-help books, workshops, or counseling. You might have seen positive change right away, or you got new tools and understanding that helped you feel you've accomplished something. You might be inspired and brimming with insights after a weekend workshop, yet these insights often have a short shelf life. Old habits, fueled by unconscious thoughts and feelings, creep back in. Then what do you do?

How do you find the time and focus necessary to create deep, lasting change when your life is already crammed full of things to do, from the time you open your eyes in the morning to when you close them at night? How do you squeeze it all into 24 hours? In your commitment to get everything done, you reach for the easiest solution, and you're not alone.

Many people look for fast and easy cures for their pain, problems, or unrealized goals. Various personal development and spiritual growth programs offer solutions requiring minimal effort. We're naturally seduced by the promise of a quick fix, yet seeking fast solutions often only hinders your journey.

Yes, it's true that transformation can take place in an instant. Grace is always available, but can instant transformation be sustained over time? You need the ability to consistently:

- Interact and communicate your needs calmly and clearly with others, even when you're angry
- Nurture and maintain healthy relationships
- Live your life rooted in your authentic self, coming from mature peacefulness

It takes time—years even—to develop a healthy and mature psyche that can sustain transformation. So as you open to greater consciousness, you can maintain the new perspective, embodying it in every aspect of life. Sometimes we think we're done; we've gone as far as we can go. We assume our struggles are normal and we'll just have to live with them. When we look at the world around us we see people with similar problems, but "normal" is relative. A label can keep you stuck in fear, resigned to struggles and suffering you don't have to continue living with.

Are you settling for less than you have to?

Life seems hard when your happiness is based upon having a good day, with no upset. Something unexpected happens—an event, loss, or unforeseen setback—and you're caught off-guard, feeling lost again. Sound familiar? You might think you're finally done with an issue, but then see more work is needed to peel away the residual and subtle layers so you feel lighter and more spontaneous.

> ❧
>
> **Are you resigned to the idea that your current level of life experience is as much as you can hope for? If so, are you settling for a pseudo fulfillment, happiness, or peace?**
>
> ❧

No matter how long you've struggled with your issues, you can mature into someone who understands and embraces important life lessons while living from your talents and strengths. You can make wiser, more effective choices, achieving goals aligned with your deepest purpose, not just your momentary ego desires. When you're at the whim of moment-to-moment hungers, you can't find peace for long; but coming from real wisdom and maturity, your experience of happiness broadens and relaxes. Even your desires shift.

Each of us has a next level of achievement, fulfillment, and happiness that's possible, but before you can change your life, embodying all you truly are, you've got to examine the issues blocking your path. Your process begins by looking at the origin of your issues, why you've held on to them, how you relate to them, and why your goals have eluded you.

Where You Get Stuck

Now let's explore where you get stuck—those persistent life issues, sometimes blatantly obvious or frustratingly subtle, that annoyingly nip at your heels. If you've been involved in personal development for a while, you've crossed paths with these issues many times. You probably roll your eyes when they reappear. In workshops, I often refer to these as the "six issues [pick any number] that we came here to work on." Like a jack-in-the-box, life turns the handle until the issue pops up again. Your job is to cycle through them until they stop showing up.

Why is it that an issue you've worked so hard and long on, to the point of feeling as though you might actually be done with it, suddenly reappears? Sometimes it seems that you can't resolve these issues, or even lessen them. To understand their stubborn nature, you must first notice when the issues arise. In my experience, issues remain because we don't believe healing is possible, we're avoiding the issue, and/or we don't know how to take it further. Just because you've covered that ground before doesn't mean you've really walked the territory. You might have developed strategies to avoid painful issues, even when you think you're dealing with them. You may need to dive deeper for lasting change, especially if you've attempted a quick fix before.

> **What are some of your issues? Why do you think they won't move?**

Our stuckness is usually rooted in feelings and beliefs formed in our past. In other words, if something feels stuck, you're probably repeating patterns from your youth that feel natural or automatic to you. We all have personal history forming much of who we are today. Those six stubborn issues can serve as the impetus to keep you searching, growing, and integrating, if you're willing to follow your wisdom. They can serve as guiding lights, but left under the rug, those issues, containing unresolved childhood adversities, remain embedded in your psyche as unconscious programming that drives your life.

Dealing With Stubborn Issues

So, you thought you'd already dealt with that issue, yet here it is again. Why?

I know it doesn't always seem this way, but when a stubborn issue blocks you, there are ways it can teach and assist you in fulfilling your potentials. As you continue your work with these issues, the meditations, exercises, and questions in this book will support your path to change, integration, and freedom. You'll understand the inherent gift of your pain, as well as the importance of confronting, exploring, and healing your fears.

Here are a few things to do if a stubborn issue comes up (again!). First, check to see how you might be avoiding thoughts, feelings, sensations, or historical patterns. There are many ways to duck and dodge discomfort. Some are trickier to recognize than others:

- You might ignore or deny the issue, or try to take your mind off it.
- You may avoid the issue by overdoing seemingly constructive activities.
- You may use substances or behaviors in an attempt to avoid deeper thoughts and feelings or alter your mindset.

It's important to learn how to self-soothe in healthy ways when faced with difficult thoughts, feelings, or sensations. Soothing yourself isn't avoiding, it's finding an observer or "adult" part of you that can acknowledge the painful feelings, and calm and console that wounded part of you. If, in any moment, you can't quite grasp the idea that healing is possible, take a deep breath and don't give up on yourself. You have far greater potential than you think!

MEDITATION: HEALING IS POSSIBLE

Take a pause after each phrase.

Deep breath. Just be with your thoughts about what you've read so far, for a moment. Notice if any issues come to mind, along with ways you put them aside, and any emotions that come up. Breathe into all of it, and let it all be just as it is. Be with your breath. Now notice any sensations that arise. Tell yourself you will dive into these issues for healing in time, but for right now only go as far as feels right. If you'd like to place your hand over your heart, belly, or anywhere else that needs your kind touch, please do. Know that your willingness to look into and be with what is coming up from the past will help you heal. Your willingness to acknowledge these issues has already begun the healing process. Even considering these again begins a deeper healing. Take another moment to extend kindness to all you are and all you do. Breathe deeply, again.

Taking It Deeper: After completing this meditation, reflect on a few of your persistent problems. Appreciate the work you've done so far in understanding and healing them. Allow your sincere desire to change and grow inspire greater freedom and happiness.

Recognizing the way you're being with stuck issues is key to shifting them, and it's what this book is all about. Of course everyone has challenges, but learning how to be with those struggles makes a world of difference. In this book, you'll learn a variety of ways to go deeper with them, lightening your load in the process.

You might say, "Well, I've tried to be with what came up but the pain was overwhelming." There are ways to be present with something difficult that's arising, and still put only your toe in the water of feelings and thoughts surrounding the issue. Breathe! You choose how fast or slow you go—but between you and me, I'm sure you'd like to change these patterns...*yesterday.*

EXERCISE: THE SIX

Do you have an idea of what your six or eight issues might be? It helps to name the issues, and if you're already familiar with them you can take them deeper.

- *Name some of the issues or themes you've dealt with throughout your life. For example, lack of money, lack of time, specific problems in relationships, etc.*
- *What, if any, connections do you see between them?*
- *What, if any, feelings run through them?*
- *How have you thought about these in the past?*
- *Add to this list as you read the next section, observing any favorite strategies.*

What Keeps You Stuck?

There are a number of subtle (and not so subtle) strategies, conscious and unconscious, that may be keeping your issues alive though you've done your best to heal them. We all have conflicting feelings and thoughts. I'm sure you recognize what seems like contradictory, internal forces pulling at you. Most of us have tried to lose weight, exercise, meditate, or achieve other reasonable goals, yet our resistance stood its ground.

In his poem, "The Song of Myself," Walt Whitman wrote:

Do I contradict myself?

Very well, then, I contradict myself;

(I am large, I contain multitudes.)[1]

Whitman spoke not only from the larger perspective of humanity, he spoke of the contradictions within ourselves. These opposing forces are usually caused by a young inner part of us. For example, this part may want to "comfort" us with ice cream, attempting to numb our feelings.

These conflicts can also have other levels. Sometimes conflicting thoughts and feelings signify something deeper calling for your attention. If you're failing to meet a goal, for example, maybe another path is using this discomfort to signal you. Your path is probably not straight or direct; growth often happens as you spiral through layers. You might have needed to walk in this direction to learn valuable skills and lessons, and now this behavior, job, or action no longer serves you.

Sometimes we misinterpret deeper desires trying to reveal themselves. As you deepen your connection with yourself, the longing of your essence emerges instead of only habitual, cultural, and programmed desires. For example, I always wanted to sing, dance, and act, and these desires were perfect for me at the time. I loved it! It trained me as a speaker and performer, and my circumstances challenged me to grow into my next level of calling, closer to the True Self. Twenty years from now I might express that connection differently (I'll keep you posted!).

As you see both the contradictions and longings emerging within you, notice the thoughts and feelings that seem to keep you holding on to your issues. You might feel discouraged and label this *self-sabotage*, and in a sense it's true. Some part of you stops you from reaching your goal. But these contradictory forces contain valuable messages, clues that show you how to reconcile them as you deepen your exploration. Many of your strategies were designed for protection and survival when you were very young, believing they'd guarantee your safety and you'd get the love and happiness you needed.

So if you recognize yourself in any of the five strategies I'm about to share, remember they began as survival and coping skills. As you recognize your participation in these strategies, you can redirect your energy toward deeper goals and healing.

Strategy 1: Reaching for Hidden Payoffs

One reason our stubborn issues change slowly, along with the unconscious programming beneath them, is because there's often a hidden value—or payoff—they provide. When you feel dissatisfied, allow it to prompt you to explore your unhappiness and what you may be getting out of it. What are the secondary gains?

Here are examples of hidden payoffs we might receive from desires or experiences:

- Do you need the world to be a particular way? Your payoff might be keeping your childhood view in place to avoid loss and pain.

- Do you continually struggle with success? Maybe you're keeping yourself small in some way because you haven't done enough separating and individuating from your parents and are perpetuating the connection, even after their death, and you could have a strong unconscious desire to be rescued.

- Are you often unhappy in relationships? You may not have done quite enough exploration of your fear of being smothered, abandoned, or hurt in some way.

- Do you struggle with important decisions? Due to some wounding, you may feel more comfortable having someone tell you what to do.

If something in your life is stubbornly refusing to change, check out the possible unconscious gain you could be getting from it. Keep in mind the one hidden payoff that most of us share: wanting to control the outcome. We often keep the status quo in place so we don't have to face our fear of the unknown.

Many of us live under the illusion we can, or should be able to, control every aspect of our experience. Some authors and teachers will tell you that if you affirm enough, or focus only on the outcome you desire, you can control everything. I've seen many frustrated people who feel that they are failures when they can't. Our unhealed egos have trouble letting go of the illusion that if we try hard enough, we can control our lives; we can have everything we want and we're completely in charge of all outcomes.

Yes, we have much more power than most of us understand and embody, yet when we're able to connect with our deepest desires—the power of life flowing through us—we feel fulfilled, living our highest and happiest life. When we're unhappy with our lives, we're either out of the universal flow and need help finding our way back, or we're in fantasy about how life should be—and sometimes both.

Strategy 2: Getting Caught Up in the Drama of the Healing or Spiritual Path

At the beginning of a healing or spiritual journey, some people hope for a dramatic experience so they know there's more to life than what their five senses suggest. Understandably, they're looking for proof of God, the spiritual realm, and the possibility of healing. I've often seen people excited, even awestruck by spiritual or healing powers.

Blissful meditation, a shaktipat transmission from a Guru, an encounter with someone who's passed, channeling, psychic abilities, the physiological event of rising kundalini, alchemical healing, and other wonderful phenomena can help us see what's possible. At the right moment, they're powerful and constructive teachers providing valuable information. If you have these abilities, you'll find comfort in a lifelong tool that will help you grow. As you go deeper and continue on your path, many of these gifts manifest naturally.

We can easily get caught up in comparing ourselves to others, placing these powers on a pedestal, as if a person who can more easily access them is better or more evolved than someone who can't. It's certainly mind-blowing to experience them, especially in the beginning, and it's easy to get sidetracked by the phenomenology of spiritual growth.

For example, if a person with "special gifts" were to tell you to get more sleep, it may sound more credible than if a "regular" person, such as your mother or yoga instructor, gave you the same advice. We can become mesmerized by the bells and whistles of spirituality, sometimes missing the meat and potatoes (sorry vegans), without knowing how to deepen ourselves and discover the richness readily available. If you've never had a paranormal experience, please remember it won't keep you from living a fulfilled life, having a fruitful spiritual practice, or experiencing a richness transcending drama and glamour.

These spiritual events and abilities inspire and increase awareness, but outside of a larger context they can distract you from healing long-held issues and reaching your fullest potentials.

Strategy 3: Wanting a Quick Fix

As I mentioned earlier, in our perpetual busyness and overwhelm we naturally gravitate toward simple solutions or quick fixes. Understandably, we want to believe the promise that transformation is easy, and sometimes happens magically.

Look at our culture: Fast camera shots in movies, fast-paced video games, high-speed Internet, cell phones, texting, and TV have all nurtured a short attention span. It's part of our cultural anxiety, drawing us farther away from our true nature. Part of the appeal of a quick fix is the promise that we can have everything *now*. In 10 minutes we can eat a full meal, sculpt a great body, and enjoy a fantastic relationship. Who doesn't want those? Add to that our physical, emotional, and mental pain and we feel we can't endure one more minute of suffering.

Instant solutions feel great for a while, but they don't usually work in the long run. It's like learning to fly an airplane by reading "10 Easy Steps to Flying." You might get the plane off the ground and think, "Sure glad I didn't spend the time and money on flying lessons!" But with your first big storm you're lost!

So you couldn't sustain the quick fix—now what? Clearly, some things need to change so you can feel peaceful, happy, free, and in the flow of life. When you take the time and effort needed to find and integrate the root cause of your suffering you can create lasting change. You'll learn to navigate through any weather, sunny or stormy. This work will keep you from spinning your wheels, and you'll reach your goals sooner than you imagined.

Strategy 4: Trying to Jump Over or Bypass Problems and Emotions

Sometimes it seems too hard to hang in there. You might try to jump over or bypass problems or feelings because you're not sure how to deal with them; they might sweep you away.

In some spiritual circles, life is compartmentalized into the higher realm of spirituality and lower realm of daily life. Some believe the icky, human issues are unimportant; but when we ignore our psychological self in favor of the "spiritual" self, we create an uneven evolution in our psyche, a gap between self-development and spiritual attainment.

Sometimes, as spiritual seekers, we assume we should be constantly blissful or enlightened. Yet our unresolved problems and unfinished emotional business inhibit our spiritual growth. The parts of ourselves we don't think are worth our time keep us stuck in the very ways we attempt to avoid.

While there's value in most spiritual approaches and experiences, without doing psychological work at the same time our efforts won't help or last. We try to bypass painful issues by using hard or soft addictions, spiritual states, philosophies and practices, excessive physical exercise, and over-intellectualizing—all for the purpose of avoiding difficult feelings. A lot of people believe positive or spiritual thoughts will save them from uncomfortable feelings.

This creates tremendous inner conflict. On some level we know we have these feelings, judge them as bad or wrong, and push them away. We try to split our humanity from our spiritual nature, choosing the impersonal over the personal, emptiness over form, indifference over emotion, and transcendence over embracing and valuing all of life. We develop a spiritual persona, but eventually the cat gets out of the bag. Our shadow selves and unconscious mind make themselves known.

Unexpressed feelings can be acted out in an inconvenient way, creating regrettable actions, or we can greet them with open arms. Historically, spiritual traditions helped people work with psychological material as it arose. As the science of psychology progressed, we found more direct ways to lessen the hold of life's challenges.

Strategy 5: Not Taking the Long View or Doing Our Psychological Healing

Many cultures, including Native American culture, hold the longer view of finding peace and happiness than we tend toward today. They see our path as a lifelong journey, or even lives-long. This fosters psychological and spiritual maturity, so we can accept reality and live fully. Many of you value staying steady, have the longer view, and are willing to do what it takes to heal.

When you feel that deep longing and begin searching, it's helpful to study a variety of modalities with highly qualified and experienced teachers. As you explore, you'll find the best fit for you. Or, you may focus on one spiritual system until another teacher or modality shifts your perspective, illuminating your studies in a new way. Steeping yourself in various schools of wisdom holds great value. You begin to see how philosophies overlap, and how they differ. I've learned from as many different teachers, healers, and modalities as I could find time for. It has provided a rich background of understanding. Remember, the most effective teachers empower people. They're kind, not shaming or brutal, and can help you see where you need to develop.

Elizabeth Lesser, cofounder and senior advisor of the Omega Institute, said spiritual awakening takes patience, hard work, and the Grace of God. She's quoted the poet-philosopher Paul Valéry: "Long years must pass before the truths we have made for ourselves become our very flesh."[2] As she so perfectly points out, 20 years of transformation—even with daily spiritual practice, excellent weekly psychotherapy, and zippy meditation methods—still takes 20 years. The psyche needs time to integrate. In the midst of psychological and spiritual work, you invite new layers to bubble up. It's a committed journey.

When people drift from class to class or book to book, sometimes they're avoiding essential emotional work. Perhaps they gravitated toward an easy solution, and when that doesn't fix things as fast as they'd like, they reach for the next solution. Even if they weren't seeking a quick fix, they wanted an easy answer. Jumping from one thing to another in a panic, approaching personal development and spiritual growth from the outside only, doesn't get you where you want to go. Often people want to be rescued from their difficult past and recurring thoughts and feelings. I have complete empathy, but it doesn't work. It just spins you around and around.

Sometimes people sincerely want to dig deep in their current practice but don't realize the power of unresolved emotional issues. They don't understand how their issues get in the way of progress with their chosen spiritual modality, as well as their life generally. It could also be that the teaching, or teacher, suggests the past, and corresponding emotional issues, can be bypassed. Sometimes the author, teacher, or guru doesn't value psychological training or embody this understanding, and can't help his or her students address or navigate their emotional lives in a way that frees them from unconscious programming.

Sometimes, as we've seen in the past, the leader/teacher/guru hasn't done enough personal work him- or herself and acts from an unhealed ego. As leaders, we can only help people walk territory we've walked ourselves. Remember, this is a lifelong journey with our humanity in tow.

As I see it, unless you do your psychological work you may not be as open to your spiritual exploration as you'd like. For in the same way that your psychological issues and unconscious programming can get in the way of your relationships, business success, and happiness, they can also prevent you from fully embracing and experiencing the depth, breadth, and beauty of your chosen spiritual path. That's why this book is so effective and powerful. When you combine psychological work with spiritual practice (from whatever spiritual path you choose), you move forward with greater ease.

That's why we leave no stone unturned.

You need to be willing to face and embrace yourself fully and let go of your desire to avoid emotional work with a quick fix, relationship, teacher, philosophy, or book. What you read can't heal you, but it can open the door to a multitude of possibilities. Put into practice, it can potentially transform you if it takes you deep enough and is based on sound psychological and spiritual principles.

- *How do you recognize yourself in these five ways of staying stuck?*
- *What ways were you familiar with and which were new?*
- *Name several issues and the strategies you've used in the past that have kept you stuck.*
- *In what ways have you successfully navigated through some of these before?*

Reaching for True Happiness

Everything is material for the seed of happiness, if you look into it with inquisitiveness and curiosity. The future is completely open, and we are writing it moment to moment. There always is the potential to create an environment of blame—or one that is conducive to loving-kindness.

—Pema Chödrön

What is happiness? Really, think about it right now. What does it mean to you? Imagine, for a moment, what happiness feels like; what it looks like. For most people, happiness fluctuates in response to their circumstances, at times disappearing altogether. Yet according to a report in the *British Medical Journal*, we have a happiness set point that remains relatively stable, made up of 50 percent genetics, 10 percent circumstances, and 40 percent intentional actions.[3] In a 20-year study, people were asked to rate their overall happiness on a scale from 1 to 10. Researchers determined that while difficult life circumstances, such as a divorce or serious injury, can lower a person's rating for about a year, it eventually returns to his or her set point. The same was found with falling in love, or winning the lottery. The person's happiness level would rise for about a year, then fall back to his or her set point. The study also found that when a slight increase in happiness was able to be sustained, the person's happiness set point changed.

When you're reaching for greater happiness, no matter your current experience or what you think it should look like, you're really trying to raise your set point. When you base happiness upon circumstances—what your boss or spouse said, the condition of your car or the economy, your hurt knee or hurt feelings—it can't be sustained. A regular spiritual practice, connection to your inner wisdom, and/or deep emotional healing loosens the grip of feelings and beliefs that block you. This creates happiness from within, raising your set point.

Take a look at your life. On a scale of 1 to 10, what is your happiness set point?

If you're like most of us, you hover somewhere around the middle—riding the pendulum of happy/unhappy. But is this all you can hope for? Yes, happiness is a choice, but how do we make that decision? We do it by acknowledging our issues and the strategies we use to keep them in place. We move our set point by healing our ego, working through our feelings, and growing strong enough to tolerate difficulty. We can't just pretend the difficulties don't exist. They do—people die, relationships end, financial meltdowns occur. As we heal enough, we can ride the pendulum swing, sustaining the bigger picture and our happiness, even in the midst of life's trials.

As with spiritual bypass, we often want only the happy moments; we just want the positive feelings. This isn't real happiness. Happiness comes when we can hold all our feelings, including grief, anger, loneliness, and shame. When we allow it all and strengthen our ego, we can relax and be truly happy. Otherwise, we remain afraid of life and painful feelings.

This book will guide you to your mature goals and longings—desires that help you appreciate everything life presents.

Marci Shimoff, in her book *Happy for No Reason*, says, "When you're happy for no reason, you bring happiness to your outer experiences rather than trying to extract happiness from them. You don't need to manipulate the world around you to try to make yourself happy. You live from happiness, rather than for happiness."[4]

- *What does happiness mean to you, right now?*
- *What areas in your life are you happy with?*
- *What areas in your life are you not happy with?*
- *Are there any areas where you feel stuck in unhappiness?*
- *What would it take for you to make a decision to be happy in those areas?*

On my Website you'll find a downloadable report that has 25 quick and easy ways to change your energy when you get stuck: *www.YourUltimateLifePlan.com/GetUnstuck.*

CHAPTER 2

Elements of a More Conscious Life

One realizes that all of existence is a manifestation of conscious-ness; that ultimately everything is made out of consciousness.
—A.H. Almaas

When you're living a more conscious life, you're being *with* yourself and *for* yourself deeply, moment by moment. No matter how attractive quick and easy solutions seem, lasting change can't happen in the time it takes to deliver a pizza. It takes time, attention, and commitment to address and heal the layers of who we are and grow in consciousness.

So, what is conscious living?

To be conscious means to observe what's present, and implies being awake or awakening to your deeper truth, an inner realization, or circumstance. Living a conscious life means having the willingness, curiosity, and courage to stay present to your thoughts and feelings, to the meeting point of body, emotion, mind, and spirit. It means staying present to the impact you have on others and your environment, as well as the choices available to you. To live a conscious life—to be awake and aware—is to be gloriously alive!

> ✑
> **Slow down, take a deep breath, and truly feel life. Every moment, even painful ones, has gifts of wisdom and joy to impart if we're willing to stay conscious.**
> ✑

We experience life in degrees. You can choose where to place your attention and intention, creating a life that feels better than it does now. You can grow, change, and deepen your ability to navigate life. You can expand and illuminate your experience of consciousness. You can mature toward greater integration and wholeness.

From the deepest sense of ourselves, our inner life longs to be experienced, understood, and validated. It's rich with nuance and complexity, and meant to be sipped and savored. It's not meant to be swallowed a week at a time, controlled by our past programming and endless "to do" lists. Slow down, take a deep breath, and truly feel life. Every moment, even painful ones, contains gifts of wisdom and joy if we're willing to remain conscious.

Living consciously includes uncovering, grieving, and working through your historical childhood difficulties, along with the programming they created. It's your job to return to your blocks, those stubborn problems that keep you from experiencing your wholeness and embracing your potentials. As you identify and heal them you create change. This opens the door to the emergence of your real self.

You might be thinking, "Grieve my childhood difficulties?! Is that even possible? Won't that take forever? Why should I go through all that effort? What problems will it solve?" To understand why it's needed, let me ask you the questions that began this book:

Are you living the life you've always dreamed of?

Often, from a young age, we have an idea of the kind of life we want to live. We have specific goals in some areas, others we paint with broader strokes, and some goals change with time. Do you feel your life expresses your deepest desire? Are you moving toward your greatest vision of life?

Are you the person you want to be?

When you reflect on who you're being in life, you may discover you're suppressing important qualities and traits while expressing others that don't feel like the real you. Are you being your authentic, empowered self much of the time?

Is there a persistent complaint, pain, or longing in your life you've yet to heal?

Sometimes, no matter how much we work on ourselves, we encounter the same inner obstacles again and again.

Are you living and feeling fulfilled by your deepest mission in life, serving others, and making a difference?

We're here to contribute to the world in our own unique way. Sometimes that contribution makes big waves, and sometimes our expression of service is quiet, subtle, or deeply personal. Each is as important in its own way. Are you making the difference you know you can?

Are you satisfied and fulfilled in your relationships?

This is an area in which we often compromise, give in to resignation, and feel we've gotten the best we can get. Are you frustrated and unfulfilled in your personal and professional relationships?

Is your work aligned with your life-path, and are you satisfied with your progress?

Are you doing what you're burning to do? Does your professional life (your job or your business) express who you authentically are in the world? Are you achieving the results you want?

- *In what ways can you say yes to these questions?*
- *In what ways would you say no to them?*
- *In what ways are you living consciously in your life, now?*

Living a conscious life changes your everyday experience in measurable ways. You'll find greater ease, resilience, contentment, and success. As you learn to be present to physical sensations, emotional feelings, and thoughts, you'll develop ego strength, and move more comfortably with the ups and downs of life. You'll be well on your way to walking the conscious life path, embodying greater freedom and happiness.

You'll relax into the most subtle and profound realms of awareness, the inner silent still point in consciousness—the silence that feeds body and soul. Father Thomas Keating, in his book *Invitation to Love*, said, "Silence is God's first language; everything else is a poor translation. In order to hear that language, we must learn to be still and to rest in God."[1]

The practices in this book can lead you into wisdom and inner silence. Some might call this opening more fully to God, Wisdom, or unified consciousness. I like to call it "enlightening-ment," meaning that for most of us enlightenment is not a destination or graduation into a permanent higher state of consciousness, but a moment-by-moment experience constantly fluctuating between degrees of wholeness and limited consciousness.

Once we've experienced and embodied this *enlightenment*, whether for a moment or more, the time spent in this impersonal state, stillness, spaciousness, silence, or wholeness leaves its mark on us forever. You probably know what I mean, and can feel it as you read. When we travel that territory, our capacity grows. We're a little more relaxed and a little less fearful, more compassionate toward ourselves and others. We're more attentive to our lives and the still small voice within.

In the book *Buddha Standard Time*, Lama Surya Das defines enlightenment as a "deep flash of awakening to the knowledge that we are much more than our time and space-bound material selves living in a material world. Some people awaken to enlightenment by Grace, seemingly without effort, but most of us stay obsessively stuck in the past or the future, running our mental trains backward and forward in that track every minute of the day." Yet, he goes on to say, "Each moment is intersected by a realm of infinite spaciousness and timelessness, known in Tibetan as shicha, the Eternal Now."[2]

It's possible to be excited about life, even on a bad day, when you're doing what you came here to do! Fulfilling your mission—the one unique to you—is possible; I'm doing it, and I've helped many others do it too. You can feel happier than you ever thought possible!

Are you ready? Take a deep breath!

Conscious Living 2.0

A kind of spiritual birth takes place when our consciousness first becomes aware of itself. Something is born in us in that same moment...

—Guy Finley

To some people, conscious living is about bringing greater awareness to every moment. To others it means making healthier and more holistic choices in their lives. *Conscious Living 2.0* goes deeper.

This book is composed of *Conscious Living 2.0* principles and practices that help you awaken more fully to who you truly are, by embracing and exploring both your messy human life and your expansive spiritual nature. It isn't exactly a linear, step-by-step process, although it contains many practical exercises and tools; it's more an approach, mindset, or way of life.

Conscious Living 2.0 combines psychological work with spiritual practice, honoring our humanity as deeply as our spiritual nature, for they are not two, but one. From the deepest context, our humanity isn't separate from, or less than, our spiritual beingness; it's an aspect of it, and deserves to be valued and fully addressed. Because of our inherent Oneness, when we honor our humanity, including any difficult psychological material that arises, our ego is able to relax and we naturally sink into our deepest self. As we do, our longing for spirit becomes more apparent, our deeper wisdom more available, and our preoccupation with winning or competing becomes irrelevant. From this viewpoint, our psychological work becomes part of our spiritual practice, empowering us to live from our essence and achieve our dreams.

The principles and practices of *Conscious Living 2.0* are based on an awareness of the Four Dimensions of Consciousness: The Action-Physical Dimension, the Formation-Emotional Dimension, the Creation-Mental Dimension, and the Emanation-Spiritual Dimension. The four dimensions are a way of framing and perceiving reality that helps you transform your life more easily. They encompass much more than the familiar concept of body, mind, and spirit, and are a powerful key to living a conscious life. We'll take a detailed look at the Four Dimensions of Consciousness in Part II: Exploring Multi-Level Consciousness.

One quick awareness and mindfulness practice is to Presence Yourself. You can do this as often as you'd like, weaving it through your day.

EXERCISE: PRESENCE YOURSELF

There is no right way to do this. Feel free to add or subtract parts of it as you see fit; try it different ways and see what's best for you. You may need different aspects of this at different times. You can begin with what's outside of you if you'd like, noticing what you experience through your five senses.

What are you seeing around you? What are you hearing, right now? What can you feel with the touch of your hand? What can you taste as you're doing this? What do you smell, right now?

Now bring yourself into Presence in all four dimensions.

Now notice what is arising for you physically. What sensations are you experiencing?

Now notice what is arising for you emotionally. What feelings are you experiencing?

Now notice what is arising for you mentally. What thoughts are you experiencing?

Now notice what is arising for you spiritually. What spiritual connection are you experiencing?

Presencing yourself before doing any of the meditations or exercises will help you connect with and absorb this material more deeply. In addition, clarifying questions are woven throughout the book, approaching a topic from many different angles as a way to lead you into the unseen crevices of your unconscious mind.

A primary practice presented in Chapter 11 is the *Multidimensional Awareness Practice*. This mindfulness practice goes a bit further than Presencing. It will give an ongoing frustration you've had a good push in the right direction. You'll use the four dimensions to examine an issue that keeps returning for further exploration.

By following the trail of information into your unconscious, you'll uncover, process, and release stubborn problems, allowing a greater opening to the True Self.

This book provides psychological and spiritual practices from a wide variety of philosophies and religions (Jewish Kabbalah, Buddhism, Hinduism, Christian Mysticism, Islamic Sufism, nondualism, and quantum physics, among others), as well as many I've developed during my 20-plus years as a practicing psychotherapist and spiritual teacher. Along with laying down a philosophical foundation for this work, there will be plenty of exercises, explorations, and meditations so that you can put this philosophy into practice, and begin embodying ever-deepening aspects of Reality. The specific skills and tools offered will also help you dive deeply into whatever's getting in the way of your happiness and success.

To begin our exploration of living a more conscious life, let's look at some of the essential elements of conscious living: meditation, being present in the moment, awareness or mindfulness, and being connected—both to your inner life and to what's in your life. We'll also look at some important qualities to cultivate on this journey, such as courage and curiosity.

Meditation

Consciousness and meditation are methods where
you can actually obtain GOD perception.
—George Harrison

Meditation is a large part of *Your Ultimate Life Plan*. There are many types and styles of meditation, as well as several dimensions of consciousness you can experience. Each perspective can potentially give you different insights. In this way, the meditations provide opportunities to broaden and deepen your experience, awareness, and healing.

The meditations in this book combine psychological and spiritual aspects, and offer different dimensions of healing that can take you to profound levels of beingness. This type of self-exploration will help you with practical goals as well as with relaxing into the spacious mystery of life. The guided meditations will assist you in examining specific aspects of your life from a deep inner landscape, prompting explicit insights and viewpoints sometimes missed in other practices.

Using the perspectives of the four dimensions gives a fresh entry point into, and expanded view of consciousness, and can be just the right tool for the job, helping you overcome long-held problems. All four dimensions have distinct value in examining issues and opening you to a larger mindset.

For example, let's say you're having trouble moving forward in your life. Feeling your way from the emotional perspective, you realize you feel overwhelmed, out of control, and fearful. Next, you allow space for those feelings, watching to see if they shift or change. From a mental perspective, you watch any pull toward thoughts or beliefs that go along with your fear and notice if you distract yourself by thinking about what you should cook for dinner.

Physically, you might allow your body to move in whatever way it needs to, unblocking energy and stimulating clarity around the issue of moving forward. From a spiritual perspective, you might sit and ask for an image of the problem as a whole, noticing patterns that show up. You might picture the issue contained in a circle, for example, looking for what keeps it in place and how it's divided. What are the sections? What happens when you hold the whole issue at once? Does it shift, and if so, what shifts? What do you see, hear, feel, think, sense?

As you can see, each dimension provides a glimpse of how and where you get stuck and what might help you move forward from a slightly different angle or view. Together, these viewpoints create an effective, comprehensive approach.

Meditation is important in helping you reach goals, but it also has a powerful effect on other aspects of living. Studies have shown it has enormous benefit to the body, and almost every aspect of our lives. It lowers blood pressure, provides pain relief, and relaxes the nervous system. Meditation is proven to strengthen the immune system, strengthen and integrate the brain, and even boost survival rates in cancer patients. It also increases creativity and productivity while decreasing worry and restless thinking. It improves your ability to focus and solve complex problems as well as allowing a deepening connection with God. It fosters an expanding capacity for love. Major religious traditions have contemplative practices that provide benefits, from a slower heart rate to deeper consciousness.

In 2004, scientists from The University of Manchester, England, studied the effects of meditation on the experience of physical pain. The study showed that long-term meditators anticipate pain less often, and find it less unpleasant. They found this was because "Meditation trains the brain to be more present-focused and therefore to spend less time anticipating future negative events."[3] In my experience, this is also true of emotional pain, and one of the reasons meditation creates an opening for emotional healing.

Being Present

Become conscious of being conscious.

—Eckhart Tolle

When you're present, you bring the fullness of your being—an awareness of all Four Dimensions of Consciousness—into this moment, this now. Feel that in your body. By practicing being more present in your life, you move into a deeper state of *Being Presence.* It helps you embrace and experience God, the Absolute, or the Universe. You're more present to your relationship with this moment, yourself, and others.

When you're present to each moment, seeing life for all it is, it's easier to open to your own joy and pain, and then you can open your heart more fully to the joy and struggle of others. You're better able to see and feel the world around you: your family, your community, your environment, your fellow humans, the planet, and beyond—and not just your own projections and historical distortions. As you practice being present, you strengthen your ability to be with whatever shows up. You can hold the paradox of allowing life as it is, while being a more active participant in the co-creation of your life.

From the perspective of *Conscious Living 2.0* and *Your Ultimate Life Plan*, being present in the moment means facing whatever arises, rather than trying to avoid or skip over it. It means looking at things from many perspectives, not just the obvious one. It means being willing to stay with an issue, allowing and encouraging it to shift, until there is some insight or movement. It means fully facing your life, inside and out, knowing your outer life continually gives you clues about what you need to be with next inside of you.

For example, years ago I brought to a client's attention that he didn't bring his irritation with people at work to his sessions. At first he thought he didn't have irritation. Then, as he became present to the question, he saw he'd brushed it off so fast, he hadn't noticed the shame, loneliness, and isolation he felt in his encounters. Now you might be thinking, let sleeping dogs lie! But if this man continued to ignore his feelings, or shove them aside, he'd have jeopardized the closeness with others he longed for. As he began opening to this, he experienced his feelings, creating more room inside of him for compassion, spontaneity, wisdom, and happiness.

Life is a constant dance between making a conscious effort to be fully present, and effortlessly surrendering, receiving, and relaxing into the wisdom and power of your deepest Self. As you do your best to be present in the moment, please know you don't need to face everything at once. You don't need to nor want to be in a state of hypervigilance. You only need to face whatever is right in front of you—the thought, emotion, or reaction that's arising now—and follow where it leads. There's no right or wrong, or some unknown perfection to attain; there's simply taking the next step and doing your best in any given moment. As you gently tread this path, remember: the potential to experience the fullness of consciousness or Oneness is present in every moment.

The goal is progress, not perfection. While commitment and consistency are essential, they need to be balanced with self-kindness and self-forgiveness for the deepest healing and change to take place. Although there will be difficult and sometimes painful moments as you journey deeper into yourself, you've chosen the path of conscious living because it's the straightest and surest road to freedom, happiness, and success.

Being Aware

To awaken is to become aware. To become aware is to put that aware-ness to work on the further awakenings that lead toward liberation.

—Stephen Levine

Being present reveals where you're aware in your life, and where you aren't. It shows where you focus your attention, and where you focus your attention is how your life goes. Your attention helps create your intention. From the metaphysical "form follows thought" to current quantum theories, it matters where you put your attention.

When looking at attention, it's helpful to break down your experience of the moment and consider your reality from the Four Dimensions of Consciousness. You can recognize the multitude of messages that surround you when you know how to see, hear, or feel them.

Awareness starts with observing your sensations, body wisdom, and the entire physical dimension. Next, you check in with your emotions. Maybe a headache (physical) is telling you to go to the chiropractor, or maybe it's telling you to at-tend to an emotional issue in your life, or both.

Next, you observe thoughts running the show, behind the scenes. When you develop awareness of your thoughts, you can change the limiting beliefs keeping your childhood historical programming in place. Then, of course, you pay atten-tion to the Grace, heart tugs, and deep stirring that form the ground you stand on, the air you breathe, and your innate knowing. It's important to notice the quality of your awareness and attention, to see whether they're steady and focused, or flitting unconsciously from thought to thought.

You're aware of your personal history and how you relate to others, as well as how and why some people and events strongly affect your thoughts, actions, and reactions. Ever notice how certain people, or certain traits in people, really bother you? This is usually rooted in your past. Maybe someone—Mom, Dad, clergy, or teachers—did something back then that brings the same feelings up in you now. When you're aware of this and work through it, you become less hooked by that circumstance.

In our everyday life, we often have involuntary reactions caused by projections from our past. These projections are the unconscious parts of ourselves we attribute to others. Imagine a stressful situation, and friends telling you, "Don't worry, you'll be fine." Maybe you aren't worried at all, yet either your friends are worried for you, or they'd be worried for themselves in your shoes. Of course we empathize with friends, but part of being conscious is not assuming we're right about the other person or totally understand him or her.

When we project, we lack awareness of the split-off, disowned, denied, or wounded part of us. For many reasons, we'd rather not see these thoughts, emotions, or traits in ourselves. Why a wounded part? If it weren't somehow difficult for us, it wouldn't split off. It would be conscious. We then project these personal interpretations into situations, conversations, and any sensory data that comes our way.

So often we assume—by projecting our thoughts, feelings, and perceptions— that we know what motivates other people. We believe we know what they're thinking and feeling. It helps to question our perceptions and the originating beliefs behind our perceptions, so our relationships grow easier, more genuine, happier, and richer.

As we open to living more consciously, we come closer to seeing the truth, not just our projections. Our awareness helps us own all of who we are, and know what's happening inside of us, outside with others, and also the difference between the two. We have a better take on what occurs in life. We can see many possible reasons someone chooses to do something we wouldn't do. Our awareness allows us to be more understanding and loving.

In *Spontaneous Evolution*, Bruce Lipton says, "We are conscious co-creators in the evolution of life. We have free will. And we have choices. Consequently our success is based on our choices, which are, in turn, totally dependent on our awareness."[4]

As we pay attention, we become aware of what we don't know, opening ourselves to the essential mysteries of life. There's always more to discover and learn, a myriad of ways we can grow and change. Life is so wonderful, and we develop a wider opening to the heart of ourselves and life. Our awareness keeps us curious, and our curiosity keeps us seeking truth. It gives us momentum to grow, allowing us to tolerate and embrace the unknown. When we're aware, we cultivate the space of not-knowing, along with the willingness to know.

Another Awareness Perspective: Mindfulness

A tradition akin to and including awareness is mindfulness, part of the Eight-Fold Path to end suffering in Buddhism. *Right Mindfulness* shows us how we conceptualize our lives. According to author, teacher, and founding member of the Cambridge Zen Center, Jon Kabat-Zinn, PhD, mindfulness is "Paying attention in a particular way: on purpose, in the present moment, and non-judgmentally."[5]

Buddhist teacher and author Jack Kornfield, PhD, says, "Mindfulness is an innate human capacity to deliberately pay full attention to where we are, to our actual experience, and to learn from it."[6] A traditional mindfulness practice teaches you to watch whatever arises in your experience. It asks you to focus attention on the present moment, on anything inside or outside of you. When mindful, you notice and observe sensations, thoughts, feelings, sights, sounds, and smells without rejecting or attaching to them. It cultivates the observer in you that notices habitual responses, bringing you closer to your actual experience, not your story about it. You learn to be with whatever comes up in each moment, the best you can. And when you can't, you be with that too!

Mindfulness is an important practice for all of us.

MEDITATION: BEING MINDFUL

Find a quiet place to meditate. Sit in an erect, yet relaxed posture, allowing energy to flow more easily through your body. Starting with only 10 to 20 minutes a day, watch your breath, your thoughts, and anything else that occurs. Allow your thoughts to be present without following a train of thought—worry, or your laundry list of things to do that invariably crops up. When you notice you're following the story again, simply bring yourself back to observing what's there. Notice what you experience after your practice.

Psychologist Britta Hölzel, at Harvard Medical School, led an eight-week study observing the effect of mindfulness meditation on the brain. After practicing 30 minutes daily for eight weeks, the meditators showed "increased gray matter in the hippocampus, an area important for learning and memory, and a reduction of gray matter in the amygdala, a region connected to anxiety and stress."[7]

The study also examined the mechanisms of mindfulness. Hölzel and her coauthors discovered that mindfulness isn't a single skill, and identified four key components: attention regulation, body awareness, emotion regulation, and sense of self. While each component has a distinct function, together they help us attend to our inner life in a way that brings attention to and moderates the activities of the physical, emotional, mental, and spiritual aspects of our being.

Whereas you can include any form of meditation that supports you, we'll explore several. Mindfulness is more than a meditation practice; it's a way of being. You can be more mindful in every moment and all your activities, such as making decisions, washing the dishes, driving, or standing in line at the bank.

Mindfulness allows a larger point of view, because you're observing what's happening, rather than being mindlessly caught in those old stories you tell yourself. This opens you beyond your ordinary perception. You can see, in the moment, the constant repetition of thoughts and feelings in response to your experience. Mindfulness keeps you attentive to life and helps you respond more consciously because you're better informed.

EXERCISE: A MINDFUL DAY

Even if you find it difficult to sit for 10 to 20 minutes every day, you can bring mindfulness to all you do. Here's what a mindful day might include (and please add to this):

- *Before your feet hit the floor in the morning, take a deep breath and feel your body for a minute: Notice any sensations, notice your emotions, notice your spiritual connection; maybe stretch a little, and notice where your mind goes. As your feet touch the floor, notice what happens.*

- *Tune in to any intentions for the day, and perhaps find your deeper connection; meditate or express any gratitude.*

- *Notice the cup you're holding, containing your morning beverage. What does that bring up for you? What is your experience of your breakfast?*

- *If you have family or pets, allow yourself to see and hear them. Enjoy them as best you can, or be with whatever feelings come up as you're with them.*

- *If you commute to work, notice what you see, hear, and feel as you travel. If not, notice your thoughts, feelings, and sensations as you start your morning's work.*

- *Stop during the day for a few moments to feel your feet and your breath. Notice these before you check your e-mail or make a phone call. What happens as you do this?*

- *Whenever you walk during the day, notice how your feet touch the ground, and remember to breathe as you walk. Feel your body as it moves through space.*

- *As you eat, stop and notice the food—the smell, the taste. Notice how you chew your food.*

- *Feel your body as you end your day. What emotions or feelings are present? What thoughts? Notice your breath.*

- *Are there any acknowledgments you'd like to make before you sleep? Is there a bigger view to help you with difficulties you had? What have you felt grateful for today? Do you have a prayer or meditation that feels right for you?*

Being Connected to Our Inner Life

Life is a process. We are a process. The universe is a process.
—Anne Wilson Schaef

When we're willing to take the time, dive deeply, and connect with our inner wisdom and divinity, we receive riches beyond anything we've imagined! We turn within, leading us to a greater connection with our essence. This makes it possible to live from intuition and wisdom. We learn to live from the silence and stillness within, from the whole of unified consciousness. We expand to know the peace, openness, love, happiness, and wisdom always available.

We connect regularly with our inner being through meditation, or other forms of focus that quiet the mind. We'll explore this later, but some include chanting, centering prayer, walking meditation, and mindfulness meditation. *(Please visit the meditation room on my Website, www.DrJenniferHoward.com, for more support. New ideas are added regularly.)*

As we learn to connect with our essence, we begin trusting ourselves. We begin to seek our own answers, rather than looking outside ourselves. Our practice maintains our connection, and helps us listen to our inner wisdom.

Essence

A big part of living a conscious life involves knowing yourself. This is the unfolding that can come with the practice of being mindful or conscious. As we open to who we really are, we naturally sink into a deeper truth about ourselves and move closer and closer to the True Self. The True Self lies beyond all personal identity, while *essence* is our individual unique personal expression of the True Self.

The word *essence* comes from the Latin *esse*, meaning, "to be." It couldn't be more primary; we're talking about existence itself. Nothing can lose its essence and continue to exist. It's our fundamental nature, and the individual part of our soul that is Divine. Dipping into our essence allows access to our very core.

Our essence is our most essential or important ingredient: the crucial element in us. It holds our unique personal and individual core qualities emerging from the deepest well within us, which is connected to God, All-That-Is, the Absolute. It's our primary essential nature, ultimately giving us our personal identity.

Our essence takes us to the nature of our deepest connection with God. When you tap into your essence, you feel it informing your body, heart, and soul. When you're connected with your essence your words and actions flow from the calling inside, allowing the foundational movement of the ongoing creation process to emanate from the deepest levels of consciousness into full manifestation. Identifying with your essence becomes the impetus for all you do. Grounded and relaxed, you enjoy greater passion and purpose.

EXERCISE: CONNECTING WITH YOUR ESSENCE

Here are some questions to deepen your experience with your essence.

- *In what ways do you experience your essence?*
- *What's essential about you?*
- *What words relate to and feel like the core or the essence of who you are?*
- *What are the five qualities that people most often attribute to you?*
- *What would you like people to say about you at the end of your life?*
- *What would you like your epitaph to be?*
- *How do you connect with your essence?*

Some ideas might be: Get quiet, meditate, do deep breathing, be aware of your inner world, witness your thoughts, check in with your feelings, go out in nature, and so on.

- *How do you recognize when you're connected to your essence?*

How do you feel physically or emotionally? How do your thoughts change? How do you perceive things differently? How do you experience your connection to Spirit or God differently? What do you say when you're connected? How do you talk to people?

> • *In what ways, if any, do you feel that you bring your connection with your essence into your everyday life?*

Conscious Living Potentials

As well as connecting within, it's important to cultivate qualities and attitudes conducive to a conscious life that lead to actualizing your potentials. As you grow and integrate, you'll see certain potentials emerge. These are latent qualities, ways to view the world. They're inherent abilities or capacities that might occur spontaneously, or you might choose to cultivate them through your psychological and spiritual work, for your betterment and the world's.

Some of these might take commitment, consistency, and focused awareness to bring fully into your life, but if you continue with the same old, habitual unconscious responses and behaviors, life won't look or feel very different in six months, or six years. The good news is some of these potentials will naturally emerge as you practice the skills and tools in this book.

As you read through the following list of potentials, notice which ones are easily accessible to you, and which ones feel more elusive.

Authenticity	Harmony	Peace
Beauty	Identity	Pleasure
Clarity	Individuality	Purpose
Compassion	Inspiration	Receptivity
Connection	Integration	Satisfaction
Courage	Integrity	Spaciousness
Creativity	Intelligence	Stillness
Curiosity	Joy	Strength
Discernment	Kindness	Truth
Empathy	Knowledge	Understanding
Endurance	Love	Unity
Fulfillment	Maturity	Value
Gratitude	Openness	Will
Happiness	Passion	Wisdom

Courage, for example, is important in facing life events, an important element of living consciously. Although **curiosity** supposedly killed some cat, it's important for deepening your consciousness. When you react to something that happens by becoming inquisitive, you create space between you and the reaction. You can ask yourself questions like, "What am I feeling and thinking? Why am I reacting this way? How is this connected to my past or a belief?" Sinking into your unconscious with clarifying questions helps you hear your inner **wisdom**, as well as develop the ability to hear others more clearly.

A client told me she noticed that as she felt less critical of herself and more open to her thoughts and feelings, she didn't judge the reactions and choices of others as much. She felt more **compassion** for all kinds of people. She expanded her tolerance, and found herself **kinder** than before. When compassion and **empathy** open, we soften toward ourselves and others, and our negative judgments relax.

As with all personal development, progress usually happens in layers or levels. Maybe you're paying attention in your day-to-day life, noticing discomfort, and as you're present with it, one of the potentials arises. Or, you're doing one of your practices and breathing into a difficult feeling, when it disappears, naturally moving into more **spaciousness**, clarity, or another potential, and nothing more is needed. To discover and work with whatever blocks you from a desired potential, you could use the *Multidimensional Awareness Practice* or another *Conscious Living 2.0* practice.

These potentials are innate in all of us, yet we don't ordinarily access them deeply. You might notice that by working toward greater clarity, your endurance increases. Then with greater **clarity** and **endurance**, as you navigate your feelings and thoughts, you might find you have less need to distract yourself. Difficulties simply don't rattle you as much.

Take **knowledge** for example; you not only have the potential to acquire more intellectual knowledge, but when you open to all the dimensions of consciousness you combine your intellectual knowing with a knowing beyond the intellect as well. You develop an intuitive knowing.

Through **steadfastness** and ruthless self-honesty, you'll begin to see more of Reality. You'll become **discerning**, seeing the difference between your stuck beliefs and what's truly possible.

With *Your Ultimate Life Plan* and the *Conscious Living 2.0* practices, you'll feel alive and **inspired**. Growing inwardly, you'll know **strength** and **gratitude**, even during hard times. This will support your spiritual and psychological **maturity**, because you don't step over anything, or leave it out. Everything's included, and you'll see the wholeness contained in all your talents and challenges. Spaciousness emerges, inside and out.

Everything's Relationship

Relationship is who we are and what we do. The whole universe is actually the sum total of our relationships with one another.

—Gay Hendricks

You're connected to all of life, as well as connected to your inner life. From a linear perspective, we live in duality, connected to everything by an infinite web of relationship. By duality, I mean day and night, you and me, pleasant and unpleasant—all relationships. Day and night are related to each other, and you're in relationship with your thoughts, feelings, and actions around day and night. So your relationships extend far beyond people. You're in relationship with everything, whether you're aware of it or not. At the most primary level, *everything* is in relationship with *everything*.

> ⊱≈⊰
>
> **At a fundamental level, everything is in relationship with everything.**
>
> ⊱≈⊰

Relationship is life; to be is to be related. Only in the mirror of relationship is the mind to be understood, and you have to begin to see yourself in that mirror.

—J. Krishnamurti

We're in relationship to the entire world, and this relatedness is life, itself. Although you might sometimes feel isolated and alone, you're always in relationship with something deeper. From the viewpoint of separateness, you might have important tasks to complete, including your life's work; but from the largest perspective you're literally sewn into the fabric of existence. From the deepest level of consciousness, we could say oneness is the marriage, or union, of duality; or that duality is the bifurcation, or branching off, of oneness.

In this way, our essential oneness is what connects us to others and to life, birthing our myriad relationships. Recent studies in consciousness, as well as quantum physics, demonstrate clearly the interrelated, interdependent, inseparable, and relational quality of the universe. Physicist David Bohm showed that the nature of physical reality, although it appears to consist of separate static objects moving through space, is, as he stated, an "undivided whole" in continuous flow and change.

Historically, various spiritual groups and traditions have spoken about direct experiences of, or union with, God. This mystical end of the spectrum allows for the experience of Oneness with the Universe. For example, Theosophy, a philosophical spiritual group, teaches reverence for all, and that the universe is contained in the "all-pervasive" whole transcending the sum of its parts. A relationship, considered a connection between two points, includes: ideas, objects, locations, thoughts, feelings, people, and more. The list is endless. Have you ever stopped to consider all your relationships in life? Besides individuals, you have relationships with your body, home, job, pets, nature, community, spirit, and planet...to name a few. It includes anything that has meaning for you or touches your life in some way.

Please take a moment to contemplate your relationships, whether friend or foe, hobby or habit. Consider the dynamics in each of the different kinds of relationships. Does the relationship give you joy, or does it challenge you to be a better person? In what ways does it help you grow? In what ways does it support you physically, emotionally, mentally, and spiritually? Be conscious of all your relationships, and deepen your awareness around them.

EXERCISE: EXPLORING YOUR RELATIONSHIPS

Write down all the relationships you can think of, starting with your family and friends, adding others as they occur to you. Think about all the people, places, things, and aspects of your life that have meaning for you. You have a relationship with your current home, whether you consider it a sanctuary or just a building. You have a relationship with your childhood home too, and your hometown, whether you continue to live there or not.

You have a relationship with your pets and garden, as well as animals and nature generally, or a single rose. You have a relationship with the earth, and your food (that's a big one for many of us). You might also feel a relationship with your scale, caffeine, carbs, sugar, and so on. And let's not leave out technology. You have a relationship with your car, and if you have a computer or cell phone, they go on your list too. (Sometimes I'd like to divorce my computer!)

This list doesn't just include who you know and what you have, it includes anything you focus on that has value and meaning, and affects your life. Add anything you have beliefs and feelings about, from politics to penguins. And don't forget to add your relationship with yourself: your body, thoughts, feelings, and spirit, as well as ideas, dreams, and goals, all of which have relationships with each other. A strong relationship with yourself helps you live a peaceful and happy life, have great relationships with others, make good choices, and reach your goals.

As you list your relationships and expand upon them, notice what comes up for you. Write this down too, and give it some thought. Looking over your list of relationships, what stands out as the most important 5 or 10?

As you contemplate each of these relationships, what comes to mind when I ask:

- *What's important about this relationship, right now?*
- *What feeds you in this relationship?*
- *What's difficult about it for you?*
- *What image comes to mind when you think about it?*
- *What do you feel in your body when you think of this relationship?*
- *What's the primary emotion?*
- *Notice any repeating thoughts or beliefs.*

Looking at what you've written, draw a picture of any images that come to mind.

Process work—whether psychotherapy, breath work, psychodrama, therapeutic body work, meditation, or something else—allows you to have a more conscious relationship with your thoughts and feelings, while learning about the mechanisms that create your life. As you build this awareness of yourself, your experience of life changes for the better.

So what happens when you don't have a conscious relationship with your thoughts and feelings? Your unconscious mind runs the show, and your unconscious childhood historical programming is in charge. This keeps you stuck and less than you really are. It's hard to access your deepest potential if you're constantly in habitual reaction to the world. For example, if you feel anxious and unable to ask a question when your boss seems preoccupied, because you're sure that it's about you, you're caught in the past and it's holding you back and work and life.

Your goal is to have an integrated life, with the many aspects of yourself and your life in harmonious relationship to one another. Then you'll have great relationships with others, along with greater health, peace, and happiness.

It's important to acknowledge, work with, and break free of any obstacles that get in the way of knowing the truth about your thoughts, feelings, and life, and therefore your existence. You can do your part to have conscious relationships with yourself, others, and God (or whatever you call the ultimately nameless One).

Relationships and intimacy are the building blocks of existence.

Be Willing to Go Deep

At the beginning of this chapter I asked you a series of questions about your life. Well, I have one more.

Are you ready to change?

If your answer is yes, be ready to dive deep.

Why?

Because although everyone experiences degrees of happiness and sees some change happening over time, to most, happiness is fleeting. It's subject to the whims of circumstance, and often the things people most want to change are the changes they most resist. But for those who lead a truly conscious life, choosing happiness is easier no matter what happens. However, it might take a little work to get there.

The same is true of change. Rather than feeling frustrated and hopeless, the person who dives deeper knows change is always possible, even on long-held issues. This knowledge helps you optimistically step further into an issue. It gives you renewed hope, and the energy needed to create lasting change. You'll develop the capacity to handle life with greater presence, and less stress. Going deeper helps you identify, let go of, or work through anything in the way of the life, success, or relationships you desire. If you're willing to dive deeper, you'll discover there are treasures to be gained. There's gold in "them thar" hills!

Going deeper means different things to different people. Yet, if you're willing to stay on your cutting edge, and build awareness toward becoming awake, you'll be happier and have more freedom. Given a choice, most would prefer to take the quick and easy path. When we see the deeper path laid out before us, it feels a bit daunting, but going deeper doesn't mean life becomes more complicated or difficult. If you make a choice to consistently apply the principles and practices of *Your Ultimate Life Plan* and *Conscious Living 2.0*, you'll reveal your deepest Reality, layer by layer, embodying more of the ever-present Wholeness, Stillness, Spaciousness, and Grace that is the truth of who you are. Every moment you spend opening to your deepest and highest consciousness is precious beyond words.

- *In what parts of your life are you more conscious?*
- *What are your favorite ways to avoid your problems?*
- *What does going deeper mean to you?*
- *What are your five greatest strengths?*
- *List the five greatest insights you've had about your life.*
- *What is the deepest calling from your essence?*

MEDITATION: BRINGING CONSCIOUSNESS TO EVERY MOMENT

Deep breath. Allow all that you read in the chapter to just be *for a minute. Notice what thoughts and feelings arise. As you breathe, notice where your attention goes. As you notice, does it change? Be with it coming up as best you can. Do you notice yourself on a familiar train of thought or feeling? If so, where are you on the trail: the beginning, middle, or end? Wherever you are, just be with what shows up. Now, again, notice your thoughts and feelings. What's the same and what's different? Now spend time with the experience of your breath in your body, as best you can, until you feel finished.*

CHAPTER 3

Everything's an Inside Job: Understanding Your Personal Programming

We are all prisoners of our own mind. This realization
is the first step on the journey to freedom.

—Ram Dass

Everything is an inside job. What do I mean by that? In the first chapter we spoke of your happiness set point, the result of the experience of your thoughts and feelings. In the same way, your interpretation of all that happens in your life—the meaning you assign to every experience—is put together by the way you "log in" that information; the way you see the world.

❧

Like a computer with default settings, our unconscious programming is our personal default.

❧

Your experience of this moment is profoundly affected by your past, as long as you perceive reality only through the lens of past experiences. It's like a computer operating system that broadcasts and interprets 24/7 in order to make sense of your life. You need this system. It's how you get things done, and how you understand what's happening in any given moment. It becomes a problem when it runs without examination or question, resulting in a life mostly ruled by your unconscious. I call this your personal programming.

Interestingly, one of the definitions of *programming*, in keeping with our computer theme, is "a sequence of coded instructions that can be inserted into a mechanism or part of an organism."[1] Your programming is the coded instructions that, in part, you brought into this life and have continued to gather from your experiences until now. The coded sequence comes from internalized interactions with your environment, especially all you saw, felt, and heard from your caregivers when you were younger. This includes their values, relationships with each other, and all the unspoken communication you could comprehend by watching their body language and feeling their energy.

We're affected by everything happening around us, both painful and pleasurable. Yet, if you've chosen to consciously journey and work on what's come your way, you can develop into much more than your default programming allows. You'll understand you're greater than the sum of these parts. You can grow and learn from your personal struggles, as well as your innate talents. You come to experience your higher self, essence, and the True Self. Even though your programming is woven into your personality, your deeper Self is always available. Wholeness or Grace is right here.

In this chapter, we'll discuss in detail the mechanisms that cause both our painful and esteem-building childhood experiences to be woven into the fabric of our body, emotions, and mind. We'll explore how they affect us, and what it will take to differentiate between the beliefs we formed as children and who we really are.

Understanding Your Personal Programming

Let's take a closer look at how the layers of unconscious programming get created.

We're influenced by everything that comes our way as we grow up. The nurturing interactions we experienced shaped us—all the affirming statements we heard, the love expressed to us, and those wonderful memories of holidays or outings we experienced. We're also shaped by any wounding interactions—all the subtle ways our self-esteem was undermined, as well as painful childhood experiences, wounding, or traumatic events. Some memories are readily available, whereas others are tucked away, deep in our psyche. It depends upon our individual history, and the degree of trauma we experienced back then.

You probably remember events that had a strong impact on you, as well as others with less. There were healthy, esteem-building events, such as when a teacher praised you for something well done, a parent took interest in your day at school, or you were asked to play a solo in the band. Of course, you may also remember difficult events, such as being pushed aside by a parent, picked on for your size or your glasses, or teased for being different. These interactions and events produced thoughts and feelings you absorbed and saved in your database. Along with other factors, they created clusters of feelings and belief structures about life and how you see yourself and everyone around you.

We see clearly that some factors arose from the environment due to circumstances, whereas others stem from something else. For example, we all see siblings with strong similarities, yet big differences between them too. Even though they share similar genetic material, experiences, and parents, there are always distinct differences. According to research, several factors are involved, including gender and birth order. For example, an oldest child and an only child share similar traits, such as the tendency to take on greater internal responsibility for their actions—the oldest because he or she was most often put in charge, and the only child because there wasn't anyone else to blame. Younger siblings tend more toward experimentation.

Siblings can also be influenced differently by circumstances. For example, if Dad gets sick or dies at age 40, leaving two kids behind, age 17 and age 7, the event will have a different impact on each child according to his or her age.

Depending upon your belief system, we can consider other factors, such as seemingly unexplainable qualities or beliefs we brought into this life with us at birth. Perhaps untraceable influences stem from past lives, creating karmic destiny, or other choices you made before this life began. As we follow our deepest soul's longing, perhaps we're led in a direction that, in the context of our current life and history, might make no sense. If we embrace this inner calling, feeling it in our bones, we begin to know it's true and right for us. Whether we view this past life information as a metaphor or reality, the knowledge we gain uncovering these untraceable influences can prove productive and healing.

Biologist and author Rupert Sheldrake talks about morphic resonance being useful in understanding what at first glance might seem to be untraceable, unknown sources influencing our beliefs and actions. According to his theory, through telepathic effect, sympathetic vibration, or collective connection, we tap into non-local fields of information.[2] Morphic resonance or fields are a kind of collective memory, a collective consciousness, patterned behavior, or energetic blueprint we pick up from each other, even from a distance. A person might conceive of an idea that alters her world view, while another, unrelated person thinks the same thought a thousand miles away. Morphic fields influence unspoken family belief systems, myths, or the collective energies around diseases. For instance, if you're told you think and act just like your grandfather who died before you were born, morphic resonance may explain the similarities.

Similarly, German psychotherapist, author, and former priest Bert Hellinger saw that people take on the unconscious connections and dysfunctional family patterns of their relatives and ancestors,[3] through fields of energy that colleague Dr. Albrecht Mahr called "the knowing field."[4] Hellinger uses a therapeutic group process known as "Family Constellations" to disentangle generations of family suffering and destructive patterns of guilt, anger, anxiety, depression, loneliness, alcoholism, and even physical illness. These unconscious connections aren't considered genetic influences or repressed memories, yet they have memory and influence in our present lives. Family Constellations demonstrate our connection to the unified field of consciousness, what quantum physics refers to as entanglements.

Fortunately, we can continue to grow and change in spite of our family patterns and other influences. The quickest way to move beyond the limitations of our programming is to examine and *decode* all the underlying mechanisms and unconscious information. We travel into the **Action-Physical Dimension** of consciousness to see our earliest programming. From the **Formation-Emotional Dimension**, we begin to uncover and release the unknown clusters of feelings. From the **Creation-Mental Dimension** we witness and disassemble our belief systems, and from the **Emanation-Spiritual Dimension** we begin loosening the wound-up energetic knots of our consciousness.

We'll explore those clusters of feelings that keep us recycling through the same old stuff, and we'll loosen the knots by thinking of them in new ways.

- *What have you read so far that stirs up any feelings or thoughts about your personal programming?*
- *What comes to mind about your family's influence, versus the influence of those outside your family system?*
- *What do you imagine it's like to live beyond your programming? Take a moment to envision your life. What's different?*
- *What would it be like to actualize more of your potential?*

The Subtle Distinctions Among Affect, Feeling, Emotion, and Mood

These words are often used synonymously, but as you understand the differences you'll deepen your exploration of the "feelings" portion of your personal programming, or the Formation-Emotional Dimension of consciousness.

The first word is ***affect***. Various schools of psychology define it differently, but for our discussion *affect* is developmentally the earliest experience of a child. *Affect* is a pre-personal, pre-verbal, biological experiential state, meaning our subjective experience of emotion. When we're affected by an incident, we register it in our body-emotion-mind-spirit more closely, whether it seems positive or negative to us. When an incident was very hard for you as a child, it stands as a painful, wounding event in your memory. This includes being affected by parents who were unable to attune to us as babies, all the way to what might be viewed as significant events or traumas. On the positive side, we're affected by having caregivers able to meet our young needs or who helped us feel deeply loved and accepted.

When you're not strongly affected by an incident in childhood, it may not register vividly in your adult memory. This means either the incident was not a trauma or milestone and it became a vague memory, or the trauma is being repressed. However, if in a present-day event you experience a distressing charge getting stirred up, then usually a past wounding has been triggered, activated, or hooked, even if you don't recall it.

When something triggers us, a definite stimulus has activated a mechanism inside of us, releasing an unconscious pattern of biological sequence. Left unexamined, each affect unfolds according to its own precise program, written from our psychological history. Affects are unidentified at this point, and feel like anything from little waves of energy passing through or something blocking us, to huge turbulence and severe "affect storms." From the perspective of affect, we don't know how to distinguish or give a name to what's happening.

A ***feeling*** is an internal sensation noted and named by the conscious mind. It's informed by previous experiences, unlike an unexplainable, unconscious affect. We move from a strictly pre-personal, biological stimulus to an internal, personal, psychological awareness. While our human inner landscapes are similar, they also vary depending upon what's happened to us and how we've interpreted the affect experience into named feelings. We move from abstract, overwhelming, affect sensation to the ability to name those affect physical waves of experience. We can label and get to know our feelings as they oscillate between our interpretations of what seems difficult or easy.

Moving from affect to awareness of feelings, we're no longer continually at the mercy of affect storms. We're able to learn from our past experiences and better navigate the complexities of life. We have less reactivity and greater empowerment. Affect is the engine for feelings, creating the intensity behind them. When you're feeling sad, naming and talking about it results in less intensity and a greater ability to move through the sadness. Similar to affects, feelings change constantly, yet when we're caught by a story from our history it can seem as though it might last forever.

Emotion is more complex, and comes from the French *esmovoir*, "to set in motion."[5] Emotions fluctuate because of outward stimulation, as well as the often unconscious inward stream of thoughts and feelings. When consciousness is present, emotion allows us to see and know these repeated affects and feelings, giving us an even greater understanding. Most data we perceive has an accompanying habitual reaction. It's our conscious attention and mindfulness that allows them to be known, helping us better navigate our thoughts and feelings in daily life. You can learn how to assimilate information in any given moment, so you don't feel "run around" by your programming.

In his book, *The Feeling of What Happens*, neurology professor Antonio Damasio suggests *emotions* are a "collection of responses, many of which are publicly observable" by others, while *feelings* are inward stirrings that cannot be observed by others.[6] Emotions display outwardly, influenced by the atmosphere and culture of our upbringing.

Determining what you feel emotionally allows you to take this amorphous, overwhelming group of sensations and have a place for them. The ability to name the affect and the feeling takes it out of the "old brain," or amygdala, which contains our fear response and childhood wounding, and helps the frontal lobe of the neo-cortex have the ability to observe and understand, as our inner adult is engaged. From this larger perspective you can integrate and communicate your feelings.

Some body-focused psychologies might have you return to an event that affected you, to help you release charged feelings embedded in your psyche and soma (body). Traumas can be released and healed all the way to the cellular level.

Many psychological modalities, as well as traditional spiritual practices, guide you to notice the sensations currently present in your body, as a way to ground you in times of emotional distress. Grounding yourself brings you into the sensations of the present moment, rather than only the memory of the event being stirred up. Noticing your body, and this moment, helps you out of the entrenched, past programming stimulated by this current incident, rather than running the old pattern working on you physically, emotionally, and mentally.

Here's an example of someone caught in the trance of past programming, and how she was able to diminish it by noticing physical sensations:

> *Sally felt extremely anxious whenever she felt the slightest bit physically ill, or experienced bodily sensations unfamiliar to her everyday life. She focused on every tiny, inner movement as proof of her impending doom. In her anxious, fearful state, her life felt overwhelming and her panic eclipsed her ability to notice what was actually happening in her body. Instead, she was in a fear story about her body.*
>
> *After she reported a particularly intense and frightening dizzy spell, I explained that tuning in to her body, and identifying the physical sensations she's **actually** experiencing, could help ground her emotionally as well as physically. Being mindful and present to her experience, not just buying into the story of*

her fear, would lessen her anxiety whenever she's feeling ill, or frightened and triggered by physical sensations. Shortly afterward, in the midst of experiencing anxiety about her body, Sally decided to stop the chain of events that usually unfolded. She chose to be with her body, and all the sensations there in the moment. She didn't attempt to address the story of her anxiety. She simply noticed all the physical sensations arising in a conscious effort to be present with her experience, rather than react to it through her habit of fear and anxiety, or escape by finding a distraction.

Doing this not only helped her calm down and soothe the anxiety, but she also connected with her body in a new and profound way. Having done soul retrieval work in the past, she also recognized subtle sensations letting her know a piece of her soul had spontaneously returned. In Shamanism, it's believed a piece of your soul or vital force can leave your body in the midst of trauma, to survive the experience. When the soul-piece returns, it's a healing that can leave you feeling more grounded, joyful, and whole.

Considering what you've read in this section:

- *In what ways did you see yourself in the description of Affects, Feelings, and Emotions?*
- *How have affect storms played a role in your life?*
- *Describe two times you've successfully navigated your emotions in past difficult situations, and the ways you did it.*

Emotional Intelligence

Experiencing one's self in a conscious manner—that is, gaining self-knowledge—is an integral part of learning.
—Karen Stone McCown

We've recognized the importance of emotions for millennia, but the idea of emotional intelligence began in the 1930s, gaining popularity in the 1990s. As we learn how to recognize, control, and evaluate our emotions, we learn to navigate our emotional stormy seas. Some people may be born with a propensity toward emotional intelligence, but it can definitely be learned and always enhanced. Edward Thorndike's theory of "social intelligence"[7] helps us get along with other people, but contributes to our inner world too.

Funny how many of us don't often think of "emotional" and "intelligence" together. In his *New York Times* bestseller, *Emotional Intelligence*, psychologist

Daniel Goleman talked about the "five elements," originally coined by psychologists Sternberg and Salovey.[8] These elements include knowing one's emotions, managing emotions, motivating oneself to marshal emotions, recognizing emotions in others (empathy), and handling relationships. Essentially, we can feel and identify our feelings and emotions as well as distinguish those of others, and we can use this information to guide our lives.

Sternberg and Salovey suggested a basic step in our psychological development is to clearly recognize emotions. We pick up on nonverbal cues, such as facial expressions, tone of voice, and body language. I've observed we also unconsciously grasp the unseen and unspoken energy of emotions. As we continue growing in our emotional intelligence, we open to other levels of consciousness, more productively using our emotions for thinking and problem-solving. Our feelings begin to guide our decisions. Recognizing emotional subtleties allows shifts, greater understanding, and appreciation within ourselves and our relationships. We learn to manage and take the helm of our emotions, so they serve our larger intentions without impeding our progress.

Unresolved Memories

What happens if memories bring up feelings and thoughts that haven't been resolved? What happens if you can't ignore this triggered material anymore?

As you explore the feelings, thoughts, and sensations arising with a memory, the intensity softens; you'll unravel the story and relax your reactions. If a current, painful situation combines with old, stored pain from the past and becomes overwhelming emotion, you succumb to what could be called mood, state of mind, or emotional atmosphere. Similar to your happiness set point, your mood or emotional set point is where you gravitate when something gets triggered. Think of people who always go to anger, no matter what difficult feelings might be sitting underneath the anger. If you continue ignoring buried pain, you're vulnerable to troubled moods lasting minutes, hours, days, or months. Once a troubled mood becomes ingrained, it takes time and work to release.

As children, most of us didn't get much help understanding or accurately naming our feelings, so as adults we often don't know what we're feeling. As adults, we can discover that feelings have many subtleties. For us to live beyond our programming with that sense of peace and happiness we all long for, we need to be able to feel, name, and process through our feelings.

A feeling, such as anger, can be unconsciously triggered many times in a lifetime; our story, or overlay of a script, may make our reactions different from another's reactions to the same stimulus. An *affect* lasts just a few seconds, a *feeling* only long enough for a flash of recognition, and an *emotion* as long as we keep finding memories that continue to trigger that *affect*.

Here's an everyday example of being triggered most of us can relate to: Your wife asks about what errands you're running today, and suddenly you feel annoyed. Because of her fear and shame, she didn't ask you directly to pick up something from the store, which might have taken you out of your way. She has trouble asking for help. You felt annoyed by her questioning, and underneath that was your unconscious fear of being controlled, because you felt controlled by your caretakers growing up. Now, you experience her questions as controlling. See how this goes?

These *feeling stories* contain layers, or clusters, of feelings. When you can distinguish one feeling from another, as well as the contents of a feeling cluster, you grow in consciousness, which aids in learning to unravel and heal your programming.

Containing and Expressing Feelings

In healthy relationships, it's essential to know how to be in touch with feelings, name them for yourself, *and* be able to hold or contain them. Containing is not the same as repressing. When you're containing, you're not reacting but responding to someone. If you can sift through the emotional briar patch and identify the underlying feeling, not just the historical story of the feeling, it's easier to understand what's happening inside you.

Someone might seem angry, but alongside or under the anger there are often other feelings, such as fear or sadness. Being with, and sorting out, the feelings helps you find the observer or adult part of you, and lets you digest whatever's going on inside. Then you're better able to contain the historical overlay of all the pain and raw feelings, and communicate a more digested version of the feeling story inside of you.

❧

In the care and feeding of healthy relationships, containing undigested feelings and expressing your needs, instead of hiding your vulnerability or dumping undigested rage, or other emotions, makes it more likely you'll be heard and truly have your needs met.

❧

Your goal is to contain your feelings and express them appropriately without acting them out. This takes practice.

Here's an example of containing and expressing your digested feelings:

Lauren used to think fighting was an appropriate response when someone said something about her she didn't agree with. After all, they had "disrespected her." This caused problems with friends, family, jobs, and life in general. She said she'd been told it wasn't good to keep her feelings inside, and she should speak her mind in any way that occurred to her. When I met her, from her childhood wounding, it felt impossible for her to stop lashing out because she didn't know what to do with her rage.

As she began to understand and differentiate the hurt feelings inside, she began to feel her rage, move into anger, and not always act it out when she heard something she didn't like. She also began to notice other feelings, for example the shame and sadness of her inner child, and then could address the situation with appropriate words, tone, and boundaries. This didn't mean she became a doormat; on the contrary, she could have her needs met, and people could finally get close, listen, and understand her. She learned to stand up for herself without rage, and began living a richer life.

The more we've processed the old anger, or any other feelings present, the more possible it is to communicate the feeling in its assimilated, digested form. This leads to more effective communication. A great way to communicate our feelings is by using the formula, "When you do X, I feel Y, and I need Z from you." This helps you put your feelings into words and talk about them. It might sound like, "When you didn't take out the garbage (X) I felt angry (Y), and I need you to take it out and keep our agreement (Z)." Remember, vomiting your undigested anger onto someone, name-calling, controlling, or manipulating people so they'll do what you want, even passive-aggressively, is not from your integrated, mature, adult self or real self. It's from a wounded, inner-child self.

Even though you've probably heard people say, "You *made* me feel X," this isn't an accurate way to communicate your feelings. I've even heard psychotherapists on TV say, "How did that *make* you feel?" Actually, no one has the power to *make* you feel anything. Everything's an inside job. Your reaction to someone is your reaction. It may seem reasonable to you, but everyone is different. You're having a feeling because a historical issue is being stimulated. Now, maybe four out of five people would feel angry at what happened, but it still relates to something inside of you and you need to take responsibility for it.

As they say in 12-Step programs, "Feelings aren't facts."[9] Emotions don't define you; they're a form of internal communication that helps you to understand yourself. They help you heal. They're a vital part of your being, part of your wholeness. It's important to own your feelings and emotions.

Through the years, different paradigms have compiled their own lists of basic emotions that are part of human experience. A healthy person knows and can properly express his or her feelings, and can work with whatever feelings need to be identified, processed, loosened, or soothed.

Naming an emotion with the accurate name helps you feel empowered and express precisely what you feel in that moment. However, to further your healing it's often more helpful to use the following 12 primary feelings to take you to the most primitive places inside of you. The most basic are anger, sadness, happiness, fear, and loneliness. I'd also add grief, shame, love, compassion, aversion, peace, and pain.

There are many subtle shades of feelings closely associated with these 12 basic emotions. Frustration and rage could be viewed as shades in the lineage of anger, for example. In Chapter 8, we'll get more specific about feelings, exploring and working with each one individually.

Considering your own feelings:

- *How have you contained your feelings in a difficult situation? When have you not been able to?*
- *What feeling stories do you notice repeating in your life?*
- *What feelings cluster together most often for you?*
- *What feeling is easiest for you to show others? What feeling is the hardest? Why do you think that's true?*

I Think Therefore I Am My Thoughts

What we are today comes from our thoughts of yesterday, and our present thoughts build our life of tomorrow: Our life is the creation of our mind.
—Buddha

Marcus Aurelius (AD 121–180), a Roman emperor best known for his Meditations on Stoic Philosophy, said it well: "Our life is what our thoughts make it."[10] This statement represents two of the ways we formulate our lives and ourselves. First, our thoughts contribute to how our lives unfold, so seeing and working with the mechanisms creating those thoughts will change our lives. Second, our perception of life, along with our ability to navigate the various twists and turns, also changes our lives. This book addresses both aspects.

Besides your emotions, a large part of your personal programming is informed by habitual and repeated patterns of thinking in your daily life. As with feelings, these patterns are formed mostly in childhood and reinforced over time. They constantly influence how you feel and live. You view reality through your unique lens, tinted by the perception of your programming that proves time and again your thoughts are true. If you think you're not very smart, for example, a glance from your teacher can prove you're not. You just know she's disappointed in you, and that glance becomes more evidence that you're not smart enough.

For the purpose of breaking down your personal programming, this chapter began looking at your feelings. Feelings and thoughts are separate, rooted in two different dimensions in consciousness. It's helpful to work with them individually, but as you start the process of unraveling your personal programming, you'll notice how they dance together in your psyche. You might start with a feeling, and then notice thoughts that come with it, and visa versa. Even though most of this chapter is about feelings and thoughts, healing our programming moves in and out of all Four Dimensions of Consciousness.

The more tightly we hold on to our stories and personal histories, and the feelings contained in them, the more likely we believe we are our stories, and the less likely we are to hear our deeper eternal truth. The good news is that the limiting thought patterns and belief systems originating from our personal history can be perceived, understood, dismantled, and transformed. Our attention begins this disentanglement process.

As with your feelings, you work with your thoughts by observing when you're triggered by a situation. When you feel triggered, consider your thoughts and thought patterns to help loosen their hold. You may have examined this pattern before, but as you begin working with it more deeply, you'll see parts of your unquestioned, habitual, limiting judgments and reactions for what they are: thoughts from your past.

Each time you work with what arises, you've freed another layer of yourself caught in the past. This helps you relax and return to the present moment, dropping into your wisdom and, eventually, the greater Reality.

The most productive way to deal with those old, habitual thought patterns lurking around is to face them head-on. Notice when you avoid, bypass, or skip over those thoughts and compassionately allow yourself to see what's there. Understanding, processing, and integrating your habitual, tightly held thought patterns helps shake up and soften those thinking and feeling constructs. We want to unearth these hidden patterns of thinking that keep us stuck and perpetuating the very things we hope to change.

EXERCISE: THOUGHTS AND PATTERNS

Think of a time, recently, when you were triggered by someone. He or she might have said something to you or behaved in a certain way. With that in mind, allow yourself to take a deep belly breath. Imagine you're there, right now, in that situation. Now notice your thoughts for a moment. Where do they go? Just notice the thought patterns for a few minutes and answer the following questions:

- *Where have I seen this thought or pattern in my past?*
- *What's the earliest memory I have with this thought or pattern?*
- *What events have occurred in my life that reinforced this?*
- *Who taught this to me through their words, energy, or actions?*

Please explore your thoughts with great compassion, and when a memory shows up, remind that younger and vulnerable part of you that it's not happening now. Although it did happen in the past, most of what happens to anyone in childhood doesn't happen again when they're an adult. The worst is over and now the healing can happen.

∼≈∘

Although some of the feelings, thoughts, and bodily sensations currently in your life are connected to your past, remember, as you bring all the different aspects of you to your conscious awareness, and begin working with them, they'll start to change, shift, and heal.

∼≈∘

The Story of the Three Selves (Real Self, False Self, and True Self)

As our sense of self is formed, a number of aspects develop to cope with life as it shows itself. Each of these aspects plays certain roles that support us and provide a lens through which to view ourselves and our world. The three aspects we're focusing on here are the real self, false self, and True Self.

After learning how to be introspective and working with your emotions and thoughts, you'll move toward an ability to be more relaxed and authentic. Sometimes this is referred to as your ***real self***. Your real self is the sum of your internal representations of how the world works, your thoughts and feelings, your belief systems, your mental images, and your cognitive content, all gained from what you've observed and learned to be true about yourself. It's your genuine feelings, needs, and desires, and as you grow, your connection deepens with time. From your real self, you're free to express yourself, live from inner strengths, and observe where your issues still hold you back from even greater freedom. It's the personal or psychological self that lets you know who you are—your likes and dislikes—and unlike some ideal of "who you think you should be," it's congruent with a deeper sense of yourself. The real self moves toward mastery of life, including personal competence, flexible ego, and living life from your highest choices. Your real self listens to what others say about you, sifts through the information, recognizes what feels true about you and what doesn't, and then knows how to respond.

The real self can identify your personal hopes and dreams, and has the self-agency to bring them into reality. It doesn't just have unconscious images running the show behind the scenes, but also allows you to observe and relate to them, which in turn changes them.

Your real self is flexible and capable of supporting you through life's ups and downs. It can experience emotions spontaneously and deeply, including joy and excitement, and have authentic, honest relationships. It has self-determination, self-motivation, and self-direction, and is self-reliant. It's creative, can be adventuresome and social, is comfortable with interdependence, and can rely on others, yet also finds solace in being alone.

Our *false self* began developing in infancy and is derived from childhood coping strategies in reaction to an environment that felt unsafe, hurtful, or overwhelming. It's the part of us that had to repress our feelings, shove our needs aside, and change our behaviors to survive our upbringing. British psychotherapist Josephine Klein says, "Other people's expectations can become of overriding importance, overlaying or contradicting the original sense of self, the one connected to the very roots of one's being."[11] Klein's "original sense of self" in the child is its essence.

The false or masked self lives from defense strategies, steering clear of painful feelings that arise as we face the truth of life. It cannot make wise choices in our adult lives because it doesn't know how to deal with present-day reality and operates using young, defensive, childlike fantasies. When entrenched in our false self, we believe our defenses are the only option and we're unable to act fully from our adult self because of the inner alienation of our body, emotions, and mind.

Often the false self is who you think you should be. Adapting to parental needs, it can show up as deflated or inflated. The codependent *deflated* false self wants to please others to protect the relationship, squashing himself or herself and abandoning any inner urges to move toward a separate, empowered, real self. For example, a person living from his *deflated* false self believes the defensive strategy that tells him he can't take care of himself in the world, and needs to be taken care of by others. In contrast, the counter-dependent *inflated* false self acts as if she has all the answers and never needs help, while all the time feeling like an imposter and fearing she'll be exposed. She keeps unmet childhood needs at bay by blocking painful feelings of shame related to parents who were either neglectful or overbearing. Unexamined, this dynamic gets re-created in our adult relationships.

Of course, the **True Self** is different from the false self, but it's also deeper in consciousness than our real self. The real self is our personal, psychological sense of self, and the True Self is transpersonal. Rather than relating only to the images or ideas we have about ourselves, the True Self is the embodiment of Spirit, Divinity. The True Self isn't known only by self-reflection and introspection, but by moving into being with the moment-to-moment, ever-changing Reality. The True Self is transpersonal and impersonal, your essence is both transpersonal and personal, and your real self is personal.

Whereas your essence is your unique individual spark of God's image, woven throughout your personal self, the True Self is Divinity, Buddha nature, or Christ Consciousness. Entering the territory of the True Self takes us into the largest context of Oneness, spiritual Wisdom, and the intelligence of the heart. To hold the compassion of heart intelligence, it helps to first know yourself from the psychological, real-self perspective. Knowing your personal "I" grows your capacity to know the "I" that's included in "We," the Ground of Being. In other words, it's necessary to explore the territory of the self, to incorporate it. This takes us into unitive consciousness.

Being gentle and kind with yourself opens the space inside for you to move toward the True, or Divine, Self. Cultivating a sense of humor is always a plus on your journey toward lightness of being.

All of this conscious journeying allows your false self to heal and integrate, your real self to actualize, your essence to emerge, and the True Self to be. It takes you beyond your programming, into an ever-present beingness. From here, you'll live your mature wisdom and bravery with kindness and wholeness. Life will feel so much easier, even though your outer circumstances haven't changed.

EXERCISE: THE STORY OF YOUR THREE SELVES

- *When and in what ways do you see your false self?*
- *What are some of the thoughts and feelings that go with that?*
- *In what ways do you see your real self?*
- *How do you see the True Self shining through your essence?*

Luminous Strands of Consciousness

As you work with the information revealed from processing your sensations, emotions, thoughts, and inner stirrings, you'll notice a shift. You might perceive a little more spaciousness inside for new ideas, greater emotional ease, and less physical tension.

What, exactly, is shifting? The answer depends on the level of consciousness you're in at the time. This is why working with the four dimensions is so powerful. You're healing and integrating your inner experience, as well as your connection with all levels of consciousness. Transforming your programming actually loosens the knots and tightness in the fabric of who you are, allowing for change. As a result, the gnarled parts of your humanity are disentangled and rectified, and then you return to being more of who you really are.

Looking from an energetic perspective, the fabric of our being can be perceived as Strands of Consciousness. These luminous Strands carry information about us, from the most basic to the most complex personal data, including physical, emotional, mental, and spiritual content. As you meet the more difficult information contained in these Strands, problems begin to unravel, the weave loosens, and you change. Issues in the forefront recede, letting you focus on other things, and return to more of the True Self.

Groups of Strands, and the programming they carry, bind together to make Slivers of Consciousness that assemble energetically. These form clusters of intertwined information, and show up in our lives as issues, or stories. These clusters resemble slivers because they cross through all the dimensions of consciousness. Following the Strands that make up a Sliver, through all four dimensions, gets at the root cause of the issue or story, and reveals all the branches of the problem. You see, feel, process, and integrate these problems from each dimension to more fully heal the issues. You start to see beyond your projections of people, life, and reality, and you become more present. We'll go into more detail about how to work with Slivers of Consciousness in Chapter 6.

EXERCISE: LUMINOUS STRANDS

Spend 5 minutes breathing and sitting with your luminous Strands of Consciousness as best you can.

MEDITATION: BEYOND YOUR PERSONAL PROGRAMMING

Deep breath. Feel your body moving into relaxation. Deeper and deeper, more relaxed. Imagine you've stopped repeating your old personal programs. No more habitual thinking. No more old feeling patterns. Breathe into all that. Be with it for a while.

Now, pay attention to any physical sensations that arise. Notice what's happening in your body. Notice your feelings. Observe your thoughts. No more habitual programming. Breathe and feel that.

Just imagine all that's possible. From here you know what you're capable of. You embrace your strengths and weaknesses. You make wise choices. You take action for your highest good and the good of others. Breathe into all of this. Sit with it for a while. This is the life you can create.

CHAPTER 4

Journeying From Wounded Ego to Sacred Self

What is it in you that brings you to a spiritual teacher in the first place?
It's not the spirit in you, since that is already enlightened, and has no
need to seek. No, it is the ego in you that brings you to a teacher.

—Ken Wilber

There's a lot of conflicting information and beliefs about the ego, so it's a confusing topic for most people. Is the ego an indispensable element of consciousness, central to healthy functioning and helping you survive as a human being with a separate self, as psychology proposes? Or, is it bent on destroying your life, sabotaging your quest for happiness and enlightenment, and something to eliminate, as some spiritual philosophies believe? In other words, should we take our ego to lunch, or kill it? This chapter will explore these questions, as well as dispel common misconceptions about the ego.

So what, exactly, is the ego? How does it develop? How does it help you survive? How does the ego become wounded, and how do you heal it?

Think of the ego as a container holding your individuality, the sum of a lifetime's personal experience, including your unresolved pain, most of which is unconscious. Briefly described, the ego is your sense of "I-ness," containing your thinking, feeling, and sensation, and distinguishing you from others. It's the part of the mind that mediates

> **There's a lot of conflicting information and beliefs surrounding the ego. So what, exactly, is the ego?** *Take a moment to feel or get a sense of your ego.*

between the conscious and the unconscious, and is responsible for testing reality and a sense of personal identity.

It helps you learn how to bring more awareness to your human journey with all its twists and turns. This conscious awareness helps you to heal and make peace with your historical pain. You can then address and heal your wounded human ego. As you continue along your path, your understanding and beliefs about who you are will present themselves for examination.

In your willingness to illuminate every dark corner of your consciousness, you'll meet parts of yourself only glimpsed before. Many spiritual circles believe you should simply let go of all the ego "stuff" without giving it your time or energy. They see the contents of the ego as unimportant to who you really are. They encourage us to bypass or jump over the personal self, believing it irrelevant to our humanity or enlightenment. This idea impedes our ability to change, and interferes with achieving our ultimate transformation. Yes, you're more than your stories, past hurts, and programming, and the more you can welcome and integrate your ego, the more fluid and flexible you'll be in your life and relationships. In time, as you become more cohesive, you'll move closer to wholeness.

As you change and grow, you heal much of your woundings and you're capable of accepting more of your humanity with grace and forgiveness. The healing allows you to sink into a more integrated ego, a personal self that's relaxed, understands its place, and opens to your sacred Self. You begin experiencing yourself as part of a bigger whole. You feel like a wave in a vast ocean. You sense the enormity of the ocean, and at the same time, you enjoy and treasure your personal *waveness*. From this perspective, you can generate gratitude for all the pleasures you've received, as well as all the difficulties.

Let's look at a few different ways to view the ego. I think this will help you begin to get a handle on the conflicting viewpoints and clear up any misunderstandings. Understanding is one of the first steps to creating more wholeness and, ultimately, more happiness.

What Is This Thing Called Ego?

Definitions of *ego* run the gamut from self-centered to self-esteem, while various philosophies go to the extreme of either deifying or demonizing the ego. Yet, at its most basic, our ego is simply our sense of self, or our consciousness of our own identity. So the ego isn't the entire picture of who you are, but a part of you that includes your individuality and helps in your individual functioning and choices.

Here are various definitions of the ego:

1.   The conscious and permanent subject of all psychical experiences, whether held to be directly known or the product of reflective thought; opposed to the non-ego

2.   The conscious mind

3.   Your consciousness of your own identity

4.   The self

All refer to our sense of who we are in the world. Lastly, it's defined as (5) an inflated feeling of pride in your superiority to others.[1] This last definition is commonly used in everyday conversations. So often *ego* equals *egotistical*.

The concept of ego dates at least as far back as 300 BC to Zeno, the founder of the Stoic school of philosophy in ancient Greece. Like the philosophy of some of the transcendentalists of the mid- and late 1800s, the Stoics believed that a good life is ethical, and empowered by knowledge of oneself, acceptance of life, and living in accordance with nature.[2] They understood that through a combination of outer experience and inner wisdom, we can influence how we perceive and live our lives. We can come to see that we have a separate self; therefore, we can take a step back, without being consumed by our suffering. We'll talk in more depth about this later. Also, in Sigmund Freud's writing the translation for the word *ego* was the German word for "I."

Whatever your belief, one thing is certain: You'll have difficult thoughts and feelings as well as pleasure and happiness, and these all are the contents of your ego. So, how do you face a distressing or painful event? For many of us, it's hard to ignore or quickly let go of some experiences. Therefore, it's not possible to escape your ego.

Whether you're aware of it or not, your unconscious, unexplored, and un-integrated psychic material is your personal programming. The ego is a mediator among the different aspects of self, and its structure is a compilation of your past—including your unprocessed thoughts and feelings. So, the ego is what keeps you running around until you can face yourself, your past, and all the unconscious content directly. You can more fully embody and live your unique expression of life with a healthy, integrated ego. As we continue our spiritual practices, and personal and psychological work, our ego naturally dissolves into its rightful place. Your ego helps you move through the world as an individual, but its integration allows you to know the Oneness and ever-present Grace that's always there.

EXERCISE: WHAT IS THE EGO?

Deep breath. Now that you've read this far, what occurs to you about your ego? The beliefs you've been exposed to about the ego may have come from a psychological or spiritual perspective, or they could simply have been presented as part of life and just how people are. Some beliefs might feel harsh and others nurturing. Write them all down.

Ego as Fundamental: The Psychological Approach

It is important, as a foundation to spiritual training and education, to learn how consciousness manifests as the ego and its mechanisms.
—David R. Hawkins

From a psychological perspective, the ego is considered the centerpiece of conscious life, something to be healed and strengthened. This is because traditional psychology looks at ego through the lens of the psychological realm only, and doesn't include a reality beyond the personal. The spiritual realm of consciousness is capable of looking at the ego from a larger context, which includes everything, and recognizes it's not the whole picture. However, pursuing insight from a psychological viewpoint helps the ego relax into its rightful place, knowing it's not all of you.

As we said earlier, when you were young, it was one of your parent's jobs to help you have a healthy sense of self. If you had "good enough" parenting you have a reasonably good sense of the "I" that's at the heart of your individuality. This enables you to move through life knowing what feels right from inside of you. You can know, from your deepest sense, where you need to be and what you need to do, rather than live from what you think you should do, which comes from a wounded sense of self. Most of us had parents who fell short in various ways, mainly because of the shortcomings of their parents.

Facing your ego means facing your stories. Consisting of thoughts and feelings, your stories often come from the words and actions of others throughout your life, such as your parents and teachers. When you understand and embrace your personal stories, an opening occurs inside, allowing you to question and discern the accuracy of all that's been reflected back to you, in order to move beyond them.

It's helpful to see the connection between Strands of Consciousness and your stories. When you see your stories as Strands of Consciousness, you can follow the Strands into the deepest reaches of your psyche, discovering and disentangling the contents and their origins, and identifying the emotional charge keeping you attached to them. Your willingness to look at the hidden parts of yourself supports you having more fulfillment, authenticity, and happiness.

From a psychological approach, the ego's journey is from wounded ego to healthy self-esteem. You individuate and become more of who you really are, and you stop acting like the puppet of your past programming. The richness of your real self informs your life and all you say and do.

When you're uncomfortable, something from the past is being triggered. If you pay close attention and process the pain from your past, you can eventually heal the ego enough so it recedes into the background. You'll use these tools: noticing discomfort; experiencing and identifying specific feelings; noticing thoughts, understanding their history, and processing them through therapy or coaching; journaling; soothing yourself; sitting with what arises. Whether using a spiritual practice or other means, doing your psychological work helps you relax and pursue connection with Spirit, while enjoying better relationships, success, and peace of mind.

How Is the Ego Formed?

Understanding how your ego is shaped and formed enhances your ability to work with it and supports your transformational journey. According to psychological theories, your ego structure is made up of your past, your identification with and experience of your body, and your inner thoughts and feelings.

The wounded ego, or human condition (like Eckhart Tolle's "pain body"), is our defense against all kinds of pain, stemming from being brought up by imperfect human beings in an imperfect world—all part of the design. Childhood leaves the deepest imprint on your sense of self, but everything you have experienced and been exposed to in your environment and culture, even energetically, affects you and how your ego is shaped. You developed these ego defensive structures for self-preservation, and from ideas of who you think you *should be*, based upon your upbringing.

Although the psychological view of the ego is relatively new, introduced by Sigmund Freud in the 1920s, the spiritual, philosophical, and personal view of the self—what it is and how it's formed—is as old as humanity's capacity for self-reflection.

Different Schools of Thought

It might be helpful to look at the ego's formation from different psychological schools of thought. When you understand how your ego is formed, it helps you see your pain differently, eventually healing it. Sigmund Freud, the father of psychology and founder of psychoanalysis, saw the ego as the part of the personality mediating between the id, the superego, and reality. In his view, our ego keeps us from acting on all the id's basic urges, and helps achieve balance with the superego's moral and idealistic standards. The ego operates in all three aspects of the mind: (1) preconscious—memories you're unaware of; (2) conscious—everything in your awareness; and (3) unconscious—buried feelings, thoughts, urges, and memories.[3]

For instance, depending on your childhood influences, the ego is what keeps you from hitting someone just because you're mad. Instead, you might deal with your frustration by writing in your journal, taking a walk, or calling your psychotherapist. Freud wrote about the ego as "the I"; one's conscious experience of who one is.

Next is Carl Jung, Swiss psychiatrist and influential thinker who founded the analytical psychology known as Jungian Psychology. He viewed the ego as our conscious sense of self, the mental story we tell ourselves about who we are. This story contains labels or ego-identifications, such as job titles, social status, possessions, and so on, which define who we think we are. Jung preferred the term *ego-complex* because it contains both the ego as a condition of consciousness, and the ego's contents. According to Jung, our self-delusions or fixed ideas are created by unresolved, long-lasting, painful events.[4] This childhood conditioning alienates our deeper self. Jung was the first in psychology to include the spiritual, a hint of the very beginning of transpersonal psychology.

Jung developed his version of psychological typology by understanding that the ego has four inseparable functions—four fundamental ways of perceiving and interpreting reality—and two ways of responding to it. The four are: sensation, feeling, thinking, and intuition, which he combined with the polarity of extraversion and introversion. The Myers-Briggs Type Indicator, a personality inventory developed by Isabel Briggs Myers and her mother, Katherine Briggs, is based on this model, and was developed to make Jung's theory of psychological types "understandable and useful in people's lives."[5] It can help you learn about aspects of yourself on a deeper level. As you grow and heal, you'll notice that you'll move toward the center of each polarity, but will usually keep your predilection toward one side.

Erik H. Erikson, a German-American developmental psychologist and psychoanalyst known for his theory on social development, coined the phrase *identity crisis*, and said, "A human being, thus, is at all times an organism, an ego, and a member of society."[6] An originator of Ego Psychology, he saw the ego as more than a servant of the id, and valued a child's environment as important in the development of identity—our vision of ourselves. According to his Eight Stages of Psychosocial Development, most of us have unfinished business in each stage.

Psychologist Abraham Maslow was a pioneer in Humanistic Psychology, and unlike most before him, he examined an individual's internal strengths, what constituted good mental health, and human potential. He's known for his Hierarchy of Needs. Maslow believed that once our more basic survival or lower needs are met, we can then desire and grow toward higher needs, like climbing the rungs of a ladder. For example, if you struggle with survival needs such as food and water, it's nearly impossible to focus on confidence and personal achievement. According to his theory, if our basic safety needs weren't met by our family, we'll have difficulty belonging, and will find love relationships challenging, because we don't feel accepted by others or ourselves. He felt that unfulfilled lower needs inhibit our search for higher meaning and fulfillment of our potential.

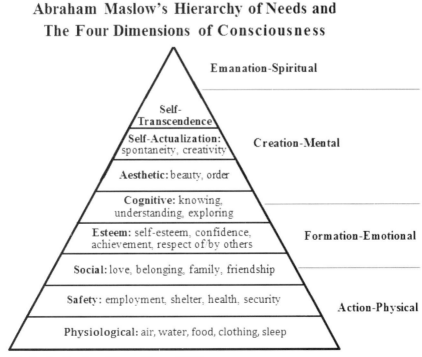

Abraham Maslow's Hierarchy of Needs and The Four Dimensions of Consciousness

The Farther Reaches of Human Nature (1971)

Maslow recognized some of the characteristics of more *self-actualized* people, including: the ability to focus on problems outside of themselves, spontaneous creativity, a clear sense of what's genuine, and less focus on social norms.[7] He spoke of the basic goodness of people, and saw "evil" behavior as a secondary reaction to human frustration. His thinking gave rise to other important therapies, including the client-centered work of Carl Rogers. Even though Maslow's list is linear, it's important to see that as we work on the ego and examine areas of arrested development in our psyche, we're more able to live from our highest/deepest selves.

Hungarian physician Margaret Schönberger Mahler turned from pediatrics to psychiatry, becoming an essential figure in the world of psychoanalysis and normal childhood development. Mahler's interest in the developing ego centered on object relationships, and how children arrive at the self. She examined the process by which an infant acquires his or her identity as separate from the primary caretaker. Her conscientious documentation of the mother-infant dyad, and her concern with the impact of early separation between children and mothers, led to her important contribution, *separation-individuation.*[8]

Mahler's work on Object Relations Theory demonstrated that people are formed and motivated by relationships, with an emphasis on how interpersonal relationships become internalized within the ego or self, and not just by Freud's internal biological drives or the need to discharge tension. In Object Relations, intra-psychic, interpersonal, and group experiences are the building blocks of an individual's identity. Our interpretation of these relationships—both conscious and unconscious—becomes the foundation for future friendships, marriage, and raising a family.

When we know our object-relations, we can better navigate our personal relationships. We'll go into more detail later, but have you noticed how your friends may have similar traits? Have you noticed how your partner can trigger your childhood issues? We're attracted to some of the good and bad qualities of our original caretakers. This attraction is nature's way of helping us grow and heal toward more wholeness.

Mahler named the process by which we acquire internal maps of self and others "separation-individuation." It's the template for our relationships with people and other aspects of our lives. These maps, or internal representations, are built up through interactions with our caregivers. In the development from birth to 3 years of age, we take in both the positive and negative aspects of relationship. You've heard of the terrible twos, when a child's favorite word is *No!* This is a child's attempt to find a self, a dynamic revisited in the teenage years. We all move in and out of aspects of individuation, or self-identity, throughout our lifetime. It's part of growing and changing. We can heal our ego enough to better navigate the frustration and pleasure within our relationships. This leads to a consistent sense of self that can tolerate shifting emotions and conditions in ourselves and others.

As we grow toward individuation and self-identity, we develop a sense for how close we can get to others, and what *we* think, not expecting or allowing others to think for us. We learn to stand up for ourselves and our rights—a dynamic also called *boundaries.*

A boundary is a limit, border, edge, or guideline that promotes integrity and defines where you end and others begin, allowing you to take better care of yourself. It's usually looked at as the amount of physical and emotional space between you and another. Creating boundaries and limits helps you hold and appropriately share your feelings, thoughts, and actions. They also help you make choices about what you will and will not accept from others. Healthy personal boundaries aren't inadequate, rigid, or fixed. They can be semi-permeable and flexible when you need or want them to be. According to author Nina Brown, EdD, there are four main types of psychological boundaries:

1. Soft—People merge with others and are easily manipulated.
2. Spongy—People fluctuate between soft and rigid, and aren't sure what to let in or keep out.
3. Rigid—People keep themselves walled-off and closed-down.
4. Flexible (the ideal)—People can evaluate situations and choose what feels appropriate to let in or keep out, and are difficult to exploit.[9]

For example, relationships need space and personal boundaries, so you can be yourself and connect with others. Sometimes setting a boundary by saying no can be strong and kind at the same time. Life becomes fuller, richer, and more relaxed when your boundaries are clear.

Here are examples of boundaries in the four dimensions.

- **Physical boundaries** involve your body, your personal space, and personal items (money, clothes, home, noise, mail), and choosing who can and cannot touch you.

- **Emotional boundaries** help create an internal sense of safety, protect us from manipulation (guilt, shame) by others, separate your feelings from others' feelings, keep you from taking too much responsibility or not enough, and won't tolerate unacceptable treatment from others.

- **Mental boundaries** allow you to have your own thoughts and opinions, and make decisions based on your beliefs.

- **Energetic boundaries** don't let anyone cross the line with their energy.

- • **Spiritual boundaries** help you distinguish and discern your will from the deep still voice within and higher/deeper Wisdom.

Sometimes it's hard to distinguish all the subtleties in navigating your personal limits and boundaries, which are informed by your upbringing and culture. By setting healthy limits and boundaries, you'll have more intimacy and fulfill your potential physically, emotionally, mentally, and spiritually.

British Object Relations theorist Donald Woods Winnicott is known for his work with the true self and false self. His true self equates more closely with what I'm calling the real self. Winnicott envisioned the ego taking shape through the baby's experiences of perceived, primitive threats to its survival, in which there is recovery. Recovery happens as the result of what he called "good enough" mothering, allowing the child to develop a "continuity of being." This is achieved when a reasonably attuned caregiver, or an "ordinarily devoted" mother, protects the baby from experiencing overwhelming extremes of discomfort and distress too often, whether emotional or physical. If the baby needs to repeatedly defend against an unsafe or overwhelming environment, his personality is formed by reacting to the "environmental impingement." He feels like his house is built on sand; the world is unsafe, and hard to be in. This promotes a split-off false sense of self that the child relies upon to create an experience of safety through what Winnicott spoke of as "compliance" and people-pleasing. This leaves no room inside the person for reasonably spontaneous expressions of one's own feelings, gestures, and ideas.[10]

Winnicott helped us understand how an infant transitions from undifferentiated unity to independence, realizing Mother is a separate person. This is how we know ourselves as individuals who can connect to our deeper self, others, and society as a whole. Otherwise, we might think we're in Oneness or unified consciousness when we're actually pre-egoic, or in pre-personal, oceanic oneness. Some spiritual seekers are confused by the differences between their pre-egoic, pseudo-oneness experiences and a more mature Oneness. There's a sense of undifferentiated unity and oceanic free-floating bliss that has a kind of selflessness that comes in the infantile state, before the ego develops. It's different from the experience of Oneness of an integrated, advanced spiritual state. I've heard many people suggest we should learn from babies in their pre-egoic state, because they have all the answers. However, their "oneness" depends upon being regulated by another person, hopefully a tuned-in caretaker.

For a spiritual seeker, seeing oceanic oneness as an answer to the spiritual search is a bypass of the difficulties of a full, adult life, and impedes spiritual growth. Bypassing is more common than you might think, but this kind of union with the Divine is a symbiotic, merged, and undifferentiated union that doesn't acknowledge or accept troubling human emotions, as if we could wish it all away.

When we're in this distortion, we can defend against the troubling feeling in a number of ways. We might replace a difficult feeling with its opposite, believing all we need to do is think positively. Or, we induce a state of numbness to escape the bad feeling. For instance, a person who deals with anger unconsciously by denying it, acting sweetly, or acting it out inappropriately (for example, by punching someone) is a person who remains in defense of the feeling. She's not facing the fear, sadness, or other feelings present. Another example is someone using drugs, alcohol, sex, or even yoga or spiritual practices to distance himself from difficult feelings. We'll talk more about this in Chapter 9.

Lastly, child development psychologist John Bowlby pioneered Attachment Theory.[11] Whereas many before him emphasized a child's fantasies, Bowlby explored the history of the relationship between child and mother. Similar to Winnicott, Bowlby looked at patterns occurring in times of the infant's perceived distress, and the response of the caregiver to the infant. These habitual parental responses lead to an imprint of attachment, ultimately influencing that infant in adult life with an "internal working model." This model of attachment creates a blueprint of feelings, thoughts, and relationships throughout a person's life. If the caregivers were sensitive, responsive, and consistent for many years, a "secure base" is developed, fertile ground for the child to explore life and flourish into a healthy adult. Later, another developmental psychologist, Mary Ainsworth, furthered this theory with four attachment styles in infants that carry forward to adulthood: secure, insecure-avoidant, insecure-ambivalent, and disorganized.

There are many more theories and great people that could be included in this section but it's only meant to be a taste of how the ego is formed.

Energy Psychology

*Your freedom is already here and now, resting just
beneath the surface of your emotions.*

—Hale Dwoskin

The former director of the Cardiovascular Institute at New York's Columbia University Medical Center, Dr. Mehmet Oz, a renowned surgeon, respected author, and Emmy Award–winning host of *The Dr. Oz Show*, announced on *The Oprah Winfrey Show* in 2007 that "the next big frontier in medicine is energy medicine."[12] Energy Psychology is a subsidiary of Energy Medicine, and combines the science of psychology with subtle energies. Even though this relatively new field employs the principles of quantum mechanics, much of it is based upon ancient wisdom. To some it means applying certain bioenergy solutions to the body's subtle energy systems, using tapping, movement, or releasing words to address specific psychological problems, or any difficult sensations, feelings, thoughts, or beliefs that arise. These techniques can be used to relieve stress, anxiety, depression, phobias, PTSD, traumas, fear of public speaking, and physical problems including IBS, headaches, muscle tension, and others. It also supports performance enhancement, whether for school, sports, or work.

When someone has done the work of becoming more conscious of his or her thoughts and feelings around a specific issue, in the right moment using one or more of these modalities to work with and move subtle energies can be a powerful transformational strategy. Keep in mind that experiencing your feelings, crying, and talking are also ways of moving and shifting subtle energy.

Energy Psychology addresses the energetic underpinnings of stuck issues, illness, or anything we experience as a difficulty in our lives. Intentionally activating your body's energetic systems while consciously processing something can be exactly what's needed to neutralize a difficult memory, changing body chemistry and re-patterning the brain.

Some ways to work with subtle energy in the realms of Energy Psychology and Energy Medicine are:

- Eye Movement Desensitization and Reprocessing (EMDR)
- The Sedona Method
- Hypnotherapy
- Thought Field Therapy
- Tapas Acupressure Technique
- Guided imagery
- Energy Healing
- Therapeutic Touch
- Emotional Freedom Technique (EFT)
- Nondual Kabbalistic Healing
- Reiki
- Matrix Energetics
- Chi Gong
- Acupuncture
- Homeopathy
- Ayurveda

When we're deeply connected to our innate wisdom, there is a bio-electric or bio-energetic intelligence that pulls us toward our physical, emotional, mental, and spiritual wholeness. Being grounded in our awareness in all Four Dimensions of Consciousness helps us create health and well-being. Drawing upon this wisdom helps us learn how to work with subtle energies, giving us answers to important questions, and guidance regarding the choices we face every day as we follow our path.

Ego as Enemy: The Spiritual Approach

One may understand the cosmos, but never the ego;
the self is more distant than any star.

—G.K. Chesterton

Ego is the biggest enemy of humans.
—The Rig Veda

Although there are many different religious and spiritual approaches to the ego, there's often a common thread—the seeming demonization of the ego. Some people think of ego and spirituality as opposites: "ego-filled" versus "God-filled." This oppositional view could be a distortion of ideas from older spiritual traditions. Maybe psychology's relatively newer definition of the ego isn't used in current spiritual approaches. It could be a problem with semantics, as some see the ego as a childlike, pre-personal, misguided, and wounded sense of self. Maybe a good conversation between the two worlds would reveal more similarities in their interpretations.

When spiritual philosophies refer to the ego, they're often referring to a symbolic representation of the finite personal, rather than the psychological construct known as the ego. It seems that *ego* has become a catchall term referring to the difficult aspects of the personal, versus the vast transpersonal, impersonal, universal, spiritual, or Godlike characteristics. It's also thought of as our limited, human perspective versus enlightenment and God.

In this context, the ego is often spoken of in an exaggerated or negative light. It's often described as self-sabotaging, the enemy within, or self-absorption, even narcissism. It's demonized for representing the opposite, or enemy, of enlightenment. From this perspective, the ego needs to be released, transcended, or killed off. Here, the ego's journey is from self-centered to no-self, pre-egoic to transpersonal, skipping the psychological and personal all together.

For the sake of argument, let's say that those who teach that the ego is our enemy are right. As military strategists will tell you, it's important to know your enemy. It's important to know the way they think and maneuver, and what they value. You know the saying, "Keep your friends close and your enemies closer." Sit down with your ego. Have some tea. Take it to lunch. Every aspect of consciousness can teach us, and there's gold to mine in every aspect of you. Let your ego talk to you. Gaze into its eyes, and journal about it.

- *In what ways have you experienced your ego as a saboteur or enemy?*
- *What, if any, are the teachings of your spiritual path about the ego?*
- *In what ways have you experienced your ego in relation to your spirituality?*

> *We do not grow absolutely, chronologically. We grow sometimes in one dimension, and not in another; unevenly. We grow partially. We are relative. We are mature in one realm, childish in another. The past, present, and future mingle and pull us backward, forward, or fix us in the present. We are made up of layers, cells, constellations.*

—Anaïs Nin

Some spiritual approaches focus upon transcending our personal issues. This can create uneven personal and spiritual development. The problem with this uneven approach is it can lead to magical thinking that continues actively solidifying childhood programming and unproductive belief systems. It fosters an abhorrence of the ego, which, because the ego is an intrinsic part of who you are, creates hatred of your own humanity, leading to the only alternative within this system: *spiritual bypass.* This misinterpreted, undifferentiated unity is an attempt to replace pain and escape difficult feelings with an immature sense of spiritual oneness, or what Ken Wilber refers to as the "Pre-Trans Fallacy."[13] Bypassing our personal or spiritual work won't get us where we'd like to go. In fact, we genuinely progress on the spiritual path by welcoming fears and enemies, or what Carl Jung referred to as our shadow, which we'll talk more about later in this chapter. Personal process work and spiritual practice cannot be separated. Both are necessary for genuine progress and integration on the spiritual path.

When we tolerate only one side of the coin, valuing the impersonal above the personal, transcendence above embodiment, and emptiness above form, we cannot truly live in wholeness. As long as we keep anything the enemy, or the "other," we live in a split consciousness that keeps us in "either/or" or "this-or-that." Keeping parts of ourselves and the world as arch rivals, we continue black-and-white thinking and will not find the peace or wholeness we seek.

Viewing the ego as the enemy, as something you have to push away or annihilate, keeps the psyche split into disparate pieces, and it's confusing. This ultimately gives the ego more power. Those unclaimed parts will eventually rear their heads. When I say to you, *Don't think of a pink elephant*, the first thing you think of is a pink elephant. Getting rid of any part of you doesn't work. It just splits off a part that comes back to bite you. Be willing to examine everything in your inner ego work, whether through psychotherapy, spiritual practice, or however you seek guidance.

Author and psychologist John Welwood says, "When we are spiritually bypassing, we often use the goal of awakening or liberation to rationalize what I call premature transcendence: trying to rise above the raw and messy side of our humanness before we have fully faced and made peace with it."[14] We then mistakenly think there's some transcendence on a mountaintop somewhere that's the answer to our difficult feelings, relationship problems, and psychological issues. Welwood also suggests that if we dismiss our human needs as just "attachments," we create more trouble for ourselves and our lives. This viewpoint won't lead to a deep, mature, embodied transcendence but keeps us caught in our childhood programming. The ego is *not* the True Self, but it helps open the door to deeper movement within us.

From the spiritual point of view, we observe the ego from a larger context. That larger context is observing all that's happening and not happening; ultimately, awareness itself, not only the contents. From this larger view, we can increasingly see things more as they are. We see our bodies as necessary, and our egos as helpful, and we recognize the limitations of both. However, if we have a pseudo-spiritual view because we're bypassing, we won't see the other layers of the self and our lives will not be as rich.

Eckhart Tolle talks about the "pain body" and how we identify with our emotional pain and our thinking. In his view, our sense of self comes from this identification, and by shifting ourselves out of psychological time we bring ourselves into the Now.[15] Wholeness, silence, and Grace are continually available. We know that what Carl Jung called the "collective consciousness" is constant, and what Rupert Sheldrake called the "morphic field" opens us to quantum leaps in consciousness. It's very important to know that you can embody your birthright at any time, and wholeness, peace, and happiness are only a breath away. Take a deep breath and feel that in your body, now.

As you read inspiring books, learn from great teachers, meditate, and pray, you'll feel this deeper state in your body. Yet how do you move toward having a steady state of deep connection and compassion? How do you stabilize it? Spiritual practice is one way and doing our psychological historical work is another.

In my many years of practice as a psychotherapist, I've noticed that as we explore the pain from our past, allowing the feelings to be identified and belief systems to be unraveled, we start to see through our own act. We loosen the attachment or identification with the story of who we think we are. Our deeper self, higher self, or essence is always woven throughout our story, but sometimes we miss it. It's often buried in the story and we have trouble accessing it. We end up thinking we're a small constellation of ideas, beliefs, and feelings, unaware we're much more.

> Choosing *not* to pay attention to your ego creates a life run by all that unconscious stuff you don't want to take the time to see.

The less you get to know this constellation of mental structures, the more tightly you hold on to your identification as the small-"s" self, get run around by the ego, and experience pain. As you continue to peel away the layers of the false self, the easier it is to live from the big-"S" Self.

I've heard people say, "I don't want to take the time to do all this work. I'm fine the way I am." On one level this may be absolutely true, but are you achieving your greatest desires and living from your deepest self? Are you truly happy, or are you settling for less?

EXERCISE: PERSONAL IDENTITY

Let's look at some of the ways you identify yourself. Complete these statements as quickly as you can, as many times as you can:

*I'm the kind of person who*_____.

I am _____.

Notice what you wrote and any feelings or thoughts that come from that.

Ego as Friend: The Integration Approach

> *Psychological development beyond ego is not a loss of ego, but transcendence of the verbal ego-mind and the existential self in a more inclusive, higher order integration....*
> —Frances Vaughn

While psychology asks us to heal our ego, and spirituality asks us to eliminate or transcend it, the Ultimate Life Plan approach guides us towards an integrated ego that's both psychologically healthy and at one with the Divine, because our personal identity and spiritual nature are two different ways of looking at the same thing. The integrated approach values the ego as a sacred aspect of our being, and as the doorway to wholeness. Yes, the ego is mediating and directing our individual physical focus, but it's also the receiver and observer of our inner perceptions. When we take on the task of healing and integrating it, the ego can correlate information from many sources, helping us walk the conscious path. Healing the wounded ego allows us to surrender into the oneness of life, the larger paradigm that holds all of us. It softens and melts our rigid stance.

So, here, the ego's journey is from wounded ego to *both* personal high self-esteem and no-self. An integrated ego is both the wave and the ocean—individual in expression, and an indivisible part of the whole.

In the 1950s there were a few psychiatrists and psychologists who started to question the status quo in Western psychology. They recognized the inherent limitations, and saw the need to include ideas, methods, insights, and teachings from the great spiritual traditions. In 1967, Abraham Maslow, Anthony Sutitch, Stanislav Grof, and others founded what became the *Journal of Transpersonal Psychology.*[16]

The transpersonal perspective integrated Western psychology and religious teachings. Its focus expanded to view human consciousness as a larger spectrum of consciousness. Other philosophers and mental health experts believed the human bandwidth included developmental psychology; self psychology; object-relations; psychodynamic psychology; and the deeper/higher, subtler stages of growth in the spiritual realm. Incorporating experiences related to reliving birth trauma, death stages, rites of passage, Shamanic realms, and transpersonal realms allowed for a depth and breadth available only in a few spiritual studies before. Scholars such as Ken Wilber, Jack Engler, Daniel Brown, Roberto Assagioli, Charles Tart, Michael Washburn, and others added valuable information.

The quickest way to begin integrating the ego is not only to make peace with it, but also to befriend your ego as a part of you. Cultivate a relationship with it—study it, get to know it, ask questions, and listen to the memories and messages it wants to impart. This way, there is no attempt to transcend the ego; rather, it's seen as incomplete and finds its rightful place. As the ego is integrated into the wholeness of who you are, you relax and can live life more fully. It naturally recedes from the foreground of your experience,

When you approach your ego with compassion and a deep desire to understand it—to understand yourself—your ego reveals its true nature.

melting into the True Self—that integrated state of being in which you experience both individuality and oneness.

Your ego is an integral part of who you are. When you fear it, you fear yourself. When you hate it, you hate yourself. That's why you can never kill your ego; taking it to lunch is the wiser choice. Welcoming your ego is your path to wholeness. It enables you to become all that you came here to be, to reach your full potential, and to relax, have some fun, and truly appreciate yourself along the way.

So your work is to deeply know your own unique combination of memories, belief systems, and inflexible, entrenched patterns. This overall patterning, or constellation of mental structures of the self within you, was organized through the processes of: introjections (internalizing your experience), identification, integration, and synthesis. The more you investigate, understand, process, and assimilate your fixated ego structures, the looser they become, and the easier it is to live from the eternal True Self.

Because most us are not completely integrated, we live in some version of the false self we spoke of earlier. The aim of our false self is to apply defensive survival strategies, avoid dealing with our real thoughts and feelings, and sidestep whatever feels like too much for our internal structure. Part of us wants to maintain our perceptions of life, keeping the same reality even if it's not working.

As long as you keep the ego at arm's length—whether out of fear, judgment, being under-informed, or lacking self-trust—you will never truly know yourself and become whole.

John Welwood says, "Spiritual practices often bypass, and thus fail to transform, the conditioned patterns and unconscious identities that arise from our personal history. Yet when we bring psychological and spiritual work together, then each approach can complement and enhance the other, creating a new synergy that increases the growth potentials in each."[17]

High-quality psychological and spiritual work, sometimes called *purification*, isn't done to attain some unreachable perfection, but to continue your growth toward more relaxation, and the ability to live with more peace, happiness, and freedom. When you notice that you're shut down, avoiding or acting out your feelings, and you see all the layers of truth, the darkness and ignorance become illuminated, opening you to all that's in you. You're actually re-patterning or re-wiring the psyche. This is how you rewrite your story.

Jalal ad-Din Muhammad Rumi, a 13th-century Sunni Islamic poet and mystic, said, "Everyone sees the unseen in proportion to the clarity of his heart, and that depends upon how much he has polished it. Whoever has polished it more sees more—more unseen forms become manifest to him."[18]

MEDITATION: HELP WITH EGO INTEGRATION

Deep breath. For a moment imagine all the parts of yourself you wish would change. As you continue breathing, name as many things as you don't like about yourself as you can. Keep breathing. Now just for a moment, allow yourself to assemble all those disliked and disowned pieces, placing them in front of you. Another deep breath, and let yourself be with them a moment. There they all are in front of you. How do you feel as you see them there? What thoughts do you have? Allow them to be, as best you can, for now. Notice what happens. If you can and it feels right for you, send compassion to all these disliked characteristics and personality traits. Remember, most of them were your coping strategies as a child. Another breath, and spend a few more minutes being with this before you continue.

Asking Your Ego to Lunch

There is psychological and spiritual work to be done, and it's your path to freedom. Whenever you experience discomfort in your life, often something from your past is being triggered. If you explore the pain arising in that moment, and see it's from the past, you'll eventually see beyond your everyday limitations. The alternative is to continue to be triggered, act out of your pain, and endlessly repeat the cycle. Until you address your past, it will keep rearing its painful head, asking for help and healing.

So, how do you continue to deal with and integrate the ego?

Start by noticing what's uncomfortable and feels unmet in you. If that doesn't seem possible, look at what doesn't work quite right in your life. This is the trail to follow. A persistent complaint is begging to be seen on a deeper level. Identify related thoughts and feelings surrounding it, and explore its origins to the earliest possible juncture. This is about clarity, not blame. Then, process what you've uncovered—write, journal, soothe yourself, or sit with it as best you can. If you find it's too much, notice what you do. Do you avoid, repress, dissociate, or shut down because of particular feelings or thoughts? Do your best to allow everything to be present consciously in your body and mind, and then see what happens. Stay open to the moment.

As you begin what could be called disassembling, or facing and freeing the ego, it might feel like annihilation, as though somehow you'll no longer exist. From one angle, we could say the annihilation of the ego is similar to integration. However, courageously following this path opens you to experience deeper parts of yourself, both psychologically and spiritually, than you might ever have imagined.

> ### Meditation: Self-Soothing and Kindness
>
> *Deep breath. Feel your breath in your body. Take a few moments to be kind to yourself, whatever that looks like to you right now. Stay here as long as you like before you move on.*

Welcoming the Shadow Self (The Shadow Knows)

Integration requires a willingness to see all that's present, at any given moment. In shining the light of consciousness on us, some of what we encounter is known to us and some is not. As we examine the contents of the ego, challenging the false self, we open the door to what's hidden in us. This is your Shadow Self, and includes everything hidden, silent, or scared in you. Like the ego, the shadow has gotten somewhat of a bad rap. Some people consider the shadow the negative side of a person. Robert A. Johnson adds to that, calling it "the despised quarter of our being."[19] The shadow contains *all* that is hidden to us.

Carl Jung introduced the concept of Shadow Self, which is often referred to as "the dark side of human nature."[20] Yet *dark*, in this case, doesn't mean evil or bad; it simply means hidden from view. The shadow is any unconscious, unprocessed, undeveloped, unexpressed, repressed, or denied part of you. What lives in your shadow can just as easily be a positive aspect of your being you've been too afraid to express, as it can be a painful feeling you're trying to avoid, or a difficult aspect of your being that you're ashamed to admit lives within you. There is much power in unearthing this material. For some folks it's anger, for others it's a hidden tenderness, and for others still, it's their authority and power.

Robert A. Johnson says, "Only awareness of your shadow qualities can help you to find an appropriate place for your unredeemed darkness and thereby create a more satisfying experience. To not do this work is to remain trapped in the loneliness, anxiety, and dualistic limits of the ego instead of awakening to your higher calling."[21]

Working with your shadow sometimes feels like the psychological equivalent of Shamanic soul retrieval. Once you've worked with the pain or fear, it's a pleasure to have the pieces back. Author Debbie Ford says, "Once befriended, our shadow becomes a divine map that—when properly read and followed—reconnects us to the life that we were meant to live and the people we were meant to be."[22]

If the ego contains our ideas, thoughts, and feelings about ourselves, what do we do with that? Clients have said to me, "So now that I see from my shadow that I feel angry, what do I do with it? Do I repress it or act it out? Should I tell those people off? Should I yell at them? How do I get rid of these feelings?"

Here's the answer:

1. Learn to identify your feelings and name them to get them out of the wordless, limbic brain only. You do this to bring the information to the frontal lobe to work with it from your adult faculties.

2. Understand the origin of these feelings from the earliest memory you can.

3. Process them—talk about them if you need to, cry about the story, and learn to soothe yourself as the adult talking to your child self.

4. Allow it to be present in your body and mind, see what happens.

This process helps begin deeper work on the ego. Repressing your feelings, or flailing them onto others, doesn't do the job.

EXERCISE: YOUR SHADOW

Deep breath. Let yourself think about the following questions.

- *What positive characteristics or parts of yourself are hard for you to claim? Why?*

- *What negative characteristics or parts of yourself are hard for you to claim? Why?*

- *Whom do you think of from your past when you think of your positive shadow parts?*

- *Whom do you think of from your past when you think of your negative shadow parts?*

- *What are the feelings that come up for you around your shadow?*

- *How do these feelings remind you of your past?*

After Enlightenment, Then What?

As you move more deeply into transformation, you welcome your fears and enemies. In the traditional story of the Buddha's enlightenment, he meets Mara, the Lord of Illusion or devil, under a tree. Mara tries to tempt Buddha back to worldliness, but it doesn't work. Buddha faces the devil. Psychologically speaking, this is an example of facing what's there. If I'm in a state of anger or attachment,

I'm limited and trapped, caught in one of Mara's snares. Mara is always around, whispering in our ears and challenging our capacity to realize our values and goals, but she also helps us continue to see what blocks our way in life. Personal process work, spiritual practice, and awakening can't be separated. It's all one thing.

We must thoroughly explore both directions. Healing the ego is a lifelong pursuit, as is spiritual practice. A productive spiritual practice can loosen the knots of both psychological imprinting and Karma. Christian mystic St. Teresa of Avila wrote about wrestling with her ego when she advises you must face all the mental obstacles as they arise in order to break through into mystical consciousness. She urges people "To have courage for whatever comes in life—everything lies in that."[23]

- *So what is your biggest encounter with Mara? How have you stared your greatest obstacles and fears in the face?*
- *What did you see, hear? What was there? What did you do?*
- *What are the ways your limitations seem to keep you safe?*
- *What is it you're trying to avoid in your life?*
- *What is your most dreaded feeling?*

What Lies Beneath the Ego

To start unraveling these internal, fixed maps of our false self and internal representations, we need to better understand what Christian theologian Paul Johannes Tillich called the "ground of our being."[24] Teacher and author Andrew Cohen says, "The ground of being is empty of everything. It's an objectless, space-less, timeless, thoughtless void. But everything that exists has come from this no-place, including you and me. This empty ground that we all emerged from is the womb of the entire universe."[25]

It's important to understand that the context from which the ego arises is the true, eternal self—our essence. It's referred to as nothingness, no-self, or Jung's collective unconscious. It's the infinite, background source, often unnoticed in our ordinary lives, and the ground on which we stand. It can be called the nameless one, YHVH, God, Allah, the heart, compassion, or love. Author and Professor Michael Washburn says that the Dynamic Ground serves as the fuel, activator, and enhancer, and is the source of psychic energy.[26]

As we covered in Chapter 2, *essence* comes from the Latin word meaning "to be," and is the deep, eternal, and primary part of you. Nothing can lose its essence and still exist. Your essential fundamental nature, or essence, is unchangeable, eternal, timeless, and wordless, and is your deepest connection with Spirit, or God, or Beingness itself

Sufi teacher Kabir Helminski says, "Only Love can tame the ego and bring it into the service of Love."[27] Feel that quote in your body for a moment before you move on.

Living in Unity, Ego and All

Ultimately, from the most profound level of consciousness, all is One. Once the "self" or "ego" has found its place, you're no longer controlled by the feelings and thoughts that come and go, but rather you can view them as part of the totality of you. You own who you are as an individual, and feel embedded in God, Spirit, or the Universe. You'll feel no need to protect yourself by controlling other people, and you won't feel compelled to practice self-denial, or subjugate yourself to someone else out of idealization or desperation.

As you integrate your ego, you'll become less defensive. You can be attacked without reacting. You're not a doormat; you can choose how to act without reacting to life. Self-protection diminishes. You've nothing to prove. You'll see through the actions of others with compassion, and you'll naturally feel more relaxed. As your essence shines through, it lightens the density of the ego. The more flexible we are, the more our inner wisdom and soul movement leads us.

We don't transcend our integrated ego. There's no need to. What we transcend are the representations and ideas revealed to be incomplete pictures of who we are. We welcome the cultivation of an empty mind, yet thoughts are not the enemy. We feel less desperate and aren't grasping at life. We're empowered and relaxed by seeing our feelings aren't facts.

Surrender is not an act of defeat—it's embracing what is; it's meeting life as presented; it's becoming whole. To live in the moment is to be with the sensations of your thoughts and feelings, but without their history, without your story, and with less of the ego's attachment to what it all seems to mean.

Wholeness is a balancing act. It's addressing discomfort and processing unresolved psychological constructs. It's individuating while surrendering into that larger sense of knowing, which you can access when you're not focused upon all the intricacies of the stories you tell yourself, about...everything! You don't have to let go of your stories, your attachments; you just need to be with them, see them, feel them, and sit with them—all of them. Even your positive attachments are to be questioned and released, because they too keep you from your deepest freedom. Facing your attachments initiates the process of freeing them, of freeing you, of living in freedom. Some work may be required, but not as much as you fear.

Integration is an ongoing process, not a one-time event. The good news is that as you get more practiced at addressing discomforts and attachments, you get faster and more efficient at facing and freeing them. As a result, you're more peaceful when an issue arises, and you acknowledge it faster. Every time you address your thoughts and feelings, you free up another Strand within yourself, relaxing you into your essence.

Buddhist teacher Jack Kornfield wrote, "When we truly sense this inner connectedness and the emptiness out of which all being arises, we find liberation and a spacious joy. Discovering emptiness brings a lightness of heart, a flexibility, and an ease that rests in all things. The more solidly we grasp our identity, the more solid our problems become."[28]

A.H. Almaas says, "From the perspective of unity, there is no such thing as dying, nor of being reborn. There is no such thing as ego death, and no such thing as enlightenment either, since you're already the unity. This is the state of affairs all the time and always—before you develop an ego, when it is dissolving, and after you are dissolved. All those parts are the unity itself, and so you are not going anywhere."[29]

Recognizing Distractions and Developing Discernment: Knowing Your Wise Inner Voice

Wisdom is your perspective on life, your sense of balance,
your understanding of how the various parts and principles
apply and relate to each other. It embraces judgment, discernment,
comprehension. It is a gestalt or oneness, and integrated wholeness.

—Stephen R. Covey

It's easy to get caught up in the details of day-to-day life: picking up the dry cleaning, doing the dishes, going to the gym, answering the cell phone, baking your best friend's birthday cake, taking the kids to soccer practice, or going to work. The list is endless. We're constantly bombarded by outer stimulation and demands, keeping us busy doing what's right in front of us—so much so, we have trouble deciding what to do next. Then there are inner conflicts, not only our thoughts and feelings about these responsibilities, but also our internal responses to life as it unfolds. This keeps the mind as busy as the body.

You've spent some time thinking about living consciously, your personal programming, and the inner workings of your ego, and you have ways to progress in Your Ultimate Life Plan. So now that you're more aware of your thoughts and feelings, how do you gain clarity about all the information you receive in a day? As you've been answering the questions throughout this book so far, how do you know when the idea, hunch, or information received is right for you? How do you know what your goals are and how to reach them? How do you know what you need to do to move forward in your life?

As you do the work laid out for you in this book, you'll become more aware of your inner promptings: go here; listen to him; do this; don't do that. You'll open to layers of your being, connecting to an inner rudder of sorts. But how do you know if this inner *voice* or sense of guidance is your deeper self speaking its wisdom, or your unconscious childhood programming, or the voice of Aunt Matilda? Discerning the difference between an automatic response stemming from family beliefs, childhood distortions, or culture, and guidance from our connection with our higher/deeper self, makes life, success, and relationships so much easier.

You'll be able to live more spontaneously, and listen to your deeper self for day-to-day decisions as well as your long-term goals and longings.

So let's journey together to understand and experience different aspects of your wise inner voice and learn to help it grow stronger.

By *inner voice*, I'm not only referring to your thoughts and internal dialogue. Because your wise inner voice can originate from slightly different internal sources, it's known by many names:

- Intuition
- Inspiration
- Hunch
- Conscience
- Knowing
- Gut Instinct
- Inner Wisdom
- Higher Self
- Essence
- Divine Core
- The Still Small Voice
- The Universe
- Spirit
- God

It comes from an integral weave between your healthy self-esteem and personal wisdom, and your transpersonal connections, or that which is beyond the physical, yet embodied within it.

This voice "speaks" to you physically through your bodily sensations. It also communicates emotionally through your feelings, mentally as ideas, and spiritually through your intuition. Your inner voice prompts and prods you in a variety of ways, sometimes simultaneously.

Aspects of your inner voice that come from your wounding or programming are also known by many names:

- Childhood Programming
- Fear, Sadness, Grief, Shame, and other combinations of unconstructive thoughts and painful feelings
- Learned Habitual Response
- Automatic Interpretations
- Past Experiences
- "Shoulds"
- Addiction-Based Cravings or Compulsions
- Negative Beliefs
- Other People's Opinions and Beliefs

These inner *voices* stem from your personal historical woundings, rather than your essence or the True Self.

These aspects of your wounding or programming give you a narrow perspective, limiting your range of choices, which often makes life more challenging. These distractions, anywhere from subtle to grand, keep you from the truth of your being and the life you're meant to be living. Although these voices can feel difficult and don't usually steer you directly to your goals, when you're able to recognize and work with them, they can lead to profound healing and insight.

What does it take to hear your wise inner voice, your inner wisdom? It takes slowing down, getting quiet, and being attentive to what's going on inside you. Sounds simple, but it's not always as easy as it sounds. There's so much going on in our lives and the world around us, pulling our attention to an *outer* stimulus, which makes it difficult to hear our own wise inner voice.

How to Deal with Distractions

Distraction cannot be seen as distraction unless there
is some central focus to be distracted from.

—Henepola Gunaratana

Some distractions are easy to spot: for example, indulging in too much alcohol, food, or TV. Others are more subtle, such as keeping busy or compulsively checking your e-mail. You might have trouble understanding your boundaries when caring for family members, or you might feel responsible for the feelings of others. There are also seemingly helpful activities we use to avoid uncomfortable feelings, such as exercise or meditation. Only a high level of commitment to yourself will enable you to see whether this is true for you.

Demands from the *outside world* can feel as though they absolutely run your life. We all have so many "shoulds" and need-to-dos that we often feel overwhelmed, like we're in an acrobatic balancing act, struggling to live a life that meets even some of our needs. Author and Buddhist teacher Lama Surya Das says in his book, *Buddha Standard Time*, "Make time for your life.... Otherwise, life can just unroll like a crazy quilt before us and we miss the best part of the ride, the soaring, magic-carpet flight to realms of self-discovery, self-realization, and connection to all beings."[1]

It's sometimes possible to ground yourself, hear your deeper self, and connect to all beings through an outside experience. Many people reach this deeper consciousness through nature. You might be moved by a stunning sunset, ocean waves lapping on the beach, or a magnificent mountain range, providing expansiveness and peace. Your union with nature can even lead to a deeper connection with Reality and Oneness with the Universe. Sometimes, from this place, you can hear the voice of your inner wisdom easily. Some people find it helpful to meditate, attend workshops, read inspiring literature, or get one-on-one support.

- *What would slowing down look like for you?*
- *What kinds of distractions are you allowing that keep you from slowing down?*
- *What is your deepest longing saying to you, now?*

MEDITATION: SLOWING DOWN

Pause after each phrase and take your time with this.

Deep breath. Just notice the speed of your breath, and, if you can, consciously slow down the pace. Notice what happens. Now tune into the rhythm of your heartbeat, and be with that for a few minutes. Now, as best you can, allow it to slow a bit. Now notice the energy in your feet. Allow all tension to flow down through your feet and into the earth. Allow mother earth to receive it. Allow your body to find its best rhythm for right now. Sit with this for a few minutes.

Even if you're highly successful, accomplished in life, and can ground yourself with the beauty of nature, you're probably not as connected to your wise, inner voice as you could be. Life is infinitely capable of being richer and fuller. Even when you're stuck in traffic you can move closer to integration, happiness, peace, and compassion.

Think for a few moments about some of the ways you allow your everyday, ordinary, outside life distractions to keep you from deeper fulfillment. Ask yourself, "What is my 'inner' experience of the outside world?"

We can all relate to feeling desperate and grasping at "the answer" in our outside world. Entangling ourselves in outer demands and continually seeking outer fulfillment only leads to more of the same, resulting in greedy behavior and insatiable hunger. Lusting after sense pleasure and fulfillment only leads to more craving. If we're reaching for this to fill our emptiness, we're in for big disappointment.

There is so much about life to enjoy. Yet, if we think enjoyment comes from the outside only, we get into trouble. It's great to appreciate something fun and new like the latest shoes, the newest cell phone, and the new travel destination, but thinking we *need* the next "whatever" is not the ultimate answer to happiness. For some it can lead to addictive behaviors and desperate actions, trying to fill an intolerable inner emptiness. Of course, life is far more meaningful and satisfying than just "wine, women, and song," or, "sex, drugs, and rock and roll."

When your life centers on trying to find fulfillment in the outside world, it's easy to focus on competition, anger, ill will, and even hatred. This is the consciousness of scarcity, the fear there's not enough to go around, and the belief that "they" have our share of life. Doubt, fear, and jealousy can overwhelm us, giving way to complacency and mediocrity. Our restless minds don't even notice our inattention and distraction. It feels natural to us. We allow ourselves to buy the story of whatever our life tells us without questioning. In 12-Step groups this is called *stinkin' thinkin'*.[2] The way out is to see that this is simply another program that blocks our way to clarity and happiness.

It's easy to stay so busy, preoccupied, and distracted that you can't hear what's going on inside. Your childhood programming can distract you through fear, pulling your attention away from a writing task or making an important call. It can tempt you to e-mail a friend instead of finishing your work. Your old, learned habitual responses—often based on past experiences stemming from negative beliefs, family dysfunctions, societal "shoulds," and opinions of past authority figures—can keep you re-creating what you don't want. These ongoing unconscious personal "news feeds" recycle previous stories and endings that don't come from your highest choices. By slowing down and spending time inside, you'll be able to know that a "news feed" is a voice of distraction and not your deeper wisdom.

George was a freelance writer who came to see me because he was running himself ragged, and getting sick all the time. He loved what he did, and even though he always worked and did quite well, his childhood fear of poverty drove him to take every job that came his way. His unconscious fear of not having enough or not being good enough kept him repeating this pattern. He was afraid each job might be the last. In our work together, he learned to discern the voice of fear from the voice of his innate wisdom, which led him to make healthier choices. He now has even more success because he chooses the projects that are best for him.

Whatever personal work and spiritual practice you choose, try to recognize any distractions keeping you from your essence and the True Self. As a part of your practice, work to dismantle the distortions of your history and connect with a state of non-clinging, forgiving mindfulness regarding whatever's arising. This will help it pass like clouds in the sky...or waves in the ocean.

EXERCISE: RECOGNIZING YOUR STORIES

Notice the stories you tell yourself and complete the following statements as many times as you can.

What are the stories you tell yourself?

- *I'll never have _____.*
- *I'm not strong enough to _____.*
- *I'm not smart enough to _____.*
- *I can't because _____.*
- *I'm too unimportant to _____.*
- *I don't deserve _____ because _____.*
- *I'm so unlovable that _____.*
- *I'm powerless to _____.*

We all have an underground current of beliefs and stories running through our lives.

Processing Outer Stimuli

Along with your inner life, you have outer influences that appear to keep you flying around the same territory in endless circles. Life is a spiral journey, and you'll continually deepen your awareness of past associations, challenge assumptions, and move toward your essential self. Some say it's like an onion and we peel it a layer at a time.

Let's think about how we process outside stimuli.

Something happens, and we first process it with our physical senses: smell, taste, touch, sight, and hearing. Our perceptions are processed through our body, brain, and nervous system. Next, we bring this external stimulus into our systems of thoughts and feelings through the filter of our conditioning and childhood shaping. This process creates a *simulation* of the world and ourselves. We create our own personal realities and myths based upon our *automatic interpretations* of the world around us. We all hear and see things differently, depending upon our internal conditioning and in consort with our thoughts and feelings. Have you ever played Telephone? Someone whispers in your ear, you repeat it to the next person, and he or she repeats it to the next...until it becomes distorted, often completely different from the original message.

Sometimes, in the midst of those automatic interpretations, we don't know we're deciding something or reacting in a certain way. Perhaps we know something's off, but we're not sure what or why. Most of us don't stop and question this either. Unknown, internal, opposing voices cause tension and stress, yet we often don't notice or question what's going on inside of us. Most of us don't pay attention until we're in real discomfort or overwhelming physical, emotional, mental, or spiritual pain. Then, we don't know how to take care of ourselves.

If you don't experience most of your life as content, joyful, and fulfilled, you might be buying into the idea that fulfillment comes from outside. Many of us neglect our inner life, because we don't want to *dwell* on things, but in revisiting our challenges we work through another layer, freeing us a bit more. Remind yourself to turn your focus inward throughout the day. As you find and follow your feelings and thoughts, they'll unravel long-held identifications and beliefs, allowing you to drop into the greater Reality. Honestly confronting your darkest shadow-self is what leads you to authentic psychological and spiritual awareness, restoring you to wholeness.

As you observe your thoughts, listen and take note of what comes to you. Perhaps you notice you breathe easier, or your belly softens. When you hear advice, does it allow you to sink into a more integrated place? Do you see more possibilities? Does an idea feel complicated and tense, or does it feel simpler and relaxing? When you connect with your inner wisdom, you'll feel more peaceful and calm, even if the answer seems difficult to hear and execute. Your belly lets go and you release the gripping around your heart. Notice if there's a sense of relief. Ask if this relief is from relaxing into a deeper wisdom, or from avoidance and escape.

EXERCISE: CONNECTING TO WISDOM

Take a few moments to breathe and connect to yourself. Sit for a few minutes and watch your thoughts. Now, think of an idea or question you have. Breathe into that for a few minutes, and pay attention to your thoughts and feelings. As you're with your thoughts, listen and feel inside. Now notice which thoughts come to you that help you relax. Notice which thoughts help you slow down and feel open. What ideas help you breathe more deeply? Perhaps an entire plan shows itself to you. If so, observe what you feel in your body. What emotions arise? Notice any images or scenes you may see, or sounds you hear. Sit quietly for a few more minutes.

Internal Rhythms & Inner Distractions

Feel the rhythm of your life without anything to do—
the undercurrents, what goes on beneath all that activity.
—Gabrielle Roth

As you grow more aware of your inner life, you can follow your internal rhythms. These include physical rhythms, such as your heartbeat and circadian rhythms (your internal clock, the 24-hour cycle), your sleeping and eating patterns, and your in-and-out breath. They also include seasonal rhythms, thought patterns, the rise and fall of feelings, activity and stillness, sound and silence, and internal resonance and dissonance. You can see the balance of doing and being, introversion and extroversion. As you align with your natural rhythms, you'll feel harmonious, relaxed, and integrated. You'll notice your communication patterns, and discover the balance between listening and speaking. This inner rhythm helps you create more spaciousness and peace.

EXERCISE: EXPLORING YOUR INTERNAL RHYTHMS

Allow yourself to sit quietly and focus inside for 10 minutes and then answer the following questions.

- *In what ways can I reduce outside stimuli?*
- *How and when do I find my internal rhythms?*
- *What rhythms are more natural for me?*
- *When and how do I need to be quiet and listen?*
- *What am I listening for?*
- *How do I know my true inner voice?*
- *What do I hear inside of me, now?*
- *What do I feel, right now?*
- *What is my deepest longing, now?*

As you explore your internal rhythms from this dualistic point of view, knowing an inside and outside, be aware of the needs of both. Stay in an investigative mode, and pay attention as best you can. As you learn which of your needs seem consistent, you can plan weeks and months ahead with these needs in mind, connected to the twists and turns that happen in life as you grow and change.

Continuing your self-exploration, ask yourself:

- *What do I need in my life right now?*
- *How might that be different from yesterday?*
- *How much exercise do I need?*
- *What kinds of foods does my body need?*
- *How much meditation do I need?*
- *What are my deepest desires today?*

Concentration: Steady and Focused Attention

> *The stages of the Noble Path are: Right View, Right Thought, Right Speech, Right Behavior, Right Livelihood, Right Effort, Right Mindfulness and Right Concentration.*
>
> —Buddha

There are different levels and kinds of attention that take us to our knowing. Your focus will remain unstable unless you practice working with all levels of attention. Our mind is like the honey bee, randomly flitting from flower to flower. We're not clear what's grabbing our attention or why. We don't know how to create a steady life, and our ability to concentrate is stunted.

Stabilizing your attention requires the ability to concentrate. Good concentration helps you cook a meal, write a book, learn to dance, and achieve your dreams. Concentration helps you make choices, and balances the left brain's rational side with your right brain's "big picture" thinking. Developing your concentration helps focus and clarify your life, lengthen your attention span, and grow your aptitude for everything.

Concentration and focus not only help you achieve and accomplish your great destiny, but provide peace and harmony.

Strengthening your attentiveness clarifies your own unique path and harnesses your mind toward a connection with unified consciousness. Meditation, in its various forms, helps calm your *honey bee mind*. Lama Surya Das talks about the practice of concentrative meditation in his book, *Buddha Standard Time*: "As we train our awareness to focus on just one thing to the exclusion of all else, our capacity to pay attention overall becomes more refined, our attention span lengthens and we more easily manage to push distractions to the side and stay fixed on the object of our interest."[3]

Observing your own honey bee experience of flying flower to flower helps you work with the hundreds of thoughts passing by. Ordinary attention flickers and wanders around. It's reactive or passive, an autonomous stream of consciousness or stream of the subconscious mind. Some thoughts get caught in loops within our mind, like the fear loop of worry. As you cultivate awareness of thought, and of the stories behind your momentary trance states, you'll blossom into the wholeness of your birthright.

MEDITATION: CANDLE FLAME

Find a darkened room and comfortable place to meditate. Light a candle that's at eye level or slightly below, and spend time concentrating on the flame. You can do this a few ways:

1. *Before you start, set an intention of something you would like to be revealed. Then begin looking into the flame.*

2. *Start looking at the flame and see where it takes you—to what images, feelings, or body sensations.*

3. *Breathing in the light, let it permeate your body. Allow it to move through you, healing and purifying your body, emotions, mind, and spirit.*

4. *Staying focused on the flame, become the flame. Get absorbed into the flame, letting the image occupy your mind. If you become distracted, bring yourself back.*

5. *With eyes open look into the flame. When it feels right, close your eyes, allowing the image to remain in your mind's eye.*

6. *Notice the smell of the candle; allow the fragrance and light to move in and out of your body as you breathe.*

Buddhist teacher Jack Kornfield says, "As we develop the ability to concentrate, our steadiness and focus grow. We find ourselves able to be more fully present with our whole being."[4]

Developing Discernment

True guidance is subtle and considers everyone, and will always lead you to the high road of personal responsibility, spiritual growth, and integrity.
—Sonia Choquette

Having true happiness and fulfillment depends upon discerning truth from fantasy, and recognizing whether your needs and actions are based upon historical programming or present-day conscious choice. You'd think it would be obvious, but the spectrum of consciousness is filled with subtlety, paradox, and illusion. To recognize when you're living from your highest self—your essence—and when you're not, you must identify the many inner signals (or the source of this inner nudge) so you know what is reliable guidance and what needs further healing.

The answers are always within you. Discernment helps you differentiate between your true wisdom and under-informed guidance. At first it might seem subtle and vague, especially as you begin learning to distinguish the differences. You'll soon realize the inner voice that says you should drink or eat too much isn't your inner wisdom speaking. Also, that voice telling you to take a certain job, or follow a certain dream, might not come from your deepest self. In time, you'll cultivate discernment and choose what's right for you.

When you apply steady attention and listen to your wisdom, your life becomes easier in many ways. You'll minimize the internal strife—although this doesn't mean life is entirely easy. Your guidance may tell you to do something very hard for your personality. Part of you might want what it wants, whether it's good for you or not. How well you've been able to listen to your "gut" or inner voice in the past determines how much you might have to change your life once you start listening. If your life is off track, you may need to jump through a few hoops, substantially disrupting your current life.

You might get contradictory messages. For instance, when someone asks you to do something, your thoughts might agree but your stomach clenches and you feel dread. Your inner wisdom may be communicating to you through your physical and emotional reaction. The fear signal in your stomach may be warning you against this action, or your fear might stem from an old, limiting belief.

Although your inner voice might seem consistent—after all, it's the voice you hear inside you all day, every day—messages can come from either your wisdom or woundedness, your highest self or your unconscious programming, or a little of both. Keep in mind, when using the word *voice*, I mean your inner signals—physical, emotional, mental, and spiritual. Those signals can lead you directly or take a more circuitous route. Even when we make what we might think of as a wrong decision, leading to, let's say, divorce court, it might be an important life lesson that we needed. At the same time, learning to *know* when our wisdom is speaking helps us move quickly toward our goals and fulfill our destiny, without spending too much time on those lessons.

Your inner wisdom is constantly available to inform every aspect of your life, if you let it. It helps you make decisions and determine your direction. It helps you connect inwardly, live authentically, and be who you really are. This is why discernment is essential. You need to recognize the difference between your trustworthy, inner wise voice and your unconscious programming that needs to be questioned and worked with.

EXERCISE: DISCERNING YOUR INNER VOICE

If you're not sure whether that inner voice comes from your wisdom or wounding, these questions can help you discern which voice is "speaking" to you.

- *Do you feel empowered or disempowered when you receive the information?*
- *Do you feel any fear? If so, what is the fear about? Or do you feel spaciousness inside?*
- *How does it inspire you?*
- *How might you avoid your feelings and thoughts by doing something else or some addictive behavior?*
- *What are the feelings and thoughts that arise out of this information?*
- *What effect does it have on you?*
- *How might this information help you? Or help others?*
- *How might it not be helpful?*

Languages of Your Inner Voice

The methods of communication from both your inner wisdom and unconscious programming are similar. Both can feel true at times. When you are present, investigate, and are discerning, you'll know when your wisdom is talking. As you learn to understand your unique internal language, becoming more sensitive to things beyond your usual range of perception, you'll move to a deeper level of self-trust and self-knowledge.

It's your birthright to feel that inner connection guiding you, but exactly how this inner wisdom, guidance, gut, or intuition speaks is slightly different for everybody. Many ways of perceiving are available to us, and the more open we are to deeper levels of Reality, the more wisdom we have access to.

There are basically six languages plus additional tools:

1. Gut feelings or kinesthetic awareness
2. Auditory or hearing answers from inside with our thoughts
3. Mental images or seeing in the mind's eye
4. Directly knowing the answer
5. Sense of smell or taste
6. Connecting with guides and angels

You might have access to a few ways or all of them, but most find one or two languages easier to access. As with everything, the signs range from subtle to obvious, but the greater your connection to your higher self, the more you automatically open to these languages.

Let's now look at each of them in depth.

1: The first language is ***bodily sensations or kinesthetic awareness***. We've all had gut feelings from time to time. It doesn't have to be a sensation that occurs literally in the gut or stomach, but your body often gives you clues. I'm sure, at some point in your life, you've experienced a visceral response to something; a feeling in the pit of your stomach. What did it mean, exactly? This is why discernment is important. All feelings have their helpful teaching. Is the message saying that this is something to avoid for your own good? Is it a fear of something that would be good for you, or is it actual wisdom about what's happening?

Is it fear or wisdom? I remember trying my hand at real estate in my 20s, and feeling a gnawing in the pit of my stomach. I didn't understand it at first, but I finally figured out that real estate wasn't my path. I quit my job, and my gut sensations quit too.

With gut feelings coming from wisdom, you'll sense that a certain person, place, or direction feels right or wrong. You breathe more easily when something feels right. Your belly relaxes, even if it seems the answer will make your life harder, temporarily. All these sensations are your body's way of communicating bits of information, and you might feel different sensations as you continue to investigate. You might feel your heart opening or your throat closing as you consider an idea. This is called *clairsentience*; a clear, conscious feeling.

As your body awareness informs you, you might sense another's energy, or feel drawn to something without logical explanation. Your emotional intelligence can attune to others, allowing you to more easily empathize. You can probably feel when someone is sad, for example, even if he or she is smiling. Of course, it's best to ask someone how he or she feels, even if you perceive it differently, and respect his or her boundaries. First of all, even if you're great at sensing other people's feelings, in certain circumstances it can be invasive to announce what you notice.

Secondly, most of us aren't free of projections, so it's best to check out what you notice. And lastly, even if the person tells you no, you still might be right—but it's important to respect other people's boundaries.

If you're having trouble making a decision, you can use your body awareness to choose. Close your eyes and imagine following the path of each option available to you. Check in with your body, and notice the sensations you feel as you picture yourself walking down that particular road. You can see what feels good to you, and what doesn't. These feelings or emotions might give you clues about something that's not quite right or a decision you need to make. Just know that all of this can be subtle *or* obvious, and it helps to meet every emotion with awareness, openness, and curiosity.

2: The second language is ***auditory***—when you hear an answer inside of you. You might perceive sounds or questions or thoughts, however fleeting, that inform you about a situation at hand. You can develop keener listening with words and dialogue, giving you perspective or new ideas. It can come as a whisper in the shower, a thought that stands out in meditation, or something that occurs to you as you're driving. It's sometimes called *clairaudience*, or clear hearing and listening. Tuning into silence facilitates this capacity opening more fully. Taking this a bit further, some might say that we can tune into our guides, our relatives who have passed, or even God, when we are deeply listening. Keep in mind, thoughts from childhood programming seem so familiar that you can misperceive them as a wise answer.

3: The third language is ***mental images***—seeing through your mind's eye, or *clairvoyance*. This isn't just normal seeing, but "having insight" beyond our physical vision. You might receive an impression or image during meditation, while daydreaming, or in another unexpected way. An image can be a literal scene with all the right players in the right places, or you might be seeing something symbolic to you. As with dream images, your internal vision can be deciphered with practice. Some people have been known to see events before or after they happened, and some see into other people's bodies to assist with healing.

4: ***Direct knowing***, even when you're not sure how or why, is another language of your inner voice. It might feel like a sudden burst of inspiration, a vehicle for creative ideas and solutions, or just a calm sense of certainty. Direct knowing is recognizing the answer, completely, and in precise detail. You might know about something small, such as that open parking space around the corner, or you might get a complete picture of someone's health you've been asked about.

5: Here we have two languages, one accessed through your ***sense of smell***, or *clairalience*, and the other through your ***sense of taste***, or *clairgustance*. Memories are connected to smells and tastes, and sometimes in deep meditation specific aromas or tastes will arise with visual images.

6: Another language through which our inner wisdom speaks to us is through *angels* and **guides**. It's said the angels were uttered into being at the beginning of creation. The four dimensions each have different kinds and levels of angels. Most of you have heard about someone having an experience receiving help from an angel. It happens more than we might think. It helps if we spend time opening our connection to them.

We also have guidance from other non-physical beings. Some might help us find things, whereas others might help with specific problems. Still others are teachers, and we also have connections with master teachers. All of this is available for our support and learning. The more you connect to the whole of you, the more available you are to receive from these other realms.

MEDITATION: OPENING TO GUIDANCE

Spend five minutes breathing and relaxing your body. Ask to receive any information from these beings in the form of symbols, signs, words, visions, or any other way they would like to show you. You might ask specific questions or just open to what they might need to share with you.

Please download a longer meditation taking you to your guidance on my Website, *www.YourUltimateLifePlan.com*.

Connecting With Your Inner Wisdom

There are tools that can help take us to our inner wisdom, such as tarot cards, a pendulum, runes, and other methods that help get the ball rolling toward tapping into your intuition.

Automatic writing and applied kinesiology (muscle testing), for example, are potentially effective, but they're only as reliable as the tester's connection to his or her own intuition. Automatic writing is when you get into a meditative state and ask for guidance and just start writing without having thoughts come first. Applied kinesiology is used by practitioners on others, as well as for personal information. It's most often used to provide feedback on the functional status of different parts of the body by asking your body a question and using your muscles to signal *weak* or *strong* for an answer. It can be used with a *yes* or *no* for other kinds of questions, from, "Is this vitamin good for me?" or "Does my body want Brussels sprouts?" to "What highway will have less traffic today?"

Journaling is very helpful for tapping into your higher awareness. If you get a hunch about something, whatever your method of tapping into it, write it down in a journal. You can look back later and see if your sense was helpful or accurate. You might discover as you practice that you'll start knowing things before they happen or know how to take care of yourself in ways you never thought of before.

This all helps you connect with your inner wisdom. If you continue doing your personal work and your spiritual practice, you'll spontaneously open to more wisdom. Just know that this wisdom is speaking all the time—it's we who need to listen better.

Decoding Messages

As I said before, all information is received and filtered through our likes and dislikes. So it's important to practice, and pay attention to your results. It's helpful to observe patterns. Keeping a diary of what you receive and its accuracy helps you interpret your internal signals. For example, say you always think of your mother when you see a flower, and then later when you're visiting a friend you see a flower in your mind's eye. Is there a connection? You don't know if this means something about your mother or her mother, your children or her children; perhaps she might be pregnant; or it could mean something entirely different. With practice, you'll learn to decode messages such as these. Until then, it's difficult to understand what it might mean for you.

Throughout the years I've noticed a growing fascination with people who appear to have a gift that allows them to offer "life readings" for others: psychics. Although it's wonderful to sharpen your intuition and guidance leading you toward the True Self, attaining these gifts can become a trap for wounded egos who over-identify with these abilities, feeling special and important. It becomes another snare for us to navigate.

As you develop your connection to your inner voice and hone these skills, what's most important is your connection to your inner life; to your thoughts, feelings, and spirituality. I've seen people get caught up in phenomena—which can, indeed, be fascinating facts and events—however, they lose sight of the greatest gift. Our connection to God, Spirit, Silence, the Universe, or whatever your name for it, will take you into the deepest, most precious waters with a compassion never imagined. Focusing on *seeing* or *hearing* without deeper spiritual practice and personal development can keep you distracted or stuck at the same level of integration.

As you discern your inner voice and wisdom, integration happens in stages. Let's do an exercise to help you with this process.

EXERCISE: ACCESSING YOUR INNER WISDOM

Choose a problem that's currently in your life. I'm going to give you a series of questions to help you work with this problem.

1. *Feel into as many of your inner wisdom's languages as you can.*

2. *You want to be able to tease out these different sensations, thoughts, feelings, images, and stirrings clearly, so take a moment to feel into this problem. What are the various sensations, thoughts, feelings, images, and overall impressions you have about this problem? Take your time.*

3. *Perhaps you see the answer already. If so, you can skip these next steps, for now. If not, see if you can notice aspects of your inner voice that are holding different points of view. Allow those points of view to speak to each other. Voice one says _____. Voice two says _____. Let them talk back and forth and see what happens. Notice if you sense or experience any sensations, images, or flashes of insight along with the internal dialogue.*

4. *After they've talked back and forth, see how it all settles down. What are you hearing? What ideas or answers help you feel more settled inside? Be patient if you haven't settled into something yet.*

5. *Allow yourself to feel into all the ideas and into your body. What is the main part of this issue for you? Allow yourself to just get a sense of the entire issue. See if a word or phrase or image comes to mind, right now. Breathe into this. Notice what's happening.*

6. *Allow whatever's happening and notice your overall body sense. Allow the word or image you've noticed to be present. See if any answers arise.*

7. *Now write what comes to mind from here, without editing yourself.*

8. *Depending on how big this issue is, you might want to sit with this information for a while—a few hours or days—and see what else comes up.*

Personal Myths

If you don't want to live in illusion and distortion, your work is to question everything, including the conditioned aspects of your mind, driven by the desires and aversions of the moment. You want to see the distorted elements of your personal myths and stories for what they are: distortions. You'll learn to maintain steady awareness through practice, unravel the childhood and incarnational mis-understandings, and avoid the mesmerizing details of illusion and the confusion of secondary interpretations. You'll move beyond the unnecessary suffering held in these stories. You'll see your story for what it is: a story.

Think, for a moment, about your childhood or family stories that generate the unique overarching template creating your life.

EXERCISE: RECOGNIZING YOUR MYTHS

Think about the family you grew up in and answer the following questions.

- *Did your parents spend much time on their inner lives?*
- *Did Mom and Dad take time to reflect on themselves and life?*
- *Did your everyday conversations involve people expressing and naming their feelings?*
- *How was the rhythm of your inner life and outer life satisfying to you as a child?*
- *In what ways was your environment safe enough for you to relax?*
- *In what ways did you have space and time to play and wonder about life?*
- *What did your Mom say about life?*
- *What did your Dad say about life?*

Complete the following statements as thoroughly as you can:

- *I struggle having a more balanced life because _____.*
- *I'm not very clear about my needs because _____.*
- *What keeps me from making my life better is _____.*

Where Outer and Inner Meet

Your blocks to deeper wisdom are located in your subconscious, or uncon-scious, perceptual programming. In fractal geometry, we see the evidence of self-similar repetitive patterning. We see this in the patterns of tree branches or the tributaries of a river mirroring the river itself. If you're conscious of the repetition of ordered patterns in the world, you can empower yourself to be awake and aware, and pay attention to what is always at work underground and out of your awareness, not only in the world but also in yourself. This helps foster the changes you desire and attract the life you long for.

Your inner wisdom and outer experience will grow more closely together, and you'll more often be living from wisdom. As you grow in your connection with yourself, you'll connect more deeply with the world. Your wisdom breathes you and you naturally move toward more stillness.

In most spiritual disciplines, including Shamanism, Buddhism, Christianity, Judaism, Islam, and so many others, you see varying degrees of emphasis on negotiating an inside and an outside life. The deeper you go into becoming one with God, or enlightenment, the more you're drawn to the quiet, internal experience. As you continue your spiritual development, the distinction between inside and outside becomes a more unified experience.

As you grow, you'll require greater stillness to live authentically. Coming to experience inside and outside as one thing, the stillness and silence feed your soul. Your spiritual practice becomes your greatest source of pleasure and you naturally follow your destiny. Being your wisdom is being with the oneness of the universe.

There's a well-known Zen Buddhist proverb that goes, "Before enlightenment; chop wood, carry water. After enlightenment; chop wood, carry water."[5] Life doesn't change after enlightening experiences, but your perception of life and your attention to life changes. We do our psychological work and our spiritual practice, and we notice what's happening during our regular daily activities. You're aware of your surroundings as well as your thoughts and feelings. Otherwise, you compartmentalize life without integrating the full tapestry of experience and existence that is your true potential.

The Great Unifier

With time and practice, meditation or any contemplative exercise will take you from inattention to the deepest source of thought—existence itself. St. Thomas Aquinas taught that God is existence, and our thoughts and words about God are insufficient.[6] The teachings of Jesus tell us we're always in God's presence.

Author and Sufi teacher Kabir Helminski says that humans are suspended in the space where the physical outer world and the mysterious inner world meet.[7] When you turn away from the demands of the physical senses, as well as the field of conventional thoughts and emotions, you'll sense an inner world of spiritual qualities. We humans stand at the threshold between two worlds. Centering yourself, and all your attention, in the reality of Divine love can unify your fragmented being, reconnecting you with the unified field of all dimensions of existence. Submerge your thinking mind into your heart, unifying reason and feeling. In this state, you'll discover your deep receptivity to infinite, spiritual Presence. Ultimately, you'll know the truth of this statement from the Qur'an (2:115): "Wheresoever you look is the face of God."[8]

PART II

EXPLORING MULTI-LEVEL CONSCIOUSNESS

CHAPTER 6

Living a 4-D Life: Embracing the Four Dimensions of Consciousness

Indeed, to some extent, it has always been both necessary and proper for man, in his thinking, to divide things up, and to separate them, so as to reduce his problems to manageable proportions; for evidently, if in our practical technical work we tried to deal with the whole of reality all at once, we would be swamped.... However, when this mode of thought is applied more broadly to man's notion of himself and the whole world in which he lives (i.e. to his self-world view), then man ceases to regard the resultant divisions as merely useful or convenient and begins to see and experience himself and his world as actually constituted of separately existing fragments.... What is needed is a relativistic theory, to give up altogether the notion that the world is constituted of basic objects or building blocks. Rather, one has to view the world in terms of universal flux of events and processes.

—David Bohm

Existence is multidimensional. There are many dimensions or levels to our known physical world. Throughout the years, we've been discovering the microcomponents of our world down to quarks, the contents of atoms. We've also been exploring our vast outer space. In our physical world there is much we cannot see in an ordinary day, but we've learned through science that it exists. From the micro to the macro, much of what exists in our physical universe is not normally detectable.

Humans exist on many dimensions too. These dimensions can be described as grades or levels of consciousness. Some levels are involved in our ordinary day-to-day lives and are very familiar to us, while other levels aren't as easily seen and can be experienced as feelings, thoughts, and connections with energies beyond our visible world. There are many degrees and layers of these feelings and thoughts that we need to discover in order to create lasting change and greater happiness. There are many layers to discover in our spiritual world as well. We are multi-dimensional beings, and in psychological terms we know we're individuals leading separate lives, yet at the same time we're part of the whole of the Universe.

From the perspective of the whole, the world is connected and all one. From our usual human perspective, we have a body, we think thoughts, we have feelings, and we can either be connected to a higher source, or not. This linear way of thinking helps us tease out our knots, difficult fixations, and painful personal issues, from the least to the most uncomfortable. An example of this is the disappointment of not getting that promotion you wanted versus the devastation of losing a loved one.

Throughout the centuries, most of the spiritual and psychological traditions have spoken of our human existence in terms of levels. Recognizing that we're multi-dimensional beings, and understanding the levels in which we can thrive is how we make the lasting changes we've been longing for, and truly reach our innate human potentials. The Yogis, the Kabbalists, the Sufis, the Christian Mystics, the Native Americans, the Buddhists, and psychotherapists all have ways of helping us work with the levels of our humanity in order to reach these potentials.

Dimensions of Consciousness

"I cannot overemphasize how important it is to know how to discriminate between the different dimensions of who we are."
—Andrew Cohen

It helps to look at transformation in the context of dimensions of consciousness, in order to frame change in the workability of these distinctions. In many schools of thought, Reality is composed of many different yet continuous dimensions that reach from lower, narrower, and denser consciousness to higher, deeper, broader, and subtler consciousness. Different paradigms break it down differently. For instance, some paradigms use body, mind, and spirit, while others begin with matter, and then separate spirit and soul.

You might have heard people talk about the auric field. They speak about different levels of their personal energy field, which often corresponds to the chakra system. The word *chakra* is derived from a Sanskrit word meaning "wheel." These chakras, or energy centers, exist throughout the body providing a framework within which much healing can take place. Most texts speak of seven primary chakras, and some mention hundreds of secondary chakras. It's said that each has frequencies of vibration as well as colors, symbols, and sounds that can help support wellness.

Whereas the Chakra system, and other paradigms, are helpful in illustrating and understanding our subtle energy systems, our primary exploration will be of the four dimensions, their transformational possibilities, and their mindsets. Although some of this is modeled from the universes in various Kabbalistic texts, our journey together will be a synthesis of psychology, spirituality, and science. Although we'll examine these dimensions separately, keep in mind the goal is integration. And as you become more integrated you'll live in ever-increasing states of wholeness for longer periods of time, which will be reflected in your life as greater degrees of calmness and peace, more loving relationships, and the ability to handle whatever arises from an increasingly stable and grounded perspective.

These four dimensions help you more accurately perceive Reality in order to more easily transform your life. Very briefly, the four dimensions include: (1) the dense and linear **Action-Physical Dimension** of matter and duality; (2) the more fluid **Formation-Emotional Dimension**, where you explore feelings and find meaning; (3) the **Creation-Mental Dimension**, where you learn to explore your thoughts and beliefs; and finally (4) the most fluid of the dimensions, the **Emanation-Spiritual Dimension**, where you recognize the Oneness of all that is, as well as Infinite Nothingness. Together these Four Dimensions of Consciousness make up a map of Reality.

This way of viewing consciousness is a linear and hierarchical model, yet all of the four dimensions are infinite, meaning you don't grow out of one and progress completely to the next. In my experience, we don't ever completely grow out of embodying Reality, connecting to our body, or doing our psychological/historical work. We simply sink deeper, unearth more subtle levels of our humanity, and travel more deeply into these simultaneous aspects of Reality.

Working on your personal or psychological issues allows more and more subtle layers of your life to be seen. This continual commitment to being aware of your human journey brings you closer to Wholeness. As you grow into all that you came to be, you notice you're more congruent and hold longer periods of cohesiveness, meaning you're less agitated by life's problems. As you become more steadfast and durable, your life can contain more fun and play.

Dimensions of Consciousness	
Adam Kadmon, Ain Sof, Godhead Pure Presence, All-That-Is Absolute, Ineffable, Unknowable Nothingness Ground of Being, Enfolded Universe	
Dimension Name	**Meaning**
Emanation-Spiritual	**Knowable/Unknowable**
Atzilut, "Nearness"	Nothingness/Somethingness, Will, Wisdom, Understanding, True Self, Essence
Creation-Mental	**Something from Nothing**
Briah, "Creating"	Origin of Thoughts, Belief Systems, Higher Self, Higher Thought, Transpersonal, is-ness
Formation-Emotional	**Something from Something**
Yitzerah, "Forming"	Personal, Speech, Emotional Realm, Journeying, Personal History
Action-Physical	**Physical Reality, Pre-personal**
Assiyah, "Making"	Affect Storms, Animal Vitality

Nested Consciousness

As well as being infinite, these four dimensions are also nested, meaning the densest and least conscious level is contained within the next higher level of consciousness, and so on. This continues all the way to the most conscious spiritual level, which means each dimension is contained in the next, all the way to nothingness or to the Godhead.

It's like a set of wooden Russian wooden dolls: When you open up the main doll, you find a smaller doll inside. Then when you open up that doll, you find an even smaller doll inside of it. So going in reverse, the Action-Physical Dimension, which is the densest and most solid dimension, would be like the smallest doll that's inside all of the other dolls. The largest doll would be the Emanation-Spiritual Dimension, which contains everything.

The Nested Nature of the Four Dimensions

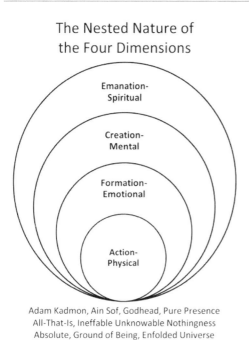

Emanation-
Spiritual

Creation-
Mental

Formation-
Emotional

Action-
Physical

Adam Kadmon, Ain Sof, Godhead, Pure Presence
All-That-Is, Ineffable Unknowable Nothingness
Absolute, Ground of Being, Enfolded Universe

Nested consciousness is called the "nested hierarchy of consciousness" by Ken Wilber. Plato referred to it as "The Great Chain of Being," in which one thing doesn't become another but is enveloped in the next level of the chain. For instance, electrons, protons, and neutrons are each discernible and distinct, yet they're the building blocks contained within an atom. Two atoms or more make up a molecule, and so forth.

Thinking of the whole of consciousness in these four nested dimensions is a great way to get started in your multidimensional understanding of the universe. I find this understanding of consciousness an extremely rich ground for exploration. We'll zoom out and get an overall view of the dimensions in this chapter, and then zoom in and explore each of the four dimensions in more depth in Chapters 7 through 10.

The Holographic Nature of Consciousness

Everything we've explored about dimensionality so far has been linear, which means progressing step by step from A to B to C. This linear perspective helps you see a path to healing, and create the lasting change and wholeness that you long for.

Yet, at the same time, this is a nonlinear, holographic universe. *Holographic* means that every part contains the whole. Or to say it differently, the whole exists within every tiny part. From the holographic point of view—from wholeness—you have access to all the dimensions of consciousness as well as all of manifestation in the present moment, in the *now*.

As you begin to think about these dimensions, it helps to remember that from the holographic perspective wholeness is always present. The word *hologram* comes from the Greek words *holos*, which means "whole," and *gramma*, which means "message."[1] A hologram is a three-dimensional representation in photographic form, recorded on film by a reflected laser beam, of a subject illuminated

⊷⊱

We understand from this perspective that in every moment we have access to everything. *Take a moment to feel and sense how this might be true.*

⊷⊱

by part of the same laser beam. If a hologram is cut into pieces, each piece projects the entire image. The well-known physicist David Bohm, who was Albert Einstein's protégé, asserts that our everyday consciousness is like a projection that's similar to a holographic image.

From the holographic nature of consciousness we've learned that information is not stored in specific places but comes together from everywhere. Bohm goes on to say, "...if you illuminate a part of the hologram you will get the information about the whole picture but it will be less detailed and from less angles, so the more of the hologram you take, the more detailed and ample the information is always going to be. But the subject or object of the information is always this one whole."[2] Stanford neurophysiologist Karl Pribram also speaks of how our brain is influenced by the holographic nature of reality.[3]

We understand from this perspective that in every moment we have access to everything. The holographic nature of reality is what allows us to know things beyond our five senses. From this way of looking at life, the entire world is available to you. The personal work that you do, which is sometimes called purification work, allows you to heal enough to hold and integrate this ever-present wholeness.

The Four Dimensions of Consciousness

The framework of the Four Dimensions of Consciousness is based in part on the four universes from some Kabbalistic texts. As we dive deeply into these four levels of existence you're going to see possibilities normally hidden from you that support deeper personal transformation.

Most religions have their mystical end of the spectrum. *Mysticism* comes from the Greek word meaning "to conceal." It's the communion with or conscious awareness of Ultimate Reality, the Divine, Spiritual Truth, or God through direct, personal experience rather than rational thought. It's an experience of the existence of realties beyond usual perceptual or intellectual comprehension. This is most often outside of your ordinary experience, hidden from usual perceptions, and is a direct embodied experience that can be felt in all four dimensions, and is not just an idea in your mind.

In Jewish mysticism the Kabbalah, which means "to receive," systematically illuminates a potential path to wholeness. The Jewish mystical tradition combines both the search for God and the truth that God is fully here, now. This could also be referred to as duality and oneness, or linear and wholistic. This path honors both your inner personal work and embraces oneness or unified consciousness. Understanding the Kabbalistic teachings of oneness and duality can help you awaken to what the Buddhists call the True Self, or what Christian mystics might call Grace or Everflow.

The four universes in the Kabbalah are part of the coming forth of creation. In the Kabbalah it says that existence began with complete and infinite light. In order for differentiation to occur in our universe God constricted God's light, allowing for all creation to be brought into being. The use of differentiation, here, refers to Reality manifesting as duality. Through life's duality we experience variety; we live in relationship with the world. That's why you can enjoy the sun, the moon, and the sky. It's why you're able to choose an apple instead of a banana. Without this constriction of light, you wouldn't exist as an individual. All would remain light.

It's important to know and embody all of the dimensions as deeply as you can. As you integrate these different parts of yourself you move closer to the embodiment of the higher, deeper dimensions, and therefore live with greater peace and freedom. Knowing and experiencing them concretely allows the integration of all the layers of self, which gives you the opportunity to experience a fully joyful life.

Many cosmologies speak of our existence from the level of God, or the Absolute, and follow it all the way through the different dimensions to full concrete tangible creation. If you understand and feel the mechanism of change, from the deepest levels of creation integrated all the way into physical reality, then you'll have an easier time creating what you want in life. Living from wholeness and a sense of balance opens up your capacity to live, and be embodied in, all these dimensions simultaneously.

From the perspective of unified consciousness, all is One. When you look through the lens of the four dimensions, you see that each distinct dimension has a unique and essential role on your path to Wholeness. When you're limited in your viewpoint, or are stuck more in one perspective or dimension, you miss the magnificent fullness available to you.

Although the framework that you're learning addresses the physical, emotional, mental, and spiritual dimensions, the contents of each isn't as clear-cut as their names would imply. Yes, in the Action-Physical Dimension you look at what's going on in your physical body, and in your life, yet there's a richness and depth in this viewpoint that goes beyond a simple consideration of your bodily reactions and physical circumstances. Each dimension has a mindset, a particular viewpoint that you'll recognize. These mindsets, or perspectives, allow you to see the pieces of arrested development in yourself on every level.

In each dimension you have the potential for understanding and growth that would be present in a developmental model, but because the dimensions are nested and holographic, you also have the potential to soar beyond the limitations of a linear model. You don't have to completely heal one dimension before moving on to the next, because you're living in them all simultaneously. In addition, there are many gradations of consciousness within each dimension, meaning Reality is a spectrum of consciousness. Speaking from a linear perspective, one end of a dimension is less integrated than the other, meaning that as you move deeper into a particular dimension you'll start to see glimpses of, and even get a taste of, the next opening into deeper consciousness.

In addition to how you move and grow through the dimensions, your relationship to a particular aspect of your life, or how you experience it, changes depending on which dimension you're in. For example, God and spirituality are viewed and experienced very differently in each of the dimensions. In one dimension it feels as if God is out there, somewhere, very far away, and you're over here. In another dimension you experience God as out there, but also inside of you, as the realization dawns that we're all made of "God stuff." And from yet another dimension's point of view, there is nowhere that God is not. From a deeper interpretation, the well-known Jewish prayer, the *Shema*, embraces unified consciousness and teaches the wholeness of life: "Hear, O Israel, the Lord our God, the Lord is One."[4] (Deuteronomy 6:4) God *and* this universe are one, and you are an integral part of this wholeness.

Embracing the depth of what the four dimensions represent has the ability to catapult your transformation. As you work with them you'll start to see how individual aspects of your personal issues, difficult historical stories, and hurt feelings are stuck in certain dimensions more than others. For example, you might notice that your confidence is shaken when you're asked to explain why you're doing something. You might notice a familiar feeling arising that takes you to an old story that you haven't completely worked through yet.

You start to see that your repeating issues have Slivers of Consciousness that pierce through—or penetrate—all of the dimensions, and affect you on many different levels of consciousness. Uncomfortable issues travel across all the dimensions, and that's why, when a difficulty appears, looking at it from all four dimensions can speed up your transformation and healing.

Let's explore the contents of this Sliver of Consciousness, *I'm not good enough*, using the framework of the four dimensions. It might look something like this:

Emotionally, a woman notices that she feels shame, and the thought that arises out of the feeling is, "I'm just no good." Mentally, she notices a constellation of negative beliefs, and that she often unconsciously says disparaging words to herself. Physically, she might not take care of herself, and might try to hide from people because she feels that she has nothing to share. Or she could go in the opposite direction, and become overly focused on her looks. Spiritually, she might not meditate because she feels unworthy of God. Or she could become obsessed with meditating, and spend most of her time trying to be good to prove her worthiness. While she longs for more, and wants to feel better about herself, she could either pull away from people, and stay isolated, or constantly surround herself with people in order to avoid her feelings.

This framework helps you see the many ways a painful feeling or belief impacts your life on every level. In your willingness to face the reality of your life, as painful as that might be at times, you have the chance to clean up your issues, and heal faster and deeper. An unexamined life can have a lot of good in it, yet unresolved issues can cause you to leave so much unlived.

The Action-Physical Dimension

The Action-Physical Dimension, or our physical world, is the densest of all the dimensions. As children, we learned that our bodies, from one view, are solid. Looking at manifestation linearly, or with the most duality, there is a this and a that. Most of us live our everyday consciousness leading with duality. This way our world feels predictable and consistent, and we don't have to face our fear of the unknown. From this perspective we tend to see everything as concrete, unchanging, and permanent. To our personality, this illusion of solidity creates a false sense of safety, and we operate solely from instinct. From this standpoint, life seems random and beyond our control. For each of us, our perception of security and strength will be challenged at some point in our lives.

When you think the material world is all there is, you naturally compare yourself to others and worry you're not good enough. When you view the world from duality only, you're looking at the part of consciousness that splits subject and object.

When you see only through the lens of the Action-Physical Dimension, you have no sense of a unified consciousness. The world is a confusing, frightening place. God is far away, out there somewhere. You don't question how life works or why things happen. You focus on your physical safety, and remain isolated and unable to connect deeply with others. You see time as linear and life as mysterious, and you're susceptible to superstition, control, and fear.

The Action-Physical Dimension has a very limited point of view. As you explore and learn to access the other higher/deeper dimensions, you can imbue the Action-Physical with greater consciousness. For instance, when you've been able to inform the Action-Physical Dimension with the next dimension, Formation-Emotional, you begin to feel into your body's wisdom. If you can also include the next deeper/higher dimension, Creation-Mental, you can learn how to heal and restore your vitality.

Slivers of Consciousness

As you come out of the Action-Physical Dimension and move toward the next higher/deeper dimension you begin to have a sense of life as more than just your tiny point of view. You move into an opening that allows for more understanding, transformation, and healing.

It might be helpful, at this point, to understand more deeply what Slivers of Consciousness are. As introduced in Chapter 3, from an energetic perspective, Slivers of Consciousness are made up of luminous Strands of Consciousness containing all of the information about us, from the most basic to the most complex personal data. These Slivers consist of intertwined Strands, which are clusters of consolidated bits of information in the fabric of who you are. They're stuck in your psyche, containing painful feelings and stories, old beliefs, and/or outmoded behaviors that beg to be healed and integrated into the whole of you. A Sliver is often something from your past you're not fully aware of, and when you bring awareness to it, it doesn't easily dissolve. It's a stubborn problem, and even when you're able to sit with it, to take the time to breathe into it and name it, the Sliver doesn't easily dissipate.

Slivers can be viewed as either positive or negative attachments that are keeping you from experiencing the greatness available to you. These Slivers keep you anchored in patterns that prevent you from fully experiencing your freedom, happiness, compassion, and peace.

To get a better visual sense of it, imagine a Sliver of Consciousness as a thorn that's causing pain as it pierces into your psyche. These Slivers slice through all four dimensions and take you on a journey into the deepest, darkest shadow parts of your soul. If they're not pursued to their origin they can fester, creating many secondary problems.

When you notice a physical, emotional, mental, and/or spiritual pain that seems to go very deep, you can begin to trace it to its deepest recesses. These deep Slivers tap into your human frailties and wounds, often causing great psychic pain. Yet once you're able to see them as concentrated Luminous Strands of information from your psyche that are woven together, there's a chance of disentangling and clarifying all that these complications hold.

Once you get that these Slivers, which take you back to your earliest childhood wounding and historical material, are the keys to your transformation and freedom, then following where they lead becomes a part of the natural rhythm of your life. Allowing yourself to follow these Strands whenever they give the slightest tug on your psyche helps you stay in integrity, and live in the truth of your journey. By touching deeply into their information in all dimensions, they begin to naturally unravel. Also touching into the Strands on a psychic and energetic level helps them move faster. When unraveled and returned to the wholeness contained within them, these concentrated bits of information help you to become more of who you're called to be in this incarnation.

Each time you discover, explore, and process one of these Slivers, you return a piece of the mosaic that is your life back to wholeness. As with all gifts and difficulties, you see them for what they really are: your teachers.

This is similar to the Shamanic concept of Soul Retrieval. In the Shamanic paradigm the shaman believes that whenever we suffer an emotional or physical trauma a piece of our soul flees the body in order to survive the experience. In the Soul Retrieval process the Shamanic healer *journeys* into non-ordinary reality to retrieve lost or stolen *soul parts* that were often split off due to childhood traumas and/or profound events or losses. Similar to *soul parts,* Slivers are aspects or fragments that when examined, explored, and reconciled, can return to wholeness and integration.

The Formation-Emotional Dimension

As we transition to the Formation-Emotional Dimension, we gain more fluidity, with an inner life of feelings. This is the beginning of psychology. From this viewpoint we learn we have an inner life and can reflect on our lives and relationships with others. Rather than reacting from a childhood place, it's possible to step back and see the emotional roots of our reactions. In this realm, we have the opportunity to see life as our own creation. We try to understand our feelings, and we search for God and meaning.

In the Action-Physical Dimension of consciousness you view life from the physical perspective only, whereas in the Formation-Emotional Dimension you develop a deeper concept of self. You begin to discern your life path, and learn to unblock the barriers to your wholeness. You can visit your *stuckness* in any area of life, and address that knot in your Strands of Consciousness. When you examine an issue and its connection to your past, you begin to gently disentangle those

Strands. Each piece of your disentangled consciousness returns your soul and psyche to a greater wholeness as you break through old patterns and create new openings for action. This means that you can see the relationship between your internal feelings and how your life manifests in the world. As you move even more deeply in consciousness into this dimension you'll begin to see glimpses of what's considered the terrain of the next dimension. You become able to perceive how thoughts and beliefs connect with your feelings; therefore, the unraveling process deepens.

The Creation-Mental Dimension

In the third dimension of consciousness, we start to bridge the more dense material dimensions with the more spiritual or subtle planes of existence. In the Creation-Mental Dimension, we begin to open to a sense of more inner spaciousness. We start to notice our thoughts, untangle our belief systems, and relax into the idea of embracing life exactly as it is, right now. From the perspective of Creation-Mental, we begin to embrace the possibility of how we could flow with the Universe without needing to reflect upon it.

In this dimension you have a more integrated, mature sense of self, and learn to tolerate all of your thoughts and feelings, omitting nothing. You begin to learn to embody unification—you're able to take in aspects of life that at first glance might seem to be different and contradictory, and discern their individuality as well as how seamlessly they fit into the wholeness of Reality.

This is the beginning of the realm of "is-ness," where you start to perceive linear time as embedded in the eternal now. You surrender to *now*, which contains both the historical past and the anticipated future. This is the level of creation. You no longer search for an external source to rescue you from your pain, but rather understand that it's all an inside job, and that inside and outside are actually one.

The Emanation-Spiritual Dimension

In the Emanation-Spiritual Dimension of consciousness, we experience Oneness. This dimension is the realm of all potentials within unified consciousness. It is pure being without concepts. It's the infinite, hidden, and unknowable nothingness.

At its deepest, the Emanation-Spiritual Dimension can be talked about as a mystery, or the unknowable dimension of consciousness. Many spiritual traditions refer to it as the vast wordless expanse. Christian Mystic Meister Eckhart often talks about what he calls the Godhead. "God is pure oneness. God...is the being of all beings."[5] All the dimensions of consciousness spring out of the primal ground of the Godhead and Divine Will.

In this dimension, you no longer identify only with your body, thoughts, and feelings, but learn to cultivate an inner stillness—the space between your thoughts and sensations. You will, as it says in Psalm 46:10, "Be still and know that I am God."[6]

> ✏️
>
> **In the fourth and spiritual dimension of consciousness we experience Oneness. It is pure being without concepts.**
>
> *Before moving on, take that in for a moment.*
>
> ✏️

Maturity

Using the Four Dimensions of Consciousness as a framework for transformation will help you grow and mature. We know we mature physically, but we don't always consider our emotional, mental, and spiritual maturity. For example, when we're emotionally mature, we can see, understand, process, and communicate clearly what we feel. We can get our needs met in our relationships, live with greater harmony, and fulfill our own needs and desires. When we lack this emotional maturity we either "throw up" our undigested feelings on other people, thinking they deserve it or that it's okay because we're venting and don't want to get an ulcer, or we might shove those feelings down inside, allowing our pain to fester and either implode on ourselves or explode in the moment because we just can't stand to keep it in any longer. Neither choice allows us to experience our life's optimum level of happiness or peace.

Spiritual maturity brings with it the firm underpinnings of all the other dimensions, allowing you to stick your toes into silence, the language of God, without bypassing, jumping over, or excluding any of your difficult sensations, feelings, or thoughts. It means you're willing to face whatever comes up and deal with it, so you can settle down inside and open to the Grace that's always there. Spiritual maturity means not using meditation as a spiritual bypass or as a pain-killer in an attempt to avoid discomfort. Instead you meditate as a way to embrace all of life and sink more deeply into the totality of existence.

You want to integrate all aspects of yourself, building a tolerance for multiple layers of existence; life's uncertainties, difficulties, and paradoxes. This is always available, and the more you embody it the more life really does feel easier!

You live simultaneously in all of the dimensions. In the next four chapters, you're going to learn how to weave this experience into the fabric of your life.

You'll begin to work with your difficulties, beliefs, and feelings. With new tools and practices, you'll see what it looks like to live consciously in the four dimensions, and create the life you want to live.

The Multidimensional Awareness Practice

One of the main tools you can use to work with the Four Dimensions of Consciousness is the *Multidimensional Awareness Practice*, or *M.A.P.* Traditional awareness or mindfulness practice consists of being aware of what's arising in your experience, both inside of you and in your life. It asks that you be an impartial observer, noticing what's arising moment to moment with great compassion and relaxing any judgment that might be present.

What distinguishes the *Multidimensional Awareness Practice* from ordinary mindfulness practice is that it asks you to not only see what's arising, but also to work with and refine what you observe. You see that what's arising is here for your transformation, and learn how to deeply engage with it. You look for and question what your experience is in all Four Dimensions of Consciousness. You then follow what arises to its source, which could be a triggering thought, uncomfortable feeling, or difficult experience. In this way you bring your awareness to the motivations, historical connections, and unconscious programming that affect your experience of life.

Doing this practice you're more able to relax, live fully, and sink into the larger context of your life—your wholeness. As you dive more deeply into each of the Four Dimensions of Consciousness, your experience of the *Multidimensional Awareness Practice* will deepen, and become broader and richer. This process gives you a *M.A.P.* for transformation.

In Chapter 11, we'll thoroughly explore the *Multidimensional Awareness Practice* and the many ways you can use it, from applying it to what feels uncomfortable or difficult as it's arising in the moment, to applying it to an aspect of your life you'd like to explore—an issue you're struggling with, a relationship you're in, or your reaction to something that's happening in your life or in the world.

Introducing the Dimension Profiles

The Four Dimensions of Consciousness are not only a *map of Reality*, they're also a portrait of your life. In the next chapters, you'll recognize many individual qualities of the four dimensions as experiences you've passed through, struggled with, are stuck in, or have mastered—or as simply who you are. To help you explore how each dimension of consciousness relates to your life, I've created five Dimension Profiles that will help you identify your strengths and weaknesses in each dimension. They'll also help you discover any blocks you may have, and give you a way to work with and release them.

There's a Dimension Profile for each of the four dimensions and one that looks at all four as a whole. The questions will be slightly different in each profile, but will identify: how you embody that dimension, where you get stuck or use that dimension for self-protection, what you need to see or ask, where you're struggling, what works well for you, and what your gifts and talents are in that dimension. The fifth profile will help you recognize which of the dimensions is your *home base* and which of them you might be trying to avoid or simply haven't developed sufficiently yet. The fifth profile will also help you discover which dimension is in the forefront of a particular feeling, belief, relationship, situation, or circumstance, and how to work with it.

The five Dimension Profiles are free to download at my Website, *www. YourUltimateLifePlan.com*. It's helpful to print out each dimension's profile before starting to read the corresponding chapter, so that as some recognition arises, you can write it down.

Self-Awareness Exercises Related to the Four Dimensions of Consciousness

EXERCISE: PRACTICE TUNING INTO ALL FOUR DIMENSIONS OF CONSCIOUSNESS

Periodically, throughout your day, stop and tune into your experience in the moment in each of the Four Dimensions of Consciousness, then try to get a sense of them all at once. Do this in a variety of situations, such as when you're at work, doing something creative, running, watching TV, spending time with your family, cooking, or meditating.

EXERCISE: A TASTE OF THE FOUR DIMENSIONS

Here's a simple awareness practice designed to help you begin getting a taste of the dimensions. The more you practice this, the easier it will be to tune into the multidimensional richness of the present moment whenever you want, and the more you'll begin doing it naturally. Answer the following questions.

1. Action-Physical Dimension

   What physical sensation are you experiencing, right now? Notice what happens.

2. Formation-Emotional Dimension

   What emotion are you experiencing in this moment? Notice what happens.

3. Creation-Mental Dimension

   What thought is going through your mind in this moment? Notice what happens.

4. Emanation-Spiritual Dimension

   What spiritual connection do you sense in this moment? Notice what happens.

5. Feel the Multidimensional Layers of the Present Moment

   Now try to get a sense of all four dimensions being present at once. Breathe deeply and let yourself relax into all of them as best you can. It's more natural than you think. Notice what happens.

MEDITATION: NESTED AWARENESS

Deep breath. Bring conscious awareness to your body. Breathe into your body, and notice any sensations. Stay with those sensations for a few minutes. See what, if anything, shifts.

Now, bring conscious awareness to your feelings and emotions. Notice what arises, and if any other feelings are present. And now notice what you feel in your body. Stay with all of that for a few minutes. See what, if anything, shifts.

Now, bring conscious awareness to your thoughts. Notice the content, and how they come and go. Notice what emotions are present, and then notice what you experience in your body. Stay with all of that for a few minutes. See what, if anything, shifts.

Now, bring your conscious awareness to your spiritual nature. Notice what arises. Next, notice your thoughts, your emotions, your body sensations. Be with all of that for a few minutes. See what, if anything, shifts.

CHAPTER 7

The Action-Physical Dimension

The possibilities are numerous once we decide to act and not react.
—George Bernard Shaw

To see your limitations more clearly, in order to grow, integrate, and move beyond your obstacles, in the next four chapters we're going to look at the Four Dimensions of Consciousness through two lenses:

1. **Mindsets:** A dimensional mindset is how we view the world, and relate to others, ourselves, and God, from the particular consciousness of that dimension. Getting a good handle on the mindset of each dimension is helpful and will give you all-encompassing tools to create the life you want.

2. **Deeper Dimensional Aspects:** Within each dimension there are levels of consciousness that become increasingly integrated by degrees and gradations in the movement toward the next dimension.

This is rich, complex material. Some of it may be new to you, and you might need to slow down, take your time, and reread parts if necessary. Please be patient and very kind to yourself.

All four dimensions are perceived or experienced differently, depending upon where you're looking from in consciousness. The dimensional mindsets described in the next four chapters are based upon two different linear movements through consciousness: ascending and descending.

In the **ascending view** we move from the narrowest, most limited mindset, toward expansion in consciousness, and open to larger contexts that include more of Reality. The ascending view from Action-Physical toward Emanation-Spiritual is called by some, "creation's attitude toward the creator," or the view from matter looking toward Spirit.

The dimensions have degrees or gradations of consciousness within them. Be aware that for the purposes of our exploration and learning, from this linear view we're giving these dimensions edges and dividing lines that might sound as if they're hard and fast borders, but they're not. As you expand in consciousness, you'll start opening to qualities in the mindset of the next larger dimension. This means the beginning of a dimension is experienced at its narrowest, most extreme view, and as you ascend into the upper reaches of that dimension, your growth is already being influenced by the next dimension.

For example, in the beginning of Action-Physical, emotions are experienced as sensations only—such as, pressure, a barrier, a block, or pain—without any realization that they could actually be related to feelings such as sadness or fear. In Action you also might quickly react to those sensations from your wounding, yelling at someone to hide your sadness, or becoming immobilized and unable to get much done because of your unrecognized fear, or believing someone is trying to control you.

As you ascend further into each dimension, openings happen, allowing you to see connections that illuminate the workings of life. For instance, as we move further into Action-Physical we start to see glimpses of the consciousness of Formation-Emotional, and begin to observe and question our sensations, instead of collapsing inwardly or reacting outwardly. As we move closer to Formation-Emotional, we start to wonder more about life. Entering Formation-Emotional, we learn we have an inner life and begin looking at ourselves with curiosity, integrating and responding more consciously.

Because of their nested nature, as you ascend from Action-Physical to Formation-Emotional, the framework of Action-Physical is completely included in Formation-Emotional. We perceive reality differently when we're in the consciousness of Formation-Emotional, which includes the more concrete perceptions of Action-Physical. So as we acknowledge our bodies and the physical world around us, we *also* notice our feelings about it all.

Next, we have the **descending view** from Emanation-Spiritual back toward Action-Physical. Some call this view "the creator's attitude toward creation" or the view from Spirit looking toward matter. Descending from Emanation-Spiritual, you experience Action-Physical differently when you're able to embody higher levels of consciousness.

We *ascend* in consciousness to expand, learn, understand, and evolve. We *descend* in consciousness to carry our bigger comprehension and awareness of life into more embodiment, freedom, love, and service, experiencing life from the mindset of embodying God's Glory. As we do, we're more present and satisfied in our everyday lives, with greater kindness and compassion toward others, ourselves, and the world.

So far, this is the **linear point of view**, and might imply that consciousness is like the rungs of a ladder—but not entirely. Yes, from one viewpoint we grow, progress, and integrate; our ego strengthens and our mindset expands, moving up the ladder to include more subtle dimensions. We then bring our new insights and consciousness down into the physical world from Emanation-Spiritual, seeing the Action-Physical Dimension in an entirely new way. But keep in mind, moving between dimensions in consciousness isn't as clear-cut as stepping back and forth over a line in the sidewalk.

Our exploration also includes the nonlinear, **holographic viewpoint** of consciousness, meaning *all* of reality is always present and available from everywhere; movement in any of the dimensions resonates in all of them. Remember, each dimension is infinite and nested, so we don't grow beyond one and move on to the next, dismissing the previous dimension. Human development is uneven. We embody and experience the pleasures and insights of each dimension, as well as explore our Slivers in each. While we're looking at four distinct dimensions of consciousness, holographically and spiritually, it's all one.

ৰ্কে

While the four dimensions are always present, we may not be adept at tuning in to all of them.

ৰ্কে

In these four chapters, you'll read about the mindsets at their most extreme to help you understand them better, but they're played out in degrees. Most of us have fixated pieces of arrested development in every dimension. These descriptions will help you see where you get stuck, especially here in Action. Understanding the dimensional mindsets will help heal those six stubborn issues, creating lasting change. They'll enrich your life, support your relationships, and create fertile ground for happiness.

Getting Oriented in Action-Physical

The whole world shrinks to the size of your pain, a very tight fit.

—Stephen Levine

When we look at Action, not only do we see our physical bodies, but we also see a mindset that's at the root of our persistent problems. Ultimately, when we embody Spirit, physical reality becomes sacred, but the Action dimension sees the world through a very narrow viewpoint. Most everyone has Slivers here. Understanding this level helps free us and resolve our Slivers, so it's worthwhile to stick with this even if it's difficult looking through such a narrow focus.

Action contains blind spots for almost everyone; it's where our deepest, pre-personal and pre-verbal traumas reside. This dimension holds our most frightening, primitive defensiveness, varying in degrees depending on our childhood wounding and how long we've worked to uncover and heal these hidden places. Our job is to strengthen our ego enough to tolerate whatever feeling arises, understand its impact, and loosen its grip on us. As you progress, you'll naturally move into higher dimensions where you can excavate it, chew on it, journal it, stomp, pull, and twist on it until it lightens...and I promise it will. Please dive into these issues and Slivers as best you can.

From this first-dimension-*only* thinking, you can't work with what arises because you haven't yet cultivated an observer or inner adult that can navigate the waters of feelings, or the thoughts and stories that go with them. That's why, in this dimension, you needed to defend yourself from the whole truth of what happened in your past. It would have been too overwhelming to see and feel everything as a child. You needed support for your ego development, and your caretakers may not have been able to provide it. So, you developed coping strategies and a pseudo adult/false self to survive and manage your life, perhaps even fooling yourself into thinking past events weren't as difficult or painful as they actually were.

You may have experienced trauma you can easily identify, such as a death or illness in the family; poverty; abandonment; physical, emotional, or sexual abuse; serious childhood illness; natural disaster; or other shocking events. Or, perhaps your parents were distracted, preoccupied, and neglectful. Maybe you needed to soothe them, trying to fill their emptiness. Perhaps you had a learning disability or other problem and didn't fit in. Teasing and bullying could have inhibited the formation of your ego. Or, maybe your wounding was less obvious, and from the outside, your childhood seemed fine. Your caretakers did their best, but your needs weren't met in a way that allowed you to build a strong enough ego to soar and reach your full potential.

Perhaps it all felt too painful, and in some ways you live with *affect storms* because it's difficult to see emotions as they are. From Action *only*, you're unable to recognize feelings, can't name the emotions, and don't connect inside to them. Maybe you shattered as a child and still do at times because you can't quite seem to get your arms around issues. In Action, and in your Slivers, you stay defended and in a false self because feelings seem overwhelming, like a force of nature—too scary to face. It probably felt normal to you growing up, and you did the best you could. Be kind—you did well, all things considered!

This book will help you build your ego so you can look directly at your pain and heal it. As you begin observing your feelings and experiencing them directly, noticing the thoughts and stories with them, you're already on your road to freedom! It doesn't help to stay in the dark, although sometimes it feels like your only option. Denial may sound better than diving in, but as I tell my clients, the worst part is over. You survived it. Now, you're returning to release anything that no longer serves you.

The Action-Physical Dimension Mindset

There are no mistakes. The events we bring upon ourselves, no matter how unpleasant, are necessary in order to learn what we need to learn; whatever steps we take, they're necessary to reach the places we've chosen to go.

—Richard Bach

When we look at our lives through the lens of the densest part of reality—the physical dimension of consciousness—we see a tangible 3-D world. Here, action is limited to your physical experience through your five senses. It's visible and concrete. In Action *only* it's not possible to know that you're influenced by unseen energy, feelings, or thoughts.

The Action-Physical Dimension is your instinctual, animal nature, focused upon self-preservation. According to Ken Wilber's developmental model, it's psychologically young, pre-personal in consciousness, without higher reason or personal self. The limitations of this dimension's mindset, or level of development, manifest throughout your life to varying degrees, depending upon your childhood and how much you've incorporated and integrated higher/deeper levels of consciousness.

In Action-Physical, we're driven by survival needs, such as safety, food, and shelter. We experience the strong, hormonal urges of sexual attraction. Yet in the higher dimensions, we think beyond purely instinctual drives, and bring meaning to our lives. We see

> ❧
>
> **When everything is seen as concrete, permanent, and resistant to change, attempts to understand life only include part of the picture.**
>
> ❧

our commitment to others, recognize the possible consequences of our actions, and discern whether or not it's wise to invite certain people into deeper levels of closeness.

While physicality includes all of manifestation, and therefore infinite possibilities, the Action perspective is shaped by biological drives and animalistic needs. Freud referred to this as the *id*, driven by the pleasure principle and wanting whatever feels good in the moment. As babies, the id helped us get our basic needs met. We cried to be fed or changed. As adults, we have low tolerance for waiting or delayed gratification. In other words, we want what we want, when we want it, the way we want it—now!

If we're blindly fixated on the 3-D perspective of physical matter, only what's visible exists. This view comes from our amygdala, the primitive, instinctual, reptilian brain, and the first part of the brain to develop. It's essential for our survival. It works behind the scenes, regulating our body functions and producing our "fight, flight, or freeze" response when it senses danger. When our amygdala is in charge, it can get us into trouble; life is difficult, and we react more aggressively. It increases our heart rate and creates adrenaline rushes. It enables us to run from a tiger, but hinders us when we feel endangered by addressing an issue with our boss, or taking a test.

With our amygdala constantly scanning our environment for danger, we're always on guard, waiting for the other shoe to drop. If we grew up in a challenging family, we tend to be hypervigilant, unconsciously scanning for emotional "danger." Eventually, this leads to adrenal exhaustion, chronic fatigue, addiction, anxiety, depression, and a host of other issues.

Through the narrow lens of Action *only*, life is not comprehended deeply, because it doesn't include an understanding of the invisible psychological, emotional, mental, or spiritual aspects of life. From this underdeveloped viewpoint, life doesn't have much meaning. We take everything literally—at face value—and life remains mysterious.

- *In what ways have you related to the Action-Physical Dimension mindset so far?*
- *What from your past comes to mind when reading about this dimension?*

Let's Get Physical

I believe that there is a subtle magnetism in Nature, which,
if we unconsciously yield to it, will direct us aright.
—Henry David Thoreau

Ultimately, your body is a living, breathing expression of your consciousness, and when you're familiar with other dimensions, you treat it as such. You listen to your intuition via physical sensations, such as a knot in your stomach or a relaxed belly; when you understand what it's trying to tell you, you move to the next dimension in consciousness.

Raw physicality is wonderful! In Action-Physical you enjoy your body. You appreciate athletic agility, a dancer's pirouette, or a runner's sprints. It connects you into your human limits and physical frailties as well as strength and prowess, teaching you to go beyond what you believed possible.

You can feel it viscerally when someone is moving from their connection with this dimension. It feels primal and alive to allow ourselves this animal power. You connect directly to nature through your body when walking in the woods, strolling along the beach, or rock climbing.

Yogi B.K.S. Iyengar understood how the body helps us toward wholeness. According to him, through the spiritual practice of Yoga, one "conquers his body, controls his energy, retrains the movements of the mind, and develops sound judgment, from which he acts rightly and becomes luminous. From this luminosity he develops total awareness of the very core of his being, achieves supreme knowledge and surrenders his self to the Supreme Soul."[1]

Yet, if we live *only* from the Action-Physical mindset, we operate as if we are only our bodies. When we equate our worth with beauty, prowess, and physical strength, we resist aging and become scared at mid-life.

EXERCISE: GET UP AND DANCE

Put on music and dance as if no one is watching.

Being Stuck

When you feel stuck, it's likely rooted in the Action Dimension. Remember, I'm presenting each mindset in its extreme form. Most of us have Slivers of Consciousness here. It doesn't matter whether you're a student, teacher, CEO, or pizza-delivery person—we all have personal programming with early childhood misses and failures. Even if you function at a high level, make tons of money, and have wonderful friends, you'll find those stuck, pre-personal issues in this dimension.

Whenever you react instead of consciously responding, you're acting out from a child inside, and not speaking from your adult feelings. You're triggered and in a pre-personal biological response that's tag-teaming with your *affects*. Your reptilian brain is automatically responding to stimuli interpreted as danger. It could be an image, sound, scent, feeling, or thought that registers so quickly, it's hard to see you're in habitual reaction. Often someone else has to point it out.

Consider the paradigm of inner child and inner adult. Our wounded, childself is triggered when we: rigidly think we're right, are stopped by fear, fight, rage, shame others, withdraw physically or emotionally, blame, punish, can't name our feelings or use addictions to numb them, dissociate, or otherwise avoid a feeling, thought, or belief. For the length of time you're caught in one of these, you're in a reaction that's anchored in your childhood wounding and the pre-personal consciousness of Action-Physical.

We might be able to give a name to the contents of our Slivers, but we don't yet know the multiple layers and topography of our emotions. We don't understand the Strands of Consciousness here. When triggered, we might say, "I'm mad," but we can't always articulate past that, and might be, ever so cleverly, blaming others for our experience. In the next dimension, we begin tracing the lineage of our feelings, seeing their layers and unearthing hidden dynamics to help free us from the constraint of our Slivers, and the Action-Physical dimension.

Sometimes our wounding leaves us with a deep emptiness that we want to bypass, jumping into pseudo-spiritual awareness, or attempting to fill it with hard or soft addictions. Alcohol and drugs are hard addictions, whereas soft addictions include culturally acceptable habits, such as surfing the internet, watching television, talking on the phone, texting, exercising, shopping, relationships, eating— any avoidance behavior that keeps our pain at bay.

Often in my practice, a client will try to push me away or distract me from a particular subject or something I've said, to avoid talking about something painful. There are many defensive behaviors that shut another person down, throwing them off track. Often unconsciously, people get angry, try to slip away, or change the subject. Offense becomes the best defense, and we attack to avoid feeling pain, shame, or fear, or being overwhelmed, like we did as children.

Sarah used the word "and" to push people away. Whenever she was asked a question she didn't want to answer, she'd distract by talking over the other person, starting her sentence with "and," then keep talking, and change the subject. She grew up with a critical father, and learned this defense to ward off the sting of his words and actions. She had no idea she was doing this. Her habitual "and" was unconscious, used when she felt others were criticizing her, even when they weren't.

In Action, the connection to your interior is limited. Life feels unexplainable and mysterious. We'll do anything to ensure our emotional and phiyscal safety, vacillating between merging with others and pushing away to avoid abandonment or isolation. We're left feeling battered by life without understanding why or how to create a better experience. The more we let go of these fixated places, the better and faster we heal.

> ✦
> **We're completely cut off and feel very alone without the depth and breadth of the other dimensions.**
> ✦

Win-Lose

We are reluctant to live outside tribal rules because we are afraid of getting kicked out of the tribe.

—Caroline Myss

Much of our thinking in this dimension is "either/or" rather than "both/and." It's a rigid, fear-based, split-off all-or-nothing, right/wrong, black/white, with very little gray. Action is essentially divided into irreconcilable opposites with no common ground, and focuses upon contrast. Because there are only winners or losers, we constantly compare ourselves to others and worry we're not enough. In our attempt to escape fear, we end up in tribal, pre-personal thinking where it's difficult to tolerate differences, much less celebrate them.

As humans, we need to belong and attach to others. We want to feel desirable, and we want others to know us. Without a strong sense of self, we might use merging with others as a substitute for inner strength, and for emotional and physical safety. When belonging becomes of prime importance, desperately trying to find safety, we can find ourselves in a tribe or group. We give ourselves over to others, and we need to remain stuck and small to be accepted.

You see this in gangs. They're indoctrinated into the tribe's specific beliefs and behaviors to engender compliance, loyalty, and obedience. As with dysfunctional families, any ideas or actions outside the tribal norm are seen as rebellion, rejection, betrayal, or abandonment. When we haven't done enough individuation, it feels scary, even impossible, to risk the isolation and pain of being cast out. We'll sacrifice anything to stay connected.

To a degree, this occurs in any group, such as families, childhood friends, religions, political parties, and nations. When we're up against someone with black-or-white thinking, it's difficult to establish common ground. Yet we must confront this tribal mindset to face our own black-or-white thinking.

As we move closer to the next dimension of emotion and meaning, we grow beyond the comfort and security of belonging at any cost. As we open to ourselves and new ideas, we gain the courage to look beyond black-or-white thinking, challenging the mentality of keeping family or group secrets, and extending beyond our limited fantasies and projections.

It takes a stronger ego to live with people different from us, without making them bad or wrong. As we develop a stronger sense of individual self-worth, we're able to trust ourselves and honor all. We open to belonging and connecting in a deeper way. We notice the similarities within the human tribe, valuing the emotional and mental worlds, and include people who look and think differently.

It takes much courage to leave our tribes, as well as recognizing other dimensions in consciousness. Once we begin to embody other dimensions, we know we must move toward the True Self as spiritual and psychological pioneers, forging new pathways.

- *Notice if there are times you exclude people who are different from you.*
- *Who are they, and how do you do it?*
- *When is tribal thinking and behavior most true for you?*
- *In what ways was your family or community tribal in their thinking and behavior?*
- *When is it easiest to accept people who are different from you?*
- *Why do you think that's so?*

Subject and Object

In Action we view manifestation from the most linear perspective and greatest sense of duality. There's an illusion of complete separateness. We see a "this" and a "that," a chair and a table, a subject and an object. When we hold ourselves separate from the world; we even treat people as things.

The Action-Physical mindset rules by brute force and magic. From here, it's easy to become too focused on the outside world, our reputation, and things. Fancy cars, the latest gadgets, good looks, income, and status are extremely important. They become magical, like an amulet, giving us power over others.

Because of our three-dimensional, physical world (the world of action and doing), what we *see*, rules. Right actions and good deeds matter most. Not only is behavior important, it's also primarily based on instinct—a world of unconscious habit and repetition. If we don't like something, we focus on changing the behavior. Sometimes it works, but it's not usually that simple.

From here, we're trapped in the magical thinking of early childhood. We parcel life into segments, without seeing how things might fit together. We have our naïve, childlike interpretation of life, and because in Action life doesn't have meaning, we can't learn from our suffering. It can only be seen as hopeless, something to avoid, and a show of weakness. We've either got to hide from it or get rid of it quickly.

In Action-Physical time is linear and travels only in one direction, from past to present to future. We think the past is over; we can't change it. We must protect ourselves from a scary future, and be rescued from our current circumstances. But in psychological time, you can always return in thought and feeling to work with memories of the past. It frees you to be here, in the moment.

Connections

When you're caught in your Slivers, your connections are based in early childhood developmental abilities, seen through the eyes of an underdeveloped ego. It's a tightly held, *self-referencing* mindset, without the interior space to step back and look at yourself. When you can't question your thoughts and feelings, you're at a disadvantage without a strong sense of self and functional boundaries.

When in our false self we vacillate between codependency and counter-dependency. We either merge with another for a pseudo-connection, or push away rebelliously to find a separate self. It's the teeter-totter of "I need you" and "Leave me alone."

We miss out on genuine connection and don't discuss anything of substance, because it seems as though the surface of life is all that exists. We don't know how to navigate conflict, and because we're in the win-lose mindset, relationships are difficult and erratic. For our safety, it feels better to overpower, placate, or just not talk. We can only speak honestly, expressing our feelings, opinions, and thoughts, when we include the consciousness of other dimensions. By stepping back, watching your urge to react, and responding instead of reacting, you're moving to the next dimension in consciousness.

There's little abstract thinking in the tangible world of biology and behavior. In this context, for example, if someone were to ask you why you like to be alone, your answer might be, "Because I'm just that way." With so little inside awareness of an inside life, it may never occur to us to question why people choose to do what they do. It might seem difficult and foreign. From here, we're not accustomed to knowing why things happen, and don't often question how life works. We were never taught, or given the space to learn how, and might not even know this is possible.

Let's look at an example of the self-referencing mindset that leaves us blind to our interior and the motives of others, and makes it hard to have empathy. This happens with many of us in our relationships with significant others, who so skillfully shine the light on our six stubborn issues for healing. We're triggered and don't know it. We jump to our own defense so fast, we can't see it.

Meet Tiffany and Brian: Brian comes home and asks Tiffany about the timing of dinner. Tiffany immediately feels he's judging her and telling her she doesn't have it ready at the right time. When Tiffany is triggered, she either responds with silence and a glance from the corner of her eye, or she launches into a long story about the crowd at the grocery store, and how the laundry took a lot longer than she thought it would. Unconsciously, she believes she's not good enough and tries to please Brian by doing more, and over-explaining to defend against her feelings of fear, hopelessness, shame, overwhelm, and loneliness.

In response to Tiffany, Brian either shuts down or rages at her. He believes she never listens to him, and is trying to control him with a barrage of unrelated details, her silence, and that look. He habitually feels anger, shame, sadness, and loneliness, believing it's hopeless and he'll never get his needs met. Thus, the dance continues in this dimension, because neither knows how to talk about their feelings, underlying wounds, and accommodating patterns.

As we do our work, these patterns change and we move into the next dimension. Brian might calm his inner part that's triggered, angry, and doesn't feel heard. He might notice Tiffany's reaction, and either explain his question—he felt hungry, and if dinner was later, he'd have a nibble—or, with a curious tone, he'd ask her what was going on with her silence and facial expression, and he'd take care of himself with a snack. He could also choose to speak from his feelings: "When you look at me that way, then I feel angry and afraid, and this triggers what happened when I asked for something as a kid."

Tiffany might observe she's triggered, calm down her inner part that's feeling scared, and answer his question. Or, with a curious tone, inquire why he asks and share that she feels she's not good enough. There are more examples, but I think you get the idea.

In the next dimension we become more self-aware, move into more individuation, and can therefore have more genuine connection and relationships. However, in Action we mostly feel disconnected from others or are disconnected without realizing it. In this case, it's easy to blame others for our problems. From here, we don't understand that as we grow and change, our relationships also change for the better, even if the other person isn't willing to budge. We think, "So-and-so won't change, so why should I?" Unless we recognize our inner life, it's difficult to navigate our feelings and take responsibility for our actions, because we don't understand how they began. We don't see that when we change, our world changes.

We don't have a sense of interconnectedness or interrelatedness, much less an integrated Oneness. It's not until the next dimension, Formation-Emotional, that we're able to observe ourselves, so in Action, relationships can feel a bit baffling.

When we grow up in families operating from a primarily Action mindset, it requires working on ourselves to move past these wounded, or unexamined places inside of us. Again, most of us have some arrested development in this dimension. It's very helpful to discover how you identify with this level. Look at your family, friends, and all these parts of yourself with compassion and possibility. **If you can see it, you can heal it!**

Our Egos

In Action-Physical, our ego is at its densest, most unconscious form, which is very delicate and fragile. This is where we're the most emotionally reactive. We focus on who and what supports our ego's primitive desires. We shut down, cut off from our feelings and from other people. Because our sense of self feels challenged much of the time, we don't trust that we can take care of ourselves in the world, or be with others effectively. We can find ourselves looping inside the "victim triangle," consisting of Victim, Persecutor, and Rescuer.[2]

From Action-Physical we keep cycling through these three perspectives, usually with a favorite, most comfortable position. This happens often with couples. They alternate among the bully (persecutor), the bullied (victim), and the one who saves themselves or the other from their feelings (rescuer). This happens in subtle ways, and empathizing becomes hard, because it requires the ability to see we have something in common with the "other."

The lack of integrated consciousness in this dimension produces a fearful undertone in life. We also cycle through our three most common reactions to fear—freezing, fleeing, or fighting. When afraid, a person may feel frozen inside, yet someone in the fearful person's presence may experience the "freeze" as aggression. In the same way, someone's fleeing may be experienced by the other person as aggression or abandonment. This is because any action by one person produces a different reaction in another, depending on the psychology of the person on the receiving end. All these habitual reactions solidify our energy into patterns of behavior that are stored in our physical bodies.

- *Notice your feelings about the victim triangle.*
- *Which position are you in most often?*
- *How do you see yourself in the other two positions of the triangle?*
- *When do you freeze? Flee? Fight?*

Where Is God?

Every man takes the limits of his own field of vision for the limits of the world.
—Arthur Schopenhauer

In Action, we might think God is influencing us, but because everything is disconnected in this dimension, it happens in some unseen, unknown gulf, where prayers are either granted, or not. God is out there somewhere, far away, hidden, and never where we are. We can't experience God or the Universe inside of us, because we have no connection to an inside life. Something is either spiritual or it's not, things of this world versus Heaven. Good and evil are far apart and everything is separate from the Divine, because our consciousness isn't whole enough to experience the extensiveness of God.

> **As we move into the other dimensions, we come to know that it's our own perception and experience of God that opens.**

From this point of view, the unseen world has power over us, and the only way to have any effect on it, or our lives, is through oversimplified, protective rituals, superstitions, and magic. This kind of magic and ritual is based in fear and the need to control, and isn't fueled from other dimensions or imbued with Spirit. For example, we might trust a lucky charm to guide us, or we might cling to the idea that a special teacher, technique, or teaching will magically save us from despair.

The Action dimension holds true and dear the fundamental end of the spectrum of religions. We see this in literal, word-for-word interpretations of scripture and doctrine, and in black-and-white beliefs. It's unimportant to consider the story's original language, type of writing (for example, poetry, parables, metaphor), historical context, or the culture and people it was written for at the time.

The good news is we don't live in Action-Physical *only*. We know all the dimensions are connected. Remember also, Action-Physical is nested and completely contained in the next dimension, Formation-Emotional.

- *Notice your thoughts and feelings in this moment.*
- *Ask yourself where they come from.*
- *In what ways do you experience God or Spirit?*

MEDITATION: GOD AND THE PHYSICAL
(Based on Cherokee spirituality[3])

First, find a quiet, private place out in nature to walk in a circle. Notice the sky. Take a deep breath. Feel your feet on the ground. Another deep breath. Find your circle. Start walking slowly, and feel the earth under your feet as if for the first time. Really take it in. Give thanks for the ability to walk, and all you see, hear, smell, and perceive in nature. Move in any way that feels good to you. If you'd like, make sounds or chant. Maybe even begin dancing. Notice what it feels like as your body moves through space. As you move or dance around the circle, keep your connection with the sky and earth.

Other Dimensions Informing Action-Physical

As you expand in consciousness, looking back at physical reality through the lens of the next dimension, Formation-Emotional, you begin to live more consciously, relating to your body in more helpful ways. When we include this next dimension in our viewpoint, instead of viewing our bodies as only objects to exercise and feed, we observe ourselves and have a relationship with our physical world. We begin to seek meaning in our world, including with our bodies. This inspires you to eat foods that support your health and well-being. Because you're connected to your feelings, you'll nurture yourself with the right amount of exercise and sleep. You'll respect and care for your body as a part of the whole of you.

Living more consciously means that you can tune in to your body in a way that allows you to distinguish between different kinds of sensations. The ability to know a tickle from a scratch in your throat, or a stabbing pain from a pinch or ache, not only helps you take better care of your body, but also gives doctors and other caregivers better information about you.

Whether you exercise, do yoga, eat well, or ignore your physical needs, it's all part of your relationship with your body, and each of your body systems is in relationship with each other. Adding the mindset of the Formation-Emotional Dimension, you see that your emotions connect with and affect your physical health. You can see that your headache might be related to a feeling, such as sadness or anger. When you know you have a relationship with your body, you can be aware of feelings associated with different physical aspects of yourself.

So many of us judge our bodies harshly, and develop a poor body image. We get this from our upbringing, as well as our culture. In some schools of thought, and some spiritual circles, we're encouraged to focus on the body rather than thoughts and feelings. Other models suggest we ignore our physical nature, focusing exclusively on the spiritual. Every dimension needs attention and care, and that's why working with all four dimensions has such transformative power.

Knowing the relationship you have to your body, and the feelings associated with different parts and systems, is important in healing the connection of your body-emotion-thought-spirit.

Now answer the following questions:

- *When you view your body, what impressions do you get?*
- *In what ways do you take care of your body?*
- *What are your feelings about the different parts of your body?*
- *In what ways do you experience their relationships with each other?*
- *What relationships, if any, stand out for you?*
- *What other feelings are arising?*
- *What happens if you invite healing energy and kindness to arise through your whole body?*

Meditation: Body Awareness

Breathe into your belly and notice what gets your attention in your body. Now feel your arms and legs and where they are in space. Notice your connection with the earth and sit with all of this for a while.

Our Cells Communicate

In her book *Molecules of Emotion* Dr. Candace Pert shares scientific research showing us that neural receptors are present on most of our cells, and our "mind" isn't just located in our head, but is present at a cellular level.[4] Although you're a product of your environment, through consciousness you can change and override the systems created by your history. We co-create our lives and our health, literally through our cells. Your body not only produces sensations, but also gives you clues about your feelings, emotionally and otherwise. You embody what you think and feel. This is the visible form of Oneness or Wholeness, and your embodiment of Spirit. As you embrace your physical body from this perspective, you relate to it as your Wholeness.

MEDITATION: LISTENING TO THE WISDOM OF YOUR CELLS

(Please download the longer version, along with an MP3, at *www. YourUltimateLifePlan.com.*)

Deep breaths. Take five minutes to relax and scan your body, head to toe. Allow yourself to go more deeply into your body and notice any part, muscle, bone, or organ that wants your attention. Now go even further into the tissues of your body and connect with your cells. Notice if any cell gets your attention and connect with that cell. Notice what feelings, thoughts, and images come up. Notice if this cell has anything to say to you. Notice if you have anything to say to it. Sit with this for a while. Then send kindness and compassion into every cell of your body. Sit a while longer and breathe in kindness. Breathe out any discomfort or pain. Take three deep breaths and let go of anything else that needs to be released.

Now, consider:

- *What did you learn from your cells?*
- *What does this show you about your connection to the physical world?*

Thoughts Have an Effect

When you go even further in consciousness to the Creation-Mental Dimension, you'll see how your thoughts affect your physical nature. Examining your thoughts and beliefs about physical reality and manifestation is helpful for creating the life you long for, as well as a healthy vibrant body.

- *What thoughts and beliefs do you have about your body?*
- *What are five things you like about your body?*
- *When might you avoid or ignore your body's signals?*
- *In what ways might you have a more conscious relationship with your body and your health?*

Healing the Physical

From a linear point of view our physical bodies are the densest in consciousness and can be the slowest to visibly change. Thinking of a physical illness, you could delve into all of the possible connections to your disease, looking at every angle of your participation, from physical, emotional, mental, and spiritual levels, and still not heal as quickly as you'd like. As your consciousness changes from your investigations and opens to new possibilities, your body might or might not reflect this immediately. Yet, as you expand, you embrace quantum reality and can heal at any moment.

In Action-Physical, you process experiences using your five senses, and your perceptions are processed through the brain and nervous system. When in our Slivers, our nervous system is so dysregulated, we can't be present to bodily sensations or emotions. It's only when working with the ego, in Formation-Emotional, that you can tap into your body's innate wisdom, listening to your gut through sensations informed by your emotions and thoughts.

When we can't process our inner life, we often try to shut down our bodies and deaden a large part of our physicality. Author and psychoanalyst Alexander Lowen, in his book *Fear of Life*, says, "...the suppression of feeling is accomplished by deadening a part of the body or reducing its motility so that feeling is diminished."[5] We often suppress feelings and memories through chronic muscular tension.

Your body naturally longs for pleasure, spontaneity, joy, and acceptance, but in Action-Physical *only*, aliveness can be frightening, and can feel out of control. As you open to your breath, you connect to your physical pleasure, as well as thoughts and emotions. Lowen also says, "It can be shown that chronic tension in any part of the body's musculature interferes with the natural respiratory movements...breathing easily and fully is one of the basic pleasures of being alive."[6]

When we feel physical sensations or discomfort, we might need a physical solution: Back pain might require a visit to a doctor, physical therapist, or chiropractor. However, your discomfort might carry a deeper message about your life—perhaps you feel burdened. Pay attention to thoughts that pop into your head, such as, "I need to take a break and walk," or a sudden inspiration you get to complete a task you've been avoiding. Sometimes, stomach tightness is telling you, "Listen to me. Pay attention to your feelings," or, "This feels like sadness from childhood, please take note." Perhaps it's saying, "This isn't the right road for you now." This is why awareness and discernment are essential to understanding the wisdom your body offers you.

Your connection to your inner wisdom lets you know when you need to address something physical, emotional, mental, or spiritual. Remember, everything you think,

> ✺
>
> **As you move into other dimensions with larger frameworks, you start to view the body not only as muscles, tendons, bones, and organs, but also as energy, prana, chi, and vital force.**
>
> ✺

feel, and do affects your health. Your perceptions and emotions affect your biology, and so with curiosity, investigation, and awareness, you open pathways to deeper wisdom, giving your life direction and affecting the quality of your health on a daily basis.

As you begin to live a more conscious life beyond Action *only*, life becomes easier. You can relax, physically and emotionally, and your meditation practice supports this. You can face whatever arises, telling the truth about what you think and how you feel. You take moments in your day to breathe deeply and connect within. Stress and difficulties still occur, but you have an underlying foundation of conscious awareness. Relaxation supports your health as well as your spirit.

Living Beyond the Action-Physical Dimension *Only*

When you know the dimensions of consciousness beyond the concrete Action-Physical Dimension, you're in touch with emotions and thoughts, as well as your energy, flow, and spiritual connection. Science tells us the universe consists entirely of energy. Beyond the physical body and included in it are levels of energy-bodies, layers of our auric field, our chakras, and the flow of the universe, all of which are constantly changing. It takes courage and fortitude to be conscious enough to stay in the flow of the River of Life, and it's absolutely possible.

The Jewish Kabbalah refers to the Action-Physical Dimension as the universe of Assiyah, meaning, "to make." This making is different from creating in the third dimension of Creation-Mental, because the Action-Physical *making* is the completion of the creative process, a final coming together, or culmination, of manifestation. The angels here are called Ophanim.

> ❧
>
> **The movement of ascending and descending continues through our growth, adding more subtle layers of consciousness in the process.**
>
> ❧

From the perspective of ascending up the ladder or expanding into more light and subtle consciousness, Action's mindset is small and un-integrated. Yet when descending the ladder, bringing with us the wisdom, knowledge, and understanding of the deepest, largest, most essential dimension—Emanation-Spiritual—we know our physical nature as more than a vehicle for consciousness, or the sum of its parts. Action becomes a vessel for everything, including receiving God's Light and the embodiment of consciousness itself.

As we work with our ego, we awaken the body to its true nature—the temple of the Spirit. Our bodies house the "indwelling God," or, from the Kabbalah, the "Shekhinah," and what Christians also call "Holy Spirit." We come to feel our body imbued with light and Divine Presence. The Divine becomes embodied in us, and, as it says in the Bible (in Isaiah 6:3), "The whole earth is full of his glory."[7]

In certain types of yoga, the body is prepared for the awakening of the sleeping, spiritual energy, called Kundalini. As our ground of being awakens, we open to the power of the Goddess Shakti, transforming our physical vehicle into an effective container for an embodied spiritual life.

Kabbalah means "to receive." From your physical body you open to your sensations, your feelings, your thoughts, and to receiving the higher dimensions and the Divine Lights.

MEDITATION: OPEN TO RECEIVING

Deep breath. Allow yourself to open to receiving as best you can. Open to the possibility of receiving the higher/deeper dimensions. Deep breath. Formation-Emotional, Creation-Mental, Emanation-Spiritual. Now, as best you can, receive all this in your body. Take it in. Breathe deeply. Open to receive the light of God, the light of the Universe. Let it illuminate you and feed you on every level, in every cell. "I receive the Divine Lights." "I welcome the light of God." "I allow the light of the Universe to warm and soothe me." The light fills all of you. And it fills the world.

The Action-Physical Dimension Profile

Reminder: You can download the Action-Physical Dimension Profile (along with the other four profiles) at my Website, *www.YourUltimateLifePlan.com.*

CHAPTER 8

The Formation-Emotional Dimension

Painful as it may be, a significant emotional event can be the catalyst for choosing a direction that serves us—and those around us—more effectively. Look for the learning.

—Louisa May Alcott

As you emerge from the Action-Physical Dimension, with its animal drives, concrete, primitive thinking, and delicate ego structure, you enter into the next largest nested dimension, the Formation-Emotional Dimension. Your solid, concrete, and fixed experience of life becomes more fluid. Time, space, and your experience of yourself are also more fluid. You recognize an inner life, with feelings, motivations, and explanations, and you can breathe more deeply and relax your body more easily.

Although in Action-Physical you may have a vague awareness of your inner life, you don't have a clue how to observe, or work with what's inside you. It's the Formation-Emotional mindset that lets you approach your inner life with enough clarity and insight to work with, process, and heal it. You now have the opportunity to develop self-empowerment and self-agency. Remember, the Action-Physical Dimension is completely contained in Formation-Emotional. It's your mindset that expands.

With this budding insight into your psychology, life has greater meaning, you realize your thoughts and feelings relate to each other, and you relate more deeply to them. You understand your motivations better, as well as those of others. As your perspective shifts from the narrow viewpoint of Action, with its black-or-white thinking, into this greater capacity for insight and understanding, "ah-ha" moments abound. Have you ever felt you understood something, and

165

in a moment of insight realized it was completely different than you originally thought? That leap of understanding, that paradigm shift, comes from moving into this larger, more expansive dimension. You see life as a journey and embark on a quest in search of yourself, and God.

You don't graduate from Action-Physical; it's the expansion of consciousness into Formation-Emotional that lets you view your difficulties, pain, and Slivers more clearly, and then process and heal them. Life begins to make more sense. You're more flexible and resilient. You're no longer blindly caught by life, as you are in Action. Instead, spending less time in automatic reaction, you have the ability to self-reflect and heal. As you move into the next-largest dimension, Creation-Mental, and then the next, you continue to develop greater capacities for understanding, healing, and embodying the True Self.

- *In what ways do you relate to the Formation-Emotional Dimension so far?*
- *What "ah-ha" moments have you had when you recognized something was different than you originally thought?*
- *How did your "ah-ha" moments change your perception or experience of yourself, others, or life?*

It's important to know that once the door of your consciousness opens and you step through it, you never completely return to your old, narrower mindset. There will be Slivers of Consciousness that cut through a few or all of the dimensions that need to be seen, processed, and released, but once your new coping strategies and capacities emerge, they can be activated whenever needed. This is why transformational work is so powerful!

Our Inner Life

The more you learn, the more you realize how much you don't know.

—Albert Einstein

In the beginning of Formation, you still have instinctive reactions, but instead of always acting on them, you recognize that they're related to something inside of you. You become curious, wanting to learn about them and from them. So, you exercise your new ability to step back, slow down, and trace the reaction to its historical cause, giving you greater understanding and freedom. Sometimes, noticing you're about to react and just taking a breath begins the shift. Eventually, you'll respond from your inner adult rather than react from your wounded inner child. This will feel like a huge victory for you. Your curiosity helps you journey inward to deeper parts of yourself, allowing you to release some Strands and integrate others.

You'll journey toward a path that gives your life significance and meaning. You'll begin to see beyond the literal, understanding your inner landscape, and exploring symbolism and dreams, which contain valuable information.

It's an exciting journey! It's the road to happiness. It can also be daunting, at times, when you see an interior life with strong desires and begin investigating, taking you into unknown territory. You can't resolve all of life's mysteries from the Formation Dimension, but your life has greater depth, and certain pieces will fall naturally into place.

Instead of experiencing over-reactivity and the inability to see outside of your insular Action-Physical mindset, in Formation-Emotional you observe your fears and longings, and how much you don't know about the world and yourself. Seeing what you don't know allows for more possibilities to bring forth your potentials as well as expanded opportunities in your relationships. Your investigations help you understand your personal history and ego; why you do the things you do. They also facilitate the healing process. You experience more space and flexibility inside you, and discover your interior has all sorts of subtle feelings with important meanings to explore. Sometimes this exploration's easy; sometimes it's harder, but it's always worth it.

For example, perhaps you discover that the reason you don't feel supported in your life is that whenever someone tries to join you and expresses empathy, you push him or her away or judge him or her, keeping one eye open for something bad to happen. You might, unconsciously, be afraid that person will fall apart like your parent, and you'll end up having to take care of him or her. If you see behind the scenes of this knee-jerk reaction of pushing people away and feeling lonely, you get to confront the scared part of you, and then actually feel the support you're longing for.

EXERCISE: JOURNEY INTO MEANING

- *In what ways have you explored meaning in your life?*
- *What have you discovered?*
- *Allow yourself to be curious about any reaction you have in the next few days. Notice where it takes you inside.*

Ego

Today, self-examination, prayer, and contemplation—the disciplines of conscious effort—are still the best ways to transfer your center of power from the external world to your interior world.

—Caroline Myss

&

The Formation-Emotional Dimension involves working with the various ego structures that make up what we call our real self.

&

You're traveling from the Action, pre-egoic, infant, pre-personal world to the more integrated, personal world of the Formation-Emotional mindset. In other words, as you move from the early childhood, split, black-or-white view of the world, with its underdeveloped and delicate ego structure, you find an ego with more stability, flexibility, and shades of grey, that includes other people's views and the ability to self-question. You can then understand and heal your historical, personal stories, embracing the real self. This offers the possibility of real happiness.

In Formation, you discover an inside life with depth and content, and an outside world connected to your thoughts and feelings. You get to look at the personal programming held within your ego, those undiscovered and unnamed feelings, under-processed fixations, and under-challenged self-identifications that keep you from changing and creating the life you came to live. Remember, from Action *only*, you don't know how to actually question or look at anything.

Beyond Tribal

In Formation, you know you have a personal viewpoint and look through your own lens at life, and that others do too. As you move more deeply into this dimension, you're willing and brave enough to leave the tribes that haven't served you, and move toward the groups you choose. You're able to make friends that have differences, but share interests such as self-discovery, growth, and change.

Connecting

With all things and in all things, we are relatives.

—Sioux proverb

In Formation you're developing the capacity to make more inner connections, to know yourself and recognize your patterns of feelings and the thoughts that go with them. You see your life as an ongoing story you learn to appreciate, and develop the capacity to empathize and resonate with the stories of others. It's an endless country to know and explore. From here, you want to understand your history and personal stories, so you can heal yourself on this journey.

In realizing you have internal space containing all your sensations, emotions, and thoughts, you're able to relate to others from your interior, and share your experiences. Here, you're able to view yourself in relationship and understand your connections to others more clearly, so you can be more open to love, compassion, and connecting in a genuine way. You feel less lonely and isolated.

Time

In the internal space of Formation, you learn that much of your present-time reaction is anchored in the past, not in the now. You begin to see that a present-day incident can *bump* into you in psychic space, touching on your past. You can see you're being triggered, identify it, and heal it. For example, when someone says something with a particular tone or expression, and you react to it, that person has activated a historical or childhood wounding in you. If Jane says, "Get in the car," and you feel angry, you might have a history with Jane and cars, but maybe she said this in the same tone of voice your mother, father, or aunt used when they told you to take out the garbage. So, this current reaction connects to feelings and thoughts that are actually about the past.

All time is available in Formation and we perceive it moving forward and backward, but we often focus on the past while aching for a future when life will be better. In Formation you don't yet have access to unified consciousness.

Subject and Object

Unlike in Action-Physical *only*, in Formation-Emotional consciousness, opposites can be held closer together. They're not as black-or-white or starkly unrelated. Even though you have greater integration and flexibility, there's still distance between subject and object. The world is viewed in distinct parts, which are not seen as parts of the whole. The vast differences in Action-Physical between subject and object become observable and understandable. Here in Formation-Emotional you still have distance, but because you can reflect upon life and be introspective, relationships among people, things, thoughts, and feelings grow more evident. You see closer associations with opposites, but they can't completely

> ❧
> **Life begins to make more sense. You begin to see your deeper motivations, can heal your childhood historical wounds, and, in turn, have more inner space and greater freedom.**
> ❧

reconcile—meaning, they don't completely transmute, become something else or another thing, but instead achieve harmony through finding balance.

In Formation, you realize you're both the observer and the observed, and experience an interior life separate from the exterior, so you're not as reactive. When in the Formation mindset, although you see connections between things, you don't yet have a place in your consciousness to experience being held consistently and completely by something larger than you. You've yet to embody Oneness, but do get glimpses of the larger context.

Our Bodies

But not only creativeness and enjoyment are meaningful. If there is a meaning in life at all, then there must be a meaning in suffering.
—Viktor E. Frankl

As discussed in Chapter 7, when you add Formation to your consciousness, the body is no longer just an object, but is related to meaningfully adding depth to life. You connect to sensations and emotions with meaning, learning to identify and name them so they're workable. But first, you must be willing to consciously feel, which requires courage and compassion.

Suffering is one of our great teachers. From Formation you're willing to walk into your suffering because you see that when you embrace it with a desire to unravel and understand its significance, you gain some relief from pain. Suffering remains part of the emotional landscape; it doesn't completely cease, but you see it for what it is. With your new understanding of pain, you develop greater empathy and compassion. Opening to life means opening to all of it. The more you open to pain, the more you open to love. You'll see the human journey is sometimes difficult, but ultimately beautiful. Father Richard Rohr says, "Love and suffering are the main portals that open up the mind space and heart space (either can come first), breaking us into breadth and depth and communion."[1] He's saying that both can take us to our knees and lift us to great heights. By relinquishing our small-self, we surrender to something beyond our comprehension.

EXERCISE: EMBRACING YOUR SUFFERING

- *In what ways have you embraced your suffering?*
- *What happened because of it?*
- *In what ways have you tried to avoid your suffering?*
- *When has suffering been more difficult for you, and why?*

The Buddhist Tonglen meditation practice has much to offer us in building our compassion muscles. Spend a few minutes breathing in the pain of the world and breathing out love. You can start with the pain of someone you want to help, and build up to the world.

God

What you seek is seeking you.

—Rumi

In Formation, you search for meaning, learning to discern and walk your life's path. It's an extremely rewarding endeavor. As you grow, each twist and turn gives you more to work with in your resolve to have a good life. This is not to be taken lightly; it helps you see yourself more accurately, and the world in greater depth.

You long for God or Spirit. There's still distance between God and self, and you don't quite feel God is always here. In your search, you develop witness consciousness and experience God both inside and outside of you, but not yet completely as One. You continue to seek in this second Dimension, but can't experience ultimate Wholeness until you move into the next dimensions.

MEDITATION: FORMATION-EMOTIONAL *ONLY*

This meditation is designed to help you experience what being in Formation-Emotional *only* is like, which includes Action-Physical because of the nested nature of the dimensions. As you read through these characteristics, notice how you feel, what you think, and any memories that arise.

Deep breath. Start by noticing what's outside of you. Things in this room, sounds, colors. Notice what draws your attention. Now notice what's going on inside of you. Your heartbeat, your breath, how hungry or thirsty you are. Notice any other sensations in your body. Observe what you're feeling emotionally. Notice anything about that feeling. A story about why you might feel that way, right now. Just notice what comes up. Notice what you're longing for in this moment. Just be with that for a while. As you breathe into your longing, notice what happens next. Notice if this longing's connected to your past. Feel that part of you that's searching for truth and honor it. Sit with this. Now, honor the journey of others for a moment. Breathe into that place. Notice if your connection with God or Spirit is more inside or outside of you, right now. Breathe into that and see what happens.

The 12 Primary Feelings

Feelings like disappointment, embarrassment, irritation, resentment, anger, jealousy, and fear, instead of being bad news, are actually very clear moments that teach us where it is that we're holding back. They teach us to perk up and lean in when we feel we'd rather collapse and back away. They're like messengers that show us, with terrifying clarity, exactly where we're stuck. This very moment is the perfect teacher, and, lucky for us, it's with us wherever we are.

—Pema Chödrön

In Chapter 3 you learned the differences between and among affects, feelings, and emotions. As you move from affect into emotion, you can name these physical sensations and the related emotions. This brings them from Action *only* into the Formation dimension, where they become more workable because you can observe and understand from your inner adult. You move beyond first dimension reactivity, no longer trapped by something unknown and scary, into feeling, naming, and processing the feelings that make up your Slivers of Consciousness.

People often mistake thoughts for feelings. When they feel a visceral response, they jump right over the feeling to a thought. Feelings can seem out of control for some, so out of fear they unconsciously jump to "safer" thoughts. Expressing your thoughts is often more socially acceptable too. Here's how you can tell which you're sharing: The word that follows "I feel..." needs to be a feeling word, such as "I feel *sad.*" If you begin a sentence, "I feel *that...,*" you aren't speaking from your feelings, but from your thoughts about them. "I feel that you didn't hear me," is a thought with an underlying feeling, maybe anger, sadness, or disappointment. When you're in touch with your feelings, and can identify your thoughts, you're freer and your relationships improve.

For example, let's say something happens. Perhaps you think, "They don't understand me," and anger comes up. Next you might notice you're feeling sad or hopeless, and think, "It'll never change." It's important to identify your feelings, distinguishing between them and the thoughts and beliefs that go along with them. Even though you might have various names for your experience, accurately identifying your feelings will bring clarity, empower you, and facilitate healing. It's a powerful way to attain mastery. Loosening and integrating your inner experience gives you the sense of peace and happiness you long for.

Most people have self-protection mechanisms that block or dampen their ability to fully know and experience feelings. Opening to the truth about your feelings empowers you. Some emotions may feel difficult at times, but all feelings communicate something to you. They're your teachers, so to speak. As you embrace all of yourself, these feelings won't be as challenging. You'll understand their messages better so you can take needed action in your life. So, here's a more in-depth look at each of the 12 primary feelings, as promised. Moving through each feeling state, one by one, allows for greater resolution of your childhood historical material.

1. Anger
2. Sadness
3. Fear
4. Loneliness
5. Pain
6. Aversion
7. Grief
8. Shame
9. Happiness
10. Peace
11. Love
12. Compassion

Anger may also be referred to as *annoyed, enraged, frustrated,* or *impatient,* to name a few. The feeling of anger can be fleeting, or linger, when the past is triggered by a current event. When we have too much unresolved anger, we end up with many angry moments that can perpetuate an angry mood.

Many of us didn't learn to express anger in healthy ways. You might show anger by shutting it down, and appearing extremely calm, whereas someone else may jump immediately to rage. This depends upon our childhood experience and the defense structure we developed. If we grew up with parents who either raged or repressed their anger, we'll have difficulty knowing how to express our own in healthy ways. Our culture generally has trouble expressing anger appropriately. Typically, women often express anger through tears and men through yelling. Remember, in Chapter 3 we learned how to communicate our feelings in more productive ways.

Sometimes anger is just one layer of feeling, clustered with other feelings. Often anger has a more vulnerable feeling underneath it, such as sadness, hurt, or fear. It's a good idea to ask yourself, *What's under this anger or rage? What is it I don't want to feel?*

It's also important to listen for what the feeling is communicating to you. Is there something you need to do, let go of, or simply feel? Sometimes anger can be a signal from your inner wisdom that something's wrong, and action is needed in a relationship or situation. Do the work of learning about your anger, then process all the associated feelings so you can contain and communicate them effectively.

In the book *Power vs. Force*, psychiatrist and spiritual teacher Sir David R. Hawkins, MD, PhD, wrote about what he called the "Map of Consciousness."[2] Hawkins delineated 17 stages of spiritual evolution, mapping out the calibration of each level's emotional tone using a scale from 20 to 1,000—the higher the number, the higher the consciousness and vibration. At the bottom of the scale is shame at 20, with grief at 75, fear at 100, and anger at 150. Enlightenment, or the ineffable pure consciousness, is 700–1,000. The good news is, as you work with your ego, your personal programming, and feelings, you heal your consciousness enough to tolerate whatever comes up. This raises your vibration so you can embody greater happiness (540) and peace (600).

You can then authentically move through the psychological realm *only*, where we're caught in our programming, and spend more time in the freedom of the realms beyond. From a more healed place you might ask yourself, *What, or whom, am I ultimately defending?*

Sadness may also be called *despair, disappointment, discouragement, gloominess, hopelessness, distress*, or *anguish*, and sometimes incorrectly named *depression*. Sadness moves through us, whereas depression comes from stuck, suppressed feelings. When we repress our sadness we might feel numb, or experience a pervasive but temporary *down* mood. Tears often help lift the feeling of sadness.

I've heard many people say they're afraid to open the door to their sadness, because they just might cry forever. When you're faced with feelings that seem too big to handle, just dip your big toe in the water. You don't have to dive in! Just one toe at a time and you'll move through your sadness.

Fear can be called *apprehension, mistrust, terror, panic, worry, dread, anxious*, or *scared*. When you defend yourself against fear, it shows up as apathy, detachment, indifference, confusion, or numbness. Fear comes from feeling unsafe physically, emotionally, mentally, or spiritually. As a baby, if you needed comfort or reassurance and your parents tuned into you, you felt safe. If your parents were able to meet most of your needs, soothing you with words and calm energy, you probably know how to soothe yourself as an adult. If you had parents who didn't respond in the way you needed—perhaps they were depressed, anxious, distracted, or very ill—you might go straight to fear when an unexpected event occurs. Many of us have a pattern of customary responses, with anger or fear as our emotional set point.

In *A Course in Miracles*, authors Helen Schucman and William Thetford speak at length about love versus fear.[3] Author and A Course in Miracles teacher

Marianne Williamson wrote, "Love is what we are born with. Fear is what we learn. The spiritual journey is the unlearning of fear and prejudices and the acceptance of love back into our hearts. Love is the essential reality and our purpose on earth. To be consciously aware of it, to experience love in ourselves and others is the meaning of life. Meaning does not lie in things. Meaning lies in us."[4]

When we live in a state of fear, we live embedded in the past, anticipating the future. We worry about what will happen, and we fear the unknown. As we heal, we grow strong and resilient enough to know we can face the unknown and deal with whatever life tosses us. From the spiritual perspective, fear is a natural reaction to moving closer to your deepest, inner truth. This fear is universal to us all. We get comfortable with how things are, even when our lives aren't working. Fear sometimes arises when we face the unknown and feel compelled to move closer to the True Self.

As with all our feelings, fear can be our teacher, supporting our psychological health as well as our spiritual growth and enlightenment. The key is to avoid copping out and settling for less than our greatest possibility. We must continue to explore our feelings at more subtle levels, so we have the ego strength to relax into deeper levels of truth.

Loneliness is an unpleasant feeling of isolation, with strong feelings of emptiness. There might be other feelings associated with it, such as sadness about being alone. Other terms that might fit are *yearning*, *pining*, *longing*, *jealousy*, *wistfulness*, *envy*, *hopelessness*, and *seclusion*. As with all feelings, if loneliness is a set point or common feeling for you, it may have begun in your infancy. You may have been left alone and unattended consistently enough that you had trouble attaching to your primary caretaker. Loneliness can be experienced in many circumstances, usually involving a childhood wounding that makes connecting difficult. This creates social difficulties and a lack of close relationships. It's also a temporary feeling for many people going through specific life transitions, such as a breakup or divorce, or loss of any significant relationship.

People who have great difficulty being alone can feel frightened and lonely. As we heal we begin to cherish alone time along with connection. Appreciating solitude is a powerful step in connecting with the True Self and in developing healthy relationships. Poet Rainer Maria Rilke said that as we learn to deal with difficult feelings, "...your personality will grow stronger, your solitude will expand and become a place where you can live in the twilight, where the noise of other people passes by, far in the distance."[5] He goes on to say, "I hold this to be the highest task of a bond between two people: that each should stand guard over the solitude of the other."[6] This creates a deep level of intimacy. Our loneliness can show us when we're disconnected from others, we have trouble connecting generally, or we're with people who just aren't right for us.

Pain can arise when life seems too difficult. This pain can involve many layers or clusters of feelings. We might call it *agony*, *anguish*, *heartbreak*, *misery*, *remorse*, or *regret*. It can accompany bereavement, shame, or hurtful events. Neuroscience research suggests emotional and physical pain share fundamental sensory components. Learning to be present to our suffering creates more inner space so we can know that we're more than our pain.

Emotional pain is often a catchall phrase for difficult feelings, and can come from childhood trauma. This distress can originate from any constant and unpleasant stimulus that activates a cluster of feelings we call pain.

Childhood trauma can come from a variety of circumstances, including verbal, emotional, physical, and sexual abuse, as well as abandonment, rejection, loss, and neglect. When the trauma is severe enough, the person can have debilitating dreams, flashbacks, dissociative problems, and intrusive thoughts and images. Any trauma with a *too much* quality to it can cause Post Traumatic Stress Disorder in people, including victims of crime, rape, war, and, depending upon your childhood, abuse, a bad divorce, or family loss.

It's sometimes difficult to get past the layers of pain an event might trigger within us. We might find ourselves reliving the event repeatedly. This is unproductive, and repeatedly looping through the past can perpetuate a cycle of blame and guilt. If you've processed an event and let go, but you find yourself in a feeling loop, ask yourself these questions: *Is it possible there's more unfinished business that needs processing and healing? What about this is so painful? What is it I'm afraid to feel? Is it possible that I'm getting some secondary gain from all this?*

Lastly, we can sometimes sink into a deeper sense of pain originating in the spiritual level. This can be soul or spiritual pain, from an untapped aspect of us stuck in the past or lacking nourishment. As with all emotions, be kind to yourself and move at your own pace.

Aversion is innate in us. As children we learn to turn our nose up at things we don't like. Often this comes from repulsion, like an unpleasant smell or sight. Events and people can also be repulsive, both physically and emotionally. Watch how you use aversion to avoid something you don't want to feel or do. If you notice you feel repelled by something or someone, stay with it long enough to see where it originates in your programming. Ask yourself, *Is this my wise inner voice, or the voice of my childhood programming?*

Grief is related to sadness. In the *Grief Recovery Handbook*, authors John James and Russell Friedman state that grief is "the conflicting feelings caused by the end of or change in a familiar pattern of behavior."[7] Grief is often overlooked and neglected in our culture. There are many obvious circumstances in which we grieve, such as the death of a loved one or loss of a job. We grieve when we experience an ending, such as divorce, retirement, graduation, the end of a holiday, or even the end of an addiction. We might also grieve when we begin something, such as a new job, a marriage, an empty nest, or with changes in our health and well-being.

We process our grief by examining our expectations, both met and unmet. We look at our wishes, hopes, and dreams. Some proved greater than you imagined and some resulted in deep disappointment. We think about what was said or not said, done or not done. When we honestly examine how something was, and is, we can heal.

Author, psychiatrist, and pioneer in near-death studies Elisabeth Kübler-Ross outlined the Five Stages of Grief in her groundbreaking book, *On Death and Dying*.[8] The stages are: **Denial** ("This can't be happening now."), **Anger** ("Why me?" "It's not fair!" "Who can I blame?"), **Bargaining** ("I'll do anything for a few more years!" "If I could go back in time, I would..."), **Depression** ("What's the point?" "I can't go on."), and **Acceptance** ("I'm going to be okay."). Although presented linearly, they generally overlap, can occur simultaneously, or you might cycle back through them. Processing and releasing our grief is an important way to lighten our load. We finally come to terms with the truth of what's happened, and come to see that life after loss is possible.

Shame is a big issue for most of us. It's also a cluster of feelings. We might refer to it as *embarrassment, chagrin, disgust*, or *being flustered, mortified*, and *self-conscious*. Shame is sometimes called *guilt*, but the two differ. Guilt is feeling remorse over something we did or didn't do, whereas shame is believing we're somehow flawed or *bad*. John Bradshaw says, in *Healing the Shame that Binds You*, "It is the believed failure of the self to the self, and the self becomes the object of its own contempt, an object that cannot be trusted. As an object that can't be trusted, one experiences oneself as untrustworthy. Toxic shame is experienced as an inner torment, a sickness of the soul."[9] Shame feels like we've alienated parts of ourselves from our real self. This begins when thoughts or feelings weren't allowed in our family and childhood. We come to believe essential parts of ourselves are wrong and bad, and nothing about us is okay.

Donald Nathanson, in his book *Shame and Pride*, says that pride is the axis of positive emotions while shame carries the negative emotions. Pride is the pleasure that arises when we're competent. Shame, he says, is the great undoing of whatever had been exciting or pleasurable.[10] When the infant experiences shame, he will impede his activity and his enjoyment. The shamed child then avoids the full expression of his positive affect and feelings. Shame/humiliation has powerful consequences for your sense of self. This shows up as either unworthiness or grandiosity, which are two sides of the same coin. Shame gives us painful self-awareness in each moment, and affects every thought, action, and feeling about ourselves. As the shame builds, we can find ourselves in a shame spiral, feeling compelled to remember every little failure, blow them out of proportion, and then worry.

> George was a very good actor. When he came to me he reported he feared auditions, and was easily distracted by any noise or movement around him. In auditions when he lost his place and needed to start over, he began to feel shame about himself, mercilessly torturing himself with his thoughts. He'd think thoughts like, "What's wrong with me? Why can't I focus like I can in acting class? I'll never be good enough." He'd feel worse and worse until he was so ashamed and scared, he felt himself watching the audition from the casting directors' table. He worked quite a bit as an actor, but knew if he had his full capacities at the auditions, he'd work much more. Even though George was very talented, his family programming had him convinced he'd never be "good enough." After we began to work with the shame and fear, he felt looser, more spontaneous at auditions, and got many more jobs.

We believe this distorted information is the truth about us. It controls the way we live our lives, and we allow it to determine our competency. We often feel separate from others, isolated, and terribly alone. Many people aren't aware of the shame running their lives. They don't see how it causes them to do sad and dangerous things, or not take important, meaningful, creative, fulfilling, and life-affirming actions.

EXERCISE: TENDERLY TOUCHING SHAME

Take three slow deep breaths. Take a moment to think about a time that you felt shame.

- *What thoughts come up for you around shame?*
- *How are you most easily shamed by others?*
- *Is there a childhood story behind your shame?*

See if you can let yourself find the shamed child inside of you. You might visualize or get a feeling for him/her.

- *Where is the child?*
- *What is she/he wearing?*
- *Can you get close to him/her?*
- *Can you connect to him/her?*

- *Will she/he allow you to be kind or soothe her/him?*
- *How does the child feel now?*
- *How do you feel, right now, doing this?*

Notice if there's a part of you that shames yourself with self-talk, or can shame others.

- *Now, how might you connect to the shamer part of you?*
- *What does it feel like to observe this shamer in you?*
- *Whom does your shamer remind you of?*
- *In what ways do you shame yourself and others?*
- *What you are feeling toward this part of yourself?*
- *How might you be compassionate toward this part of you? Notice what comes up.*

EXERCISE: EXPLORING YOUR FEELINGS

Do the following exercise, starting with <u>anger</u>, and then repeat it with the feelings of sadness and fear. Please take a moment to write what comes to mind, and then repeat the exercise with loneliness, pain, aversion, and grief (or any other feeling). Then repeat this exercise with your positive emotions. You don't have to do this all in one day!

Take yourself into the feeling and physical sensations, only as far as it feels safe to you. If a memory's too strong or this starts to seem like too much, stop, breathe, feel your feet on the ground, and look around you. Remember today's date and know these painful events are in the past. Please be kind to yourself, and only put your big toe in the feeling if this is new for you.

Take three slow deep breaths in and out. Ask yourself:

- *When was the last time you felt <u>angry</u>? What were the circumstances? What happened?*
- *Now think of a time that you felt very <u>angry</u>.*

As you remember this feeling, go inside and be with what is happening, right now, as you feel it.

- *How intense does it feel right now on a scale from 0 to 10, if 10 is the worst/strongest (or best if it's a positive feeling)?*
- *Where in your body is it located?*

- *What physical sensations are present? Notice where they are. Is there tightness anywhere, heaviness, fluttering, trembling, physical pain, or burning? Pay attention to your entire body—chest, stomach, jaw, shoulders, throat, and check yourself head to toe. (If doing positive emotions, notice where you feel relaxed, expanded, and settled.) Be with what's there.*
- *What color does it bring up? Notice what happens.*
- *Does any shape come to mind? Notice what happens.*
- *Do things shift or move?*
- *What images come up for you?*
- *What smells, sounds arise?*
- *What other feeling, if any, are you aware of right now?*
- *What thoughts or beliefs come to mind as you're with this feeling?*
- *Are any of these thoughts or beliefs a pattern for you? If so, what pattern do you see?*

Breathe into all that's there for a moment and then continue.

- *What circumstances do you notice habitually trigger <u>anger</u> in you?*
- *What other feelings come up for you when you're feeling <u>angry</u>?*
- *What thoughts did you have during your last experience of <u>anger</u>, or afterward?*
- *What thoughts or beliefs do you have about <u>anger</u>?*
- *What thoughts or beliefs do you notice habitually trigger <u>anger</u>?*
- *How do you contain, express, or repress your <u>anger</u>?*

Now, looking at your history with this feeling:

- *As you grew up, in what ways were you discouraged from feeling and expressing <u>anger</u>?*
- *In what ways were you encouraged?*
- *Are you "allowed" to feel <u>angry</u> now in your life? If not, why?*
- *When in your life do you push <u>anger</u> away? How do you push it away?*
- *Who, if anyone, do you think of when you have this feeling?*
- *What is your earliest memory of <u>anger</u>?*
- *How did your parents or caregivers contain, express, or repress <u>anger</u>?*
- *What happened inside of you when your parents contained, expressed, or repressed <u>anger</u>?*

- *What did your parents tell you about <u>anger</u>? How did they respond when you got <u>angry</u>?*
- *What would you say about this feeling and its place in your life?*

Now go back and allow yourself to hold this <u>anger</u> as vividly as you can. See what happens as you allow it to be there. What do you notice? How might it shift or change? Stay with the process as best you can and allow it to unfold. As you feel ready, take a deep breath and let the anger go. Notice what happens. Perhaps you want to hold on to this feeling or push it away. Take some time, write, and move on to the next feeling.

(A set of these questions for each of the 12 primary emotions are free to download at my site, *www.YourUltimateLifePlan.com*.)

Opening to Positive Feelings

Neuroscience has shown that joy decreases neural brain activity, leaving us feeling more relaxed and open. Working with your feelings allows you the space inside to unlock life's possibilities. You naturally open to positive feelings, such as excitement, and find interest in what emerges from your deeper longings. You open to the process of asking questions, allowing discoveries that fuel your life and creativity.

Creative folks such as painters, choreographers, writers, musicians, and other inspired individuals experience a love and happiness for what they do. Yet even though they have these positive feelings, because of life's complexities, they often deal with struggle and frustration at the same time they're enjoying the moment-to-moment unfolding and flow of the creative process.

Happiness! Most of us would like to feel more *excited, fun, amazed, lively, passionate, joyful, blissful, ecstatic, enthusiastic,* and *relaxed.* As you learn to open yourself to your full range of feelings, even those that seem difficult, happiness becomes a steadier state and encompasses your ups and downs.

In her book *Real Happiness* Sharon Salzberg states, "Conventional happiness—the consolation of momentary distraction—is not only transitory, it can be isolating, shot through with an undercurrent of fear." She continues, "Real happiness depends on what we do with our attention."[11]

Peace is a state of tranquility or quiet, having a sense of *freedom, harmony, centeredness, fulfillment,* and *serenity.* When peaceful, you feel satisfied and content. To find peace you must learn to be present, in this moment, with all your feelings and without depending upon external circumstances. To feel more peaceful, it helps to have completed some historical childhood investigation, bringing your feelings from the unknown into the known. Then you can sit and be present with all that's happening inside of you, with more buoyancy and resilience. This is how you can *be* peace, and not just have peace.

I love what Buddhist teacher Thich Nhat Hanh says in *Being Peace*: "Breathing in, I calm body and mind. Breathing out, I smile. Dwelling in the present moment I know this is the only moment."[12]

Love, as with peace and happiness, easily moves to a transcendent level of consciousness. It's also called *loving-kindness, devotion, admiration, fondness, adoration*, and *veneration*. You feel a personal love for people, animals, and things. You have an encompassing, spiritual love for all and for God. You feel generous and accepting toward yourself and others. Christ spoke often of love, and when you live in Christ Consciousness, embracing the Cosmic Christ, you turn toward what John of the Cross referred to as the "fire of love," living in this divine fire with thought, word, and deed.[13]

Philosopher, theologian, and Christian mystic Meister Eckhart says, "What a man takes in by contemplation, that he pours out in love."[14] As you move into silence—the language of God, higher vibratory levels, and desired emotions—you begin to claim your birthright of Wholeness.

Christian mystic Hildegard of Bingen wrote, "May the Holy Spirit enkindle you with the fire of His Love so that you may persevere, unfailingly, in the love of His service. Thus you may merit to become, at last, a living stone in the celestial Jerusalem."[15] She also wrote,

Love abounds in all things,
excels from the depths to beyond the stars,
is lovingly disposed to all things.
She has given the king on high
the kiss of peace[16]

Compassion and *empathy* naturally arise as you do your personal work. You create greater space and openness to see a world beyond your judgments and narrow view. You can be both for yourself and for others. You drop into spaciousness taking you to acceptance and a rich, inner emptiness—not the wounded, fearful emptiness but the emptiness paired with fullness.

Father Matthew Fox, PhD, writes, "Compassion is another word for the unitive experience and therefore is another name for mysticism."[17] And according to Meister Eckhart, "You may call God love, you may call God goodness. But the best name for God is compassion."[18]

The Journey

As we walk the path, we mature, ever enriching our lives. It takes dedication to stay on the journey and isn't always a path of rose petals. Author and counselor Mariana Caplan, PhD, wrote, "Rumi has a quote about 'fools gold exists because there's real gold,'...less people are going to go for the real gold. Because the real gold requires mining, and you'll get dirty, and you'll go to uncomfortable places, and you work tirelessly, often for no response and no payoff."[19] She also wrote, "If the road to truth means having to learn what is untrue and to face unconsciousness and obstacles within ourselves, the lover of truth gladly accepts this challenge. Each time we expose and face that which is untrue, we are that much closer to what is true."[20]

Walking our path toward truth and healing with tenacity, commitment, and skillful means, things shake loose, shift, and change. At some point, you realize you're no longer involved in an unwanted pattern, unconsciously repeated. You might not have noticed you were healing, but suddenly the old pattern is gone. This is the alchemy of transformation and healing; we work and work on something, and suddenly we notice it's shifted.

As you journey, there may be times you want support. The role of the psychotherapist, spiritual teacher, or coach is to help extend the horizons of self, and to shepherd the awareness brought forth by the inner real self into our lives. Moving into the third or Creation-Mental Dimension, you venture beyond the personal *only*. From the transpersonal perspective, you endeavor to create a new synthesis. From the psychological perspective, you connect all the teachings about the ego with teachings from spiritual traditions. You bring all of yourself—your sensations, feelings, and thoughts—and grow stronger, more resilient and flexible, helping you explore and eventually embody the mystery of life.

Psychotherapist Dr. Diane Shainberg wrote, "Healing arises by confronting what is taking place and seeing that we are changing moment by moment when we let be what is and do not cling to certain thoughts or feelings."[21]

Beyond the Psychological Realm

Meditation is not a means of forgetting the ego; it is a method of using the ego to observe and tame its own manifestations.

—Mark Epstein

Yes, wholeness is always available; it's our ego fixations that keep us from experiencing this from an embodied place. It's very important, in your spiritual pursuits and practices, that you return to your stuck places as they arise. You can use your spiritual practices to inspire you and give you a larger perspective as you tap into the underpinnings of Reality.

In the Kabbalah, Formation-Emotional is called Yitzerah; it means "to form" and is sometimes referred to as speech. It's the speech that comes from thoughts inside us, rather than thoughts from higher consciousness, which we'll explore in the next chapter. The angels here are called Chayot and cherubim.

In Formation, we grow and get to know ourselves. Our relationships improve, we grow more fulfilled in our work, and we make the world a better place. We feel connected to something beyond us, but we can't yet hold the ever-present Wholeness, the Now, or experience clearly defined guidance.

❧

Remember, Formation-Emotional, containing Action-Physical, is completely contained in the next dimension, Creation-Mental.

❧

Remember, from the holographic perspective, God or Spirit is available to you wherever you are. But from Formation *only*, you experience endless longing, a desperation to fix and heal yourself, and you get caught in the loop of seeking without finding. Understanding the Four Dimensions of Consciousness, using the exercises provided in this book, and having a good spiritual practice, excellent spiritual teacher, or skillful transpersonal psychotherapist can help lead you out of these loops. You can then seek, grow, and change while knowing at the deepest level, you're held by God, the Universe, and Silence in every moment.

The desire to know truth never ends. It's a humbling and sweet element of the journey. Moving into the next dimension, Creation-Mental, allows us to drop into a deeper sense of life and the world.

- *What have been the five biggest turning points in your life?*
- *How and when might you have found yourself seeking and not finding?*
- *In what ways do you search for truth?*

Spend 10 minutes meditating on what comes up for you after reading this chapter before starting the next.

The Formation-Emotional Dimension Profile

Reminder: You can download the Formation-Emotional Dimension Profile (along with the other four profiles) at my Website, *www.YourUltimateLifePlan. com.*

CHAPTER 9

The Creation-Mental Dimension

Life isn't about finding yourself. Life is about creating yourself.
—George Bernard Shaw

The Creation-Mental Dimension is your next leap in consciousness and goes from the observation of thoughts and seeing their origins to tasting a larger Reality. The spectrum of inner dimensionality is even more evident in the Creation-Mental Dimension than in the first two dimensions. From the linear perspective, this dimension is more than examining and unraveling thoughts and belief systems; here we find the bridge between the inner and outer realms, holding the space where implicate and explicate, potential and manifestation, personal and impersonal, undifferentiated consciousness and individuality all meet. Creation-Mental introduces us to the continual, moment-by-moment, dynamic process that is the underpinnings of ongoing creation.

In this bigger picture of Reality, we participate at the level of creation, forming something from nothing, not simply forming something from something that already exists, like a cup from clay. As you're about to move into Emanation-Spiritual from the uppermost reaches of Creation-Mental, you're poised on the threshold between inner and outer, manifest and un-manifest, and the perception of intelligence beyond the intellect.

Beyond Action-Physical, you come to see that you're not just a body, physical power, and concrete mindset. When you get triggered and aren't in the narrowly focused, physical world *only*, you begin to question life, learn there's more, and your body settles a bit from your investigations. In Formation-Emotional, you can navigate what once seemed like the turbulent waters of feelings and the

185

thoughts that drive them. You recognize your sense of self is more than feelings about your life. In Creation-Mental, you face all that arises, tuning in to the continuous mental chatter in the background you didn't hear before. You realize you're more than your belief systems and ego structures. As you sink further into this third dimension, you get tastes of the Silence that feeds you, anchoring the embodiment of Spirit. You see who you really are, as the stream of consciousness moves to the forefront.

In each larger, deeper, and more essential dimension we experience greater spaciousness, fluidity, and integration. By integration I mean we're more formed. We've moved away from the pre-personal, where our beingness was split and in pieces, toward an internal coherence where we start to make sense as a being and all the pieces of our lives connect. We have greater unity and wholeness within ourselves. Consequently, we have fewer internal conflicts, and if a conflict does arise, it's resolved more quickly and smoothly.

Remember, because of the nested nature of the dimensions, Creation-Mental contains both Formation-Emotional and Action-Physical. It's a much bigger mindset. We're able to hold more Reality; we can see the "win-win" in our circumstances, reconcile opposites, and move beyond our projections, seeing others for who they are. We can see and process childhood wounds to the point that the Strands return to spaciousness, or we can let them be. We return to more wholeness and are able to rest in our personal self without remaining caught in our history. Through the journeying and internal work we do in Formation-Emotional, we become cohesive enough to relax and drop into Creation-Mental.

At the same time, Wholeness or God is available to us in every moment through our ever-present, holographic reality. On some level, we long for our connection to the Mystery, and our DNA resonates with this. As you read, allow your DNA to awaken to the bigger truth of who you are, not merely the stories you have told yourself or been told.

The fluidity of the Creation-Mental Dimension doesn't refer only to our selection of the thoughts darting quickly across our field of consciousness before disappearing, nor does it simply refer to the internal mechanisms that cause thoughts to slow down and solidify into beliefs, or the process of deconstructing those beliefs; it also refers to the fluidity between the spiritual and material worlds.

Mature Oneness

When you've done the work to stabilize your ego, you experience greater differentiation between yourself and others. You also have greater psychological maturity, your ego integrates into your being, and you experience the two as one. As your inner cohesion increases, you're better able to contain this level of consciousness consistently, seeing what's true and facing the thoughts and feelings that arise. When the body, emotions, and mind are not caught in habitual reaction, you can make richer, more relaxing, satisfying, and fun choices. These choices may be made unconsciously, as well. With your vibration higher, you naturally find yourself in healthier, more promising situations.

You're more integrated with a mature oneness that includes all of life and all levels of being, not the split-off oceanic pre-personal merged oneness, which is actually a form of spiritual bypass, that keeps us reaching for the wholeness we long for without attaining it.

Oceanic oneness (an experience of bliss) is the aliveness and state of being we felt as infants, when allowed to experience fusion or merging with a "good enough" mother. This is so important for developing young nervous systems and healthy attachment, and experiencing the world as safe. If a parent couldn't attune to his/her child sufficiently, perhaps because he/she was preoccupied and ignored the child, or intrusively wanted the child's attention, the child develops a false self. If we have the coping strategies of an inflated or devalued false self, then we grew up too fast and used doing (or were frozen, and unable to do anything) as an attempt to cover over the fear and anxiety of this hypervigilant pseudo-adult self. This false self can't negotiate the unfinished separation and individuation process with our parents that everyone needs to do.

Oceanic bliss in adults is sometimes called spiritual bypass, a distorted attempt to heal ourselves. It's a split-off version of a true experience of living in the oneness and two-ness of a mature adult spiritual life. It's tenuous and conditional, easily ruffled depending on circumstances, and therefore depends on the environment and others. It's not self-generating. It's looking to alleviate difficult feelings in an attempt to feel better rather than searching for truth, which can be scary and painful at times, yet ultimately leads us to freedom, happiness, and spontaneity.

The felt sense of an integrated, mature, adult self chooses to see the world as it is, good and bad, difficult and easy. It can weather the ups and downs of life. Meditation teacher and author Jack Kornfield says, "True maturation on the spiritual path requires that we discover the depth of our wounds: our grief from the past, unfilled longing, the sorrow that we have stored up during the course of our lives."[1] He goes on to say that he refuses to distinguish between psychological and spiritual development, as both can be seen addressing places of spiritual ignorance and

> **Here in Creation-Mental, autonomy is one of the real, actualized, God-given states. The self is part of everything and it stands alone.**

entanglement. Both these levels of self-examination are important and allow us to be fully in Creation-Mental and not in fantasy.

Mature oneness is a grounded state of being, an overall quality of consciousness, not a fleeting experience. This doesn't mean we aren't sometimes in other dimensions. If you want to know whether you're experiencing oceanic bliss or true, mature oneness, see how you are when someone confronts you, or something difficult comes up. In a more mature oneness you're able to stay with the larger context and flow with what is, rather than defensively react to momentary pain. You may have pain, but it doesn't take you over. It's not bigger than you.

It's not necessary to strive for unattainable perfection, or wait until all your historical or childhood wounding is completely healed, before you can know the upper reaches of Creation-Mental. Yet the more healed and coherent your ego, the more self-accepting and freer you are to see the world and Reality as it is.

Now, I don't want you to think we're taking a strictly linear view here. From this larger and more fundamental perspective, in the depths of this dimension you aren't always the observer. You can observe whenever the need arises to solve any personal issue, even a small one, but you can also be with what is. You're in the flow of the universe, not always reflecting upon it. The observer and observed become one. This mature oneness doesn't obliterate separateness, and separateness isn't foreign to or cut off from oneness. Here, our integrated oneness leaves nothing out. Jack Engler writes about this kind of experience in the book *Transformations of Consciousness*: "Life becomes multidimensional and multi-determined in its dynamism and manifestation. This mode of perception leads to a deeper acceptance of human life and death, now set within the context of an unfolding universe in which there is both form and emptiness."[2] Remember, each dimension of consciousness is infinite in depth.

Holding Opposites

Mature oneness entails being with everything. This means we tolerate and hold opposites, seeing them as two sides of the same coin within the larger context that holds all. When holding opposites, we not only find healing, integration, and balance as in Formation-Emotional, but here in Creation-Mental a deeper shift happens, allowing a change into something new, fresh, and distinct that transcends these two—a third entity—creating an entrance into nondual consciousness.

Author Marion Woodman says about opposites, "Life's great challenge is in developing an integration between the spirit and the body. From this integration there arises a divine 'tension,' allowing for a new consciousness to unfold. Why is this integration so difficult?"[3]

Carl Jung spoke of the Transcendent Function. He said if opposites were held in an oscillating tension, a "third thing" appears that is not a blend of the opposites but is qualitatively different. Through this shift in levels of consciousness, a portal opens to a deeper, more fundamental Reality. It's a reconciliation that allows us to drop into more spaciousness. Jung also says, "From this reconciliation a new thing is always created, a new thing is realized."[4]

We transcend dualistic thinking *only*, to nondual. From one direction, we see that opposites can coexist without a problem and from the other direction everything is connected and ultimately one. Opposites also co-arise, as we can't have down without up. In Buddhism it's called the middle way.

Adyashanti, in his book *Emptiness Dancing*, says, "The Middle Way has nothing to do with the notion of being halfway between two opposites. Spirit and matter are not two different things, they are two aspects of the One."[5]

From this level of embodied unification, we see contradictory aspects of Reality as part of the whole of Reality. Because of this synergy, we experience the whole as more than the sum of its parts. Through this union of opposites, we find greater peace, creativity, and the True Self.

Take *contain* and *flow*, for instance. *To flow* is to move steadily and continuously in a current or stream, whereas *to contain* is to control or restrain. Yet a river needs banks to contain its flow, making it a river. And a garden needs to be trimmed, or restrained, to grow well.

If you were to hold both *contain* and *flow*, with one in each hand, as you move your focus back and forth finding a rhythm that's right for you, you don't end up holding half *flow* and half *containment*; you end up with the alchemical fusion of both and an embodied experience of what they produce and how they affect you.

EXERCISE: HOLDING OPPOSITES

Breathe deeply. Spend a few minutes relaxing your body. Begin by holding the concept of "contain" in your right hand. Take some time to be with what this feels like. You can repeat the word to yourself. Now hold the concept of "flow" in your left hand. Take some time to be with what this feels like. Now move your attention back and forth between the two, finding the right rhythm for you, until you notice a shift. Just allow what's there to be.

Repeat this exercise using *light* and *dark*.

So, What's a Thought?

For our purposes here, a thought is a unit of information recognized by the mind and arising out of the unfoldment of all possibilities. Most thoughts don't just pop up out of thin air; instead, something happened that brought the thought to you. Some stimuli, whether visual, auditory, tactile, olfactory, memory, sensation, emotion, or another thought, is perceived. We then create a mental representation of what we perceived, logging it in as a thought. Primarily this is done from past associations, helping us make sense of life. This is why, when you find yourself thinking about something or feeling something that seems unrelated to what's happening in the moment, it's valuable to trace the sequence or train of thoughts back to where they just came from. So, starting where you are, what was the last thing you thought? And what was the thought before that? And the one before that?

Unresolved issues aren't waiting for a quiet moment to sneak up on you and say, "Remember me!" Although a thought might appear to come out of nowhere, because you're not conscious of the sequence of thoughts that led up to it, when you trace your thoughts back you'll understand how you got there, and receive valuable insight for your healing journey. For example, suddenly you notice you're caught in a loop of repeatedly thinking about that hurtful thing your father said to you years ago, and you have no idea why it's here, again. Tracing that back to the thought before, perhaps your roommate questioned you about something, and you unconsciously felt a flash of shame about it. Before that, you felt some anxiety about the possibility of not completing a project, and that reminded you of your dad's definition of failure. One thought and association led to the next until you got caught in a particular thought loop fueled by unresolved feelings from years ago. When you're conscious of your thoughts and feelings, following your thoughts back can help you break free from your negative programming and childhood wounding at any time.

So it helps to see which stimulus brings you into certain thoughts and stories in order to more easily deconstruct them. Thoughts are associative, and if we're deeply embedded in our past programming, our thoughts will most likely be linked to past difficulties. As we evolve, fresh thoughts can arise from a deeper source such as Great Mind. Here are three ways to trace back a thought or Strand:

1. Follow it back to the thought before and then follow it back to the thought before that, and so on.
2. Follow it back to a childhood memory.
3. Follow it back to its origin, seeing it arise from deeper Reality.

The Tales We Weave

In Creation-Mental, we begin to know the impersonal, going beyond the stories we tell ourselves, knowing we're not just the wave, or personal, but also the ocean, the impersonal. We can *experience* there is only water, and we're always swimming in God, Universe, or the Absolute. Spiritual practice helps cultivate our connection and receptivity to the impersonal. Because everything is contained in the highest/deepest dimension, from the integrated Emanation-Spiritual Dimension we embody both the impersonal and personal. This is the human journey.

Since you're more cohesive having done some work in Formation-Emotional, you naturally move into more spaciousness taking you to Creation-Mental. You've seen the thoughts connected to your feelings and have unraveled some of the difficult historical material of your life, but haven't focused on thoughts directly nor known the thoughts that come from Creation-Mental or Higher Mind. Here, you start to see behind the scenes of the entire panorama of structures that make up you.

In the beginning of Creation-Mental you learn to be with thoughts as they arise and start more clearly seeing the thoughts and patterns that form your life as you know it. These patterns are the subtle details of you, the ways you consciously and unconsciously choose the positive and negative thoughts and feelings that create your life. They contribute to the ego structure you've built your life around.

As we observe the tales we weave, we learn to question, feel, and grieve the stories comprising our beliefs. This allows us to reach a level of Presence where our beliefs begin to deconstruct, and the Strands of Consciousness loosen, returning us to the wholeness that's always there. To see more of the truth, sometimes it takes conscious processing, perhaps with the *Multidimensional Awareness Practice*. Our practices help us notice the subtle ways we stay in reaction, enabling us to see it for what it is, work with it, then let it be. This loosening allows brief glimpses into the next dimension of consciousness, Emanation-Spiritual—the emptiness, openness, and spaciousness out of which everything arises, including thoughts. All this can eventually happen in an instant, as you work with it.

Many of these thoughts speed by so fast we don't even notice, and often people run their lives according to these patterns without knowing it. Buddha called our easily distracted, continuously moving mind, "Monkey-Mind." Like monkeys swinging from tree to tree, our mind keeps grabbing the next thought, often craving something to fill our wounded emptiness.

With meditation you begin to slow your thoughts, and see the layers of thoughts and beliefs that keep a coherent self intact. It takes facing the unknown and all you *think* is you, to begin unraveling those tightly held ideas about yourself.

Some of those stories are true and some are not. Seeing these fixed ideas and mental constructs for what they are helps you reach the largest context.

Our nervous system relaxes so we can walk into the Mystery and settle into closeness with the Divine, God, or the Absolute. We're able to travel into uncharted waters, facing the fear that accompanies the unknown, moving us toward the fourth dimension where there's no language, pointing us to what lies beyond words.

Belief Systems

A thought is received information that becomes a representation. A belief is an acceptance that the representation/thought we just perceived is true and exists. When a thought becomes charged with emotions as a result of some story we were told or deduced from what we experienced, a passing thought is turned into a belief we hold as true.

A thought might be, "I want to take a walk," but a belief has commentary on the thought, based on history, and is usually beyond our awareness. For instance, the thought, "I want to take a walk," may activate or trigger the belief that "I *need* to walk [with an underlying *because*...]," or "I *don't want* to walk [with an underlying because...]." Whether beliefs are life-enhancing, "I can do this," or limiting, "I can't do this," each has its underlying *because*.

As we try to make sense of the world, we construct *belief systems*, networks of interconnected beliefs. Belief systems are webs of individual beliefs composed mostly of unconscious thoughts coming from spirit and soul, along with our childhood history and our interpretations of what we encounter. Over time, belief systems create automatic pathways in consciousness, making it appear that this is how the world operates. These act as vibrational magnets helping us attune to or attract certain people, places, and things. As we change, our attunement changes, and suddenly the same kind of folks don't show up in our lives anymore, or if they do, we respond differently.

> Remember, at any point in time and in any dimension you can make a quantum leap or new choice. The more you integrate, the easier it becomes.

To take our lives to the next level requires becoming aware of our limiting beliefs, and meeting them with compassion and acceptance. We learn to slow down, quiet the mind, and practice deep awareness.

Neuroscience suggests we have about a half second between when a stimulus arrives and our response. Quantum Mechanics teaches us we have many quantum choices in that span of time, but we "collapse the wave" according to our personal programming or our ego's habitual response from childhood, or past-life familiarity. When you do the work to hold this level of consciousness, you create space to choose something new and different. It happens as we grow and change. We can step out of the way, allowing a higher sense and deeper Mystery to unfold. We're led by something beyond our ordinary mind.

Working with our ego and doing spiritual practice refines us, helping raise our vibration and growing our capacities. It feeds and strengthens the causal or soul body, our vessel for the Divine breath of God, Temple of the Soul, or Super-Conscious Mind. This is where we connect with that kernel of our karmic material, and face current belief systems that keep us recycling old behaviors.

EXERCISE: EXPLORING YOUR BELIEFS

- *Name five of your life-enhancing beliefs.*
- *Name five of your limiting beliefs.*
- *Which beliefs seem to cause you the most difficulty, and why?*

Take one limiting belief and explore its origin by asking:

- *Where have I seen this in my past?*
- *Did someone I know live this in his/her life or teach it to me?*
- *What events either introduced or supported this belief?*

Things

Liberation can only be gained by practice, never by mere discussion.
—S.N. Goenka

In Action-Physical, Formation-Emotional, and very early in Creation-Mental we're concerned with our separate sense of self. In establishing this sense of separate self, we develop internal structures—an internal system, consisting of a combination of thoughts and feelings from childhood programming overlaid on the True Self. This is the scaffolding or framework we carry inside to create consistency in our everyday lives. This ego or self structure is put in place to get a sense of who we are in the world. It's where we develop preferences about whom we like or don't like, and what we choose to do or not do. This structure keeps us from feeling as though we're about to fall apart. Our personal work helps us harmonize and assimilate the ego contents of our programming with our essence. Then we can relax our defenses, see our programming for what it is, and form a more cohesive, integrated structure. As we grow, we become conscious of certain aspects of this structure that no longer contribute to our highest good and transform them. We continue to examine and purify the structure for greater spaciousness, and deeper connection with the Divine.

To see through the ways we've organized our lives, we use psychological and spiritual processes to unwind and deconstruct beliefs we think are us. This structure, out of which we live, is the coalescing of everything—thoughts, feelings, and ego. In Creation-Mental, you begin to view the patterns and structures directly.

Deeper consciousness helps us see "behind the curtain." In our effort to create a coherent self, we hold our beliefs so tightly; we solidify them, making them *things*. Life no longer flows; we're stuck with the same behaviors and life we don't want. We limit our possibilities and stop the flow of the stream, once again picking up our favorite six issues and the stories that go with them. Keep in mind that we evolve in stages, and fluctuate between change and homeostasis.

In *Wholeness and the Implicate Order*, David Bohm wrote that through philosophy and science, his understanding of the nature of reality and consciousness is "an unending process of movement and unfoldment." He goes on to say, "Whenever one thinks of anything, it seems to be apprehended either as static or as a series of static images. Yet, in the actual experience of movement, one senses an unbroken, undivided process of flow...in the 'stream of consciousness' not dissimilar to the sense of flow in the movement of matter in general."[6]

In codifying our perception of life through thinking, we create separate *things* out of these passing images. From this perspective we're not seeing the world as it is, but as our projections, representations, or symbols. These representations— ideas of the world based upon our projections and interpretation of reality— become our idols, standing between us and God. We can't stay in the flow of life because we think our representations are the thing, itself, mistakenly believing our representations/idols *are* Reality.

The purpose of doing our personal work and spiritual practice is to wake up, see the beauty that's actually here, and not get caught by false images. In British Philosopher Owen Barfield's book, *Saving Appearances: A Study in Idolatry*, he spoke of smashing idols, saying that Western reality consisted of objects—"hollow pretenses of life"—and we're lost in the representational world.[7] We then stay stuck in what we think is true, without questioning our life. This affects our personal fulfillment, our understanding of life, and our relationships with others, ourselves, and God.

Origin of Thoughts

We've talked about many ways of questioning our automatic thoughts and behaviors. Observing the contents of the mind helps us see we are more than our thoughts. We *have* thoughts. Noticing and questioning our beliefs, or sitting with whatever comes up, can begin smashing those idols. It really helps to sit in meditation and watch these thoughts. Mindfulness meditation is great to practice here. Doing your practices helps you more clearly see the many choices you have, leading you to expanded consciousness.

As we calm our mind and nervous system, we use spiritual practices to help us sink down into more subtle levels of thought. We expand our consciousness to include the stirrings at the source of our thoughts in the unconscious, as they percolate up from Greater Mind.

Yogi Maharishi Mahesh says, "A thought-impulse starts from the silent creative centre within, as a bubble starts from the bottom of the sea. As it rises, it becomes larger; arriving at the conscious level of the mind, it becomes large enough to be appreciated as a thought, and from there it develops into speech and action."[8]

9 MEDITATIONS

The following meditation practices can be done to help stabilize your focus, see the origin of your thoughts, and move toward more inner silence. You might want to read the instructions and then sit quietly with your eyes closed to do the practices.

1. *Notice your thoughts and let them pass like clouds in the sky. You can start by focusing on your breath. After a thought passes, come back to your breath, or feel the sensations in your body until you notice another thought. It might help to practice both focusing on the breath and noticing sensation.*

2. *Notice the monkey mind or mental chatter that goes from thought to thought and desire to desire, and like the swinging monkey, be conscious of each branch or thought as it comes. What happens as you're simply with the passing thoughts?*

3. *Notice your thoughts and let them go, but if you're caught in a story take note of the content. Use any material from this—thoughts or feelings—to do your Strands of Consciousness exercises.*

4. *Be with a thought and see if you can drop into it more deeply. Allow it to expand. You might notice it begins to dissipate, dissolve, or get*

you started down a trail following a story. Bring yourself back to that thought, notice the sensations and emotions connected with it, and notice what happens.

5. *Notice any repeating patterns in your thoughts and feelings. You might repeat phrases, stories, sounds, or images. Write about or draw what you see, hear, or feel.*

6. *Slow your thoughts down by breathing into them. You'll start to experience some rumblings behind your thoughts, then more spaciousness. You may have different kinds of body sensations, pranic movements, or kriyas (we'll explore this further in the next chapter). You might find yourself doing spontaneous body movements, yoga positions, or mudras. As you breathe into your thoughts, you'll continue to experience more and more spaciousness taking you to the origin of your thoughts or patterns. You may start to experience thoughts as they arise out of awareness itself.*

7. *Notice a thought and allow it to move into a shape, color, or image. Allow it to move into the stream of consciousness. Be with whatever comes up.*

8. *Repeat the mantra* Hum-Sa. *Recite* Hum *on the inhale and* Sa *on the exhale, then reverse it for a while. It's Sanskrit, meaning, "I am that" or "I am that I am."*

9. *Centering prayer: Choose a sacred word. Keep thinking of it in whatever form it arises, relaxing with it. Use this as a pointer for your inward movement toward the indwelling presence of God. When your mind wanders, return to your sacred word and relax. Allow yourself to open to the Ultimate Mystery, Divine Presence, Source, or resting in God.*

Suffering

In Formation-Emotional, we learned to walk into our suffering, knowing it contains insight and wisdom that deepens our humanity and makes us more loving. Creation-Mental views both suffering and joy as fundamental to human existence. You become willing to experience suffering head-on, without any preoccupation with a secondary story, or preferred suffering. You know that problem that pops up again and again? Even though it causes some pain, it may feel safer than facing another, more difficult issue. As you stay with your suffering, you discover it can be the very catalyst facilitating your transformation and happiness.

Because you finally know everything is an inside job, and inside and outside are one thing, you've stopped looking outside yourself for the source of pain and the rescue from pain. You learned from Formation-Emotional that you're resilient, and there's great freedom in knowing you don't need to be rescued from difficulties. You've experienced a shift, and now see that both problems and solutions come from inside. You can ride life's ups and downs more easily, and be present for all of it. You know Grace is your bedrock as you move through life.

In Creation-Mental we brush up against nonduality, called *advaita* in Sanskrit. Whether you choose to call these upper reaches Awareness, Nirvana, Consciousness, Spirit, God, Cosmic-Christ, Brahman, or Tao, this takes you into the richness of the fourth dimension, Emanation-Spiritual, where you know the constant, nondual, ever-present, unchangeable Is-ness of all existence.

Metaphor

In Creation-Mental we begin to hold paradox. We realize that subject and object become one, recognize the patterning of reality, and begin to embody quantum theory. We begin experiencing the duality of wave and particle as the dance of oneness, and the mind as existing throughout non-local consciousness. At the upper reaches, we begin touching intimate awareness of the Divine.

In the English language there are different definitions for similes, metaphors, and parables; however, spiritually they all help point to that which is beyond intellectual comprehension. Throughout history many great religions and sages from all traditions have called these three *metaphor*, using it to convey their transmissions of the deeper, wordless, ultimate Reality.

Metaphor is the language of the upper reaches of Creation-Mental. Metaphor compares two seemingly unrelated subjects, and can be worded in three ways:

1. In a simile, using the words *like* or *as*. For example, "Life is like a roller-coaster."

2. The first subject described as being the second subject, as in Shakespeare's "All the world's a stage."

3. As a parable, an extended form of metaphor.

Unlike metaphor, symbols are objects, signs, or images that relate to what they're representing, more the language of Formation-Emotional. We can use symbols and metaphor to inform us in deeper ways.

The Bible's book of Matthew includes the parable of the mustard seed, wherein Jesus used a metaphor to teach about faith. Jesus said that if the people had faith even as small as a mustard seed they could tell a mountain to move and it would move. He was helping people see that a small amount of faith was all they needed to experience God.[9]

Light and Dark are often used as metaphors in spiritual teachings. Dark represents evil, or ignorance preventing us from seeing the truth, whereas Light signifies God, knowledge, possibility, comprehending truth, and walking the righteous path. Even a tiny light in a dark room illuminates the darkness, making everything visible and allowing us to see clearly.

In metaphor, we can point to that which is beyond words, not only showing us unconscious information, but releasing us from our usual belief systems and old patterning. We don't just rehash old programming, but bring in a new perspective. We also begin to understand words have power, and language helps us embody deeper truth. In Creation-Mental we discover that we, indeed, create our lives every day. The answer lies in our personal metaphors. They show our view of the world, and help deconstruct beliefs while constructing something new and distinctive. With this knowledge, we manifest our highest purpose.

EXERCISE: METAPHORS

Complete the following statements. Move quickly, without thinking, allowing your unconscious to inform you. You'll be looking at your view of yourself and your life, who you think you are and what you do. Notice both the positive and negative ways you see yourself and experience your day-to-day life. See if any images or bodily sensations come up for you and write those down also.

I am _____. *Examples: a survivor, a tiger, a bear, a helper, a lover, a spiritual warrior, a healer, a writer, a loser, a winner, lazy, a hard worker, strong, a moving river, a stop sign, etc.*

Life is _____. *Examples: easy, hard, fun, a struggle, magical, a dance, funny, an adventure, a game, a sunset, a rainstorm, etc.*

Write, draw, paint, or dance several empowering metaphors for your life. *Example: Life is a dance, and I find the ways I move with it and enjoy it.*

The "I" Maker

In Creation-Mental, we learn we're more than our thoughts and ordinary mind. We're part of the Great Mind and can live our lives embedded in a larger truth about us.

We know, from psychology and spirituality, the ego is our sense of personal identity. Looking at the view from matter, we know that to stop re-creating our unwanted programming, we need to question our unconscious routine, and challenge false beliefs about ourselves and life. But how do we choose something different from all the quantum choices?

We've learned about the *personal* from a psychological perspective, and now we're beginning to see, from the upper reaches of Creation-Mental consciousness and the view from Spirit, where our personal self arises out of the *impersonal* Plenum, Wholeness, implicate order, quantum field, or all possible options. This is where something comes out of nothing; your "I," or personal self comes into your essence from the impersonal no-self. Let's look at the existence of the personal "I," and question, who is this "I," this personal self?

Continued questioning of the "I" behind everything helps us see the "I" maker, or the thought creating the personal "I," that's our separate sense of self. This thought springs from that which is beyond logical intellectual thought: Supermind, Great Mind, Mind of God, All-That-Is.

Deep into Creation-Mental, you finally see that the ego, with all its gyrations, and the True Self are two faces of the One. The "I" is the personal nature of the deeper "I Am" Presence, encompassing all opposites, seeing them as dualistic impressions of a unified consciousness. Looking from the upper reaches of Creation-Mental, Wholeness views opposites as intrinsic to the whole and we have more space for compassion. Remember, from your holographic nature you always resonate with the deeper "I Am" Presence, because it's ever-present.

Sri Ramana Maharshi, a Hindu teacher of awakening, talked of how we recreate ourselves from the lower, fixed, mental concepts. He said, "You are now identifying yourself with a wrong 'I,' which is the 'I'-thought. This 'I'-thought rises and sinks, whereas the true significance of 'I' is beyond both." He said, "The true 'I' is not manifest and the false 'I' is parading itself. This false 'I' is the obstacle to your right knowledge. Find out wherefrom this false 'I' arises. Then it will disappear. You will be only what you are—i.e., absolute Being."[10]

He taught people to question this personal "I"-thought by constantly asking, "Who am I?" Am I my body? Am I my thoughts? Am I my feelings? And who is the "I" asking the question? As much as you may identify with your body, thoughts, and feelings, when you say, "*my* knee hurts," who is the "I" claiming possession of the body? Or when you say, "I'll think about that," who is the "I" that thinks? Even when you say, "I'm sad," what you're really saying is, "I feel sad." Who is this "I" that feels?"

In Sanskrit this can be referred to as *neti, neti*: "I am not this, I am not that." Putting this all together, Sri Ramana said, "The 'I'-thought is therefore the root thought. If the root is pulled out, all others are uprooted at the same time. Therefore, seek the root 'I,' question yourself 'Who am I?'; find out its source. Then all these [thoughts] will vanish and the pure Self will remain."[11]

EXERCISE: WHO AM I?

Deep breath. See what arises with these questions:

Ask: Who am I? If the answer is your name, or "me," ask yourself, *Who answered?* If the answer is your name or "me" again, ask again, *Who is that?*

Remember to also ask, in the face of any physical sensations, feelings, or thoughts: *Am I my body? Am I my feelings? Am I my mind and thoughts? Then, who is the "I" that's thinking?*

Ask again: *Who am I? Who is the "I" that's answering? What is the source of this somebody?*

Now notice your thoughts. As each thought arises ask, *Who is thinking this thought?* Wait for the answer, and if it is "I am," then let that lead you back to, *Who am I?* Again, wait for the answer, and as you notice it arising, ask, *Who is the "I" that's answering?* For the next few minutes, keep asking *Who am I?* or *Who is that?* with each new thought that arises.

Quietly sit with this for a while.

Falling into the Gap

Every time you create a gap in the stream of mind, the light of your consciousness grows stronger.

—Eckhart Tolle

Living in this mature relationship with Presence brings us to the moment of relaxing into the ever-present Grace, or what Father Thomas Keating calls "resting in God."[12] Franciscan Priest and author Richard Rohr says, "Mature Transcendence is an actual 'falling into'.... What we fall into is what Christianity would call both 'an abyss' and an 'utter foundation.'"[13] It seems like a paradox, but from the embodiment of Creation-Mental, it's not. This Dimension teaches through paradox, metaphor, and actually tasting the Divine.

To "fall into" this dimension of consciousness you must be willing to face yourself, by being with everything that presents itself—what you thought would be, what you were taught was supposed to be, what society says must be, your ideology, and every other idea you have about life. It means being willing to fall into the abyss, the mystery of life, trusting something is there. Maybe you won't be who you thought you'd be. Maybe there's something bigger and greater, but perhaps it will look nothing like you thought it would.

We experience "falling into" the gap between thoughts. It takes us below the surface of the mind to Great Mind, guided by the True Self. We're drawn to the power of silence, and our choices become clear.

MEDITATION: THE GAP BETWEEN THOUGHTS

Notice the gap between your thoughts, and allow yourself to drop into that gap. As you notice your thoughts, keep bringing yourself back to the gap. You might find you're able to stay in the gap for a while, then a thought, emotion, or sensation might bring you back to your stories and personal agendas. Again, bring yourself back to the gap. Notice any spaciousness present.

Existential

Inner adventures and peak experiences often propel us into deeper and deeper territory. If we're seekers, even if we've only managed to open the door a crack, we're fueled toward nondualistic, full-bodied consciousness.

There are different kinds of opening experiences, as well as varying degrees. You may have had: a revelation about your life's work; a realization about how to manage a very difficult situation; a heart-opening burst of understanding while in therapy; a sense of timelessness in meditation; a deep, spacious connection with nature; a feeling of great stillness with a spiritual teacher; a mind-opening experience during a Zen Koan practice; a spontaneous movement into yoga postures from a meditative state; an unshakable, enriching silence during a retreat; a sudden epiphany about the marriage of twoness and unified consciousness; etc.

❧

We are led to a felt sense of embodied Wholeness.

❧

If these inner adventures go well, they can lead directly to opening into the deepest waters available to us in any given moment. If they don't go as well as you'd hoped and it seems that you took a detour in your growth in consciousness, remember you can always reach out for support. And anyway, everything is grist for the mill of learning and growing. Life is a journey.

As we move into these deeper, spiritual realms through our studies and experiences, a new set of issues arises. If we keep our eyes open, new levels of self-development and inner work will appear. These apply not only to the six issues we continue to refine, but to subtle, new issues about our existence, as well as existence itself.

When a new level opens, you may experience existential anxiety, or psycho-somatic symptoms such as headaches, fatigue, or odd physical sensations. Some people face the "dark night of the soul," a period of doubt, confusion, and frightening emptiness. After tasting the Divine, experiencing ecstasy or sudden clarity, people sometimes regress and suffer a spiritual crisis or spiritual depression, which we'll discuss more in the next chapter. It feels different from neurotic depression, yet can include pre-personal Slivers that need healing. It's important to examine these issues. Otherwise, in my opinion, you'll never reach your deepest truth or live as freely as you'd like.

From here, you're less reactive and less inclined to use avoidance behavior, and you can relax and drop into being with life as it is. From this bigger picture, you don't feel so desperate. You don't dissociate from a thought or feeling. You may prefer a certain outcome, but aren't attached to an idea of what must happen. Father Richard Rohr says, "...you surrender to the naked now of true prayer and full presence."[14]

Some powerful questions to ask yourself that will help you access these deeper levels are: *What do I avoid?* Sit with this question and take some time to explore it fully. *Do I ever use any seemingly positive activity, to escape or avoid something I don't want to face or feel? Am I using anything—any action or habit, feeling or mood, thought or belief—to shield me against the pain of living? Am I avoiding my feelings, or my body, or my relationships, or my work in the world?*

For most of us, living from an embodied, deeper consciousness in Creation-Mental takes commitment and personal truth-telling. Doing your Formation-Emotional healing work furthers your dedication and steadfastness in your commitment to clearly seeing the truth. It helps to notice what in your life is not working as smoothly as you'd like it to.

❧

It's the Oneness containing everything—duality and unitive consciousness. You're free to be the wave and the ocean. The conflict between separateness and oneness is nullified. It's finally seeing Reality in its entirety.

❧

Bigger Reality

Deep into Creation-Mental is the realm of "Is-ness," where God is a verb, because we're living in the now of each moment. Eternity and linear time come together. We surrender to right now. For *now* contains all possibilities, the present moment as well as the historical past and anticipated future. It's the level of creation where everything is distinct, individual, and itself, without any interest in comparing and contrasting.

It's in the upper reaches of Creation-Mental that we look at our ultimate metaphors and the "I"-thoughts that create our lives. We're *in* reality, not observing it. Because of this, here we don't create *things*, objectifying reality. We see life and people as they are, experiencing the depth and poignancy of life's beauty. God-connectedness is exactly where we are. When the light of God shines through, everything seems exquisitely vivid and imbued with luminous transparency.

We're guided by clear intuition. Our life is a response to a calling from our true nature and the true nature of God, which is the same thing. From these upper reaches of Creation-Mental, we see the beauty of, and are not frightened by, the duality of Action-Physical, nor the emotions, meanings, and suffering of Formation-Emotional. We begin to sense that we're one of the faces of God.

In the Kabbalah this dimension is named *Briah*, meaning "to create," and is considered the bridge connecting the upper dimension of the ineffability and "nothingness" of Emanation-Spiritual and the lower dimension of Formation-Emotional. The threshold between Creation-Mental and Emanation-Spiritual is the ever-constant origination point where nothingness is unfolding into somethingness.

Creation-Mental links us with universal patterns and sacred geometry. When embodied, we can feel and experience these patterns as the actual fabric and foundation that literally connects us all, the matrix that holds the entire creation.

The Angels here are called seraphim and archangels, the embodiment of pure intelligence, consciousness, and comprehension.

From the Vajrayana Buddhist text, the Hevajra-tantra:

The great awareness exists
In the bodies of all sentient beings,
Neither as duality or non-duality
Neither as substance nor non-substance
But as the supreme state
Pervading all things, dynamic and static.[15]

The Creation-Mental Dimension Profile

Reminder: You can download the Creation-Mental Dimension Profile (along with the other four profiles) at my Website, *www.yYourUltimateLifePlan.com*.

Chapter 10

The Emanation-Spiritual Dimension

*Emanation is the process in which the One pours
over into all of the realms of being.*

—Plotinus

The Buddha said the True Self can be seen, at least for a moment, in the space between thoughts. As you may have noticed, words become increasingly inadequate the further you go into Wholeness. Words point to the Emanation-Spiritual Dimension, but ultimately you understand through experience that moves you toward a fully embodied life. The process of learning, understanding, and moving toward embodiment opens you to guidance and connection beyond your wildest dreams. This chapter could just say, "Sit in silence, and be nourished by the language of God." But this is a book, so here we go.

Early in Emanation-Spiritual, we continue where Creation-Mental left off, being the interface between the infinite and intimate, God and creation, the Absolute and relative. Like mind-bending explorations of a Zen Koan, we've ascended into the depths and mystery of the outer reaches of consciousness where we simultaneously move inward, outward, and sit still. This transpersonal dimension is difficult, if not impossible, to comprehend logically. It's beyond intellect; it's an experience. Here we have the deepest intimacy with God, receiving our existence from pure Presence. It includes both fullness and emptiness, and contains all potentials. We cultivate the ability to embody this fluid dimension

❧

From the holographic, quantum-reality, and nondual perspectives, all is one.

❧

205

by working with all the dimensions, leading us to a state of inner stillness that is our birthright.

Emanation-Spiritual cannot be reached through intellectual reasoning, understanding, or sentiment. This level of undifferentiated mind isn't divided into concepts or ideas. Although the embodiment of Emanation-Spiritual is Supra or Higher Mind, Understanding, Wisdom, the Will of God, or the Universe, it's revealed through compassion, truth, strength, harmony, endurance, empathy, receptivity, and all the other potentials that become realized when we embody God. Remember, all dimensions are contained within this dimension.

Physicist David Bohm stated that deep within the implicate order—an undivided and enfolded wholeness that is the infinite background source from which the material world of our everyday visible lives unfolds—thought and language fail us. He says whereas thought can grasp the unfolded material world, only something beyond thought, such as intuition, unmediated insight, or sacred silence, experiences the enfolded.[1] Bohm goes on to say that some background source underlies our everyday perception. We might call it the experience of Wholeness, or the Godhead.

Coming forth out of Nothingness, the enfolded, is creation, going all the way to Action-Physical, the unfolded. From the Emanation realm, we experience ourselves as more than our linear thoughts and feelings, more than who we *think* we are. In fact, letting go of who we think we are, with our limiting beliefs and childhood programming, opens us to experience who we truly are.

In Emanation-Spiritual our awareness, and the state in which it arises, cannot be separated. It's one. It's like the Advaita teaching about Gold in the sacred Hindu text, the Chandogya Upanishad. Although Gold may be fashioned into different shapes and have different appearances, such as a bracelet or a ring, it's still Gold. Here, Gold is a metaphor for Brahman or God. It's as if a gold bracelet (someone) goes to a guru and asks where to find Gold (God.) Yes, we are separate bracelets and rings, but we are all Gold.

Some spiritual practices can help us get a taste of the ultimate Divine stillness, the Absolute, Brahman, or God, and we build upon that taste. These practices help us explore internal territories, develop our inner observer that sees and works with our difficulties, and experience the observer and observed as one, which seats us in the largest possible context, so we can integrate and live from an intuitive connection with our essence.

Opening to Emanation

Faith takes us to deep places, to the ruptures in our self-confidence and our lives. Do not settle for spiritual comfort all the time.... Darkness is divine also. Faith is not about positive thinking so much as the perseverance that kicks in when we are weak, sick, and full of doubt. The via positiva never stands alone. The via negativa is always with us on our faith journey as well.[2]

—Matthew Fox

We could say that everything written so far in this book helps you to heal, open, and attune to this dimension. By looking at our early, stuck places, embracing our feelings and examining our thoughts, we clean out our psychic cobwebs, creating more space inside to receive the ever-present Grace and "Breath of God." We need this space, or emptiness, to better discern and receive the deepest Wisdom, Beauty, and Glory. All this prepares us for inviting, allowing, and surrendering to the Ground of Being.

We open to receive the revelations available from Emanation, so we're able to live from our essence, and the True Self, in our everyday lives. Rabbi Rami Shapiro says in his book, *The Divine Feminine*, "I believe revelation comes to you when you slip from narrow mind, what the Jewish sages call mochin d'katnut, to spacious mind, mochin d'gadlut."[2]

Looking at the view from Spirit, from All-That-Is, we descend into Emanation, into a level of knowable velvety sparkling nothingness, a nourishing emptiness moving into somethingness. We're moving into a dimension of consciousness that we're capable of brushing against or cleaving to, that informs and bathes us, and all of creation, with Divine Lights.

This profound sparkling emptiness includes everything, even all our feelings—good and bad—but we experience it differently than deficient and fearful psychological emptiness. Notice what comes up for you as you read about emptiness and nothingness. We'll address it in more detail at the end of the chapter.

> ❧
>
> **This deeper Reality is sometimes referred to** as *God cleaving* in **Judaism,** *the ocean of compassion, Buddha nature, Reality-as-it-is,* or, in **Contemplative Christian terms,** the *Cosmic Christ* or *Logos.*
>
> ❧

Now, looking at the view from matter, in Emanation we're receptive to all possibilities and potentials, and we consent to God. This dimension receives its light directly from Divinity, the Godhead, Adam Kadmon, Pure Presence, Emptiness, Nothingness, or Spaciousness, which exist everywhere.

In the Bible, Genesis 1:2–3 says that the spirit of God hovered over formless void and chaos. Then God said, "Let there be Light."[3] The light of God illuminates and creates the world. At the outer reaches of Emanation, undifferentiated light begins emanating toward embodiment, becoming increasingly differentiated as it passes through each dimension, until God's light is the most veiled, or hidden, in Action-Physical.

Kabbalistic texts say that the ongoing creation process begins in the fertile, black nothingness. All potentials and possibilities originate from this nothingness. Emanation begins with God's loving act of constricting God's light, the first act of "Will." It's where nothingness and the Will of God come together, the original impetus for creation.

> ⚘
> **Remember, the word *Kabbalah* means "to receive."**
> ⚘

God partially withdrew God's light to create the universe, allowing God to be in the world without obliterating or overwhelming it. This leaves room for choice and our own free will. We experience this creation process daily. Without the space created by the constriction of light, matter wouldn't exist. There would be no table, no chair, no you or me.

The Kabbalah calls this dimension *Atzilut*, meaning "nearness," and says at this level of nearness to God "no thought can grasp Him." God is infinite, and therefore cannot be characterized or defined. God is limitless Being and Existence, as well as limitless Nonexistence.

- *In what ways does the idea of opening to Spirit or God seem easier or harder than opening to other aspects of your life?*
- *When you think about opening to receive, what images or thoughts come up for you?*
- *What might receiving look like for you, from Emanation?*
- *What internal cues let you know you're in the process of receiving?*
- *From what you've read about Emanation-Spiritual so far, what do you notice physically? Emotionally? Mentally? Spiritually?*

MEDITATION: THE GATES OF MERCY AND LIGHT

Deep breath. Sit quietly and feel yourself moving into relaxation. Focus on your breathing. Now open to the gates of Mercy, the gates of Light. Consent to receiving Source pouring Mercy over you and through you, filling you with the everflow of unending Mercy and Light. Allow Spirit to bestow Mercy and Light upon you. Bathing you. Relaxing into the Light and Mercy. Feel the Light warming your face, your entire body. Bathe in this Light and Mercy. Feel the Mercy blessing you, warming you, healing you. Bathe in this Light and Mercy for a while.

Embodying Spirit

We continue opening to greater intimacy with God through spiritual disciplines such as prayer, contemplation, chanting, meditation, yoga, Sufi whirling, and other spiritual practices. Father Thomas Keating says in his book *Open Mind, Open Heart*, "The interior experience of God's Presence activates our capacity to perceive Him in everything else—in people, in events, in nature...as well as in prayer."[4] He goes on to say, "Interior silence is the perfect seed bed for Divine love to take root.... Divine love has the power to grow and to transform us."[5]

In our embodying process, vital energy emerges from the source of Emanation and flows from the spiritual to the physical. From the perspective of the Godhead, this vital energy pours into us and imbues us with Divine Lights. From the perspective of the human body, we receive vital energy from Emanation descending through the dimensions, moving through the human energy body into our physical body. This ever-present vital energy is called many things: prana, chi, Shakti, ruach, life force energy, mana, pneuma, bioplasmic energy, orgone, and others. As we open in all dimensions, channels and centers of subtle energies open called meridians, chakras, nadis, bindu, sefirot, or other names depending on the paradigm.

Sometimes, when these energy channels and centers open, people manifest certain experiences, behaviors, and existential issues. Whereas some openings feel good, others might feel confusing or scary. Some spiritual teachers believe that continuing to rely on the more naturally open energy channels without learning how to open the other channels impedes your spiritual growth and causes certain health problems. We can unwind psychic knots, called *granthis* in yoga traditions or *stuck places* in our Strands of Consciousness, and return them to Wholeness.

In the paradigm of Kundalini Yoga the clearing or purification of these blocks manifests in certain spiritual experiences. It might feel like a spiritual emergency, as Kundalini energy awakens, uncoils, and rises. Kundalini-Shakti energy is a primal, spiritual life force lying dormant at the base of the spine, which begins to rise when we open to Divine Energy. As the energy rises, it flows through the nadis or energy channels. You don't need to be a Yogi to experience this rising. You might notice a manifestation through any form of an opening process. Some of these include meditating, receiving or giving energy work, doing breath work, discovering a past life, receiving a transmission from a spiritual teacher, and many others.

You might also feel the urge to physically move in some way or make sounds. Following these urges could be guidance and might be an opening for you, but please be wise. If it doesn't feel right, get support with your transformation. You might have experiences that are difficult or painful physically, emotionally, mentally, or spiritually. If you have any concerns that these might be indicating other problems needing attention, please consult an appropriate professional.

Here are some of the experiences that can occur as we are awakening:

❧

Signs of Kundalini Awakening

Here are some of the experiences that can occur as we are awakening:

Physical issues and energetic blocks: Anything from heat, burning, heart pounding, spinal pain, gastrointestinal discomfort, headaches, extreme tiredness, change in your libido, expanded senses or sensitivity, and others.

Emotional issues: One of your six issues might show up in a big way, or you might feel anxiety, anger, or other emotions. You could have out of body experiences, profound compassion, or an outpouring of unconditional love and other experiences.

Kriyas or pranic movements: These are experiences of involuntary shaking, waves of energy, vibrations in your body, or an urge to move in unusual ways like spontaneous yoga postures, rocking, or mudras you don't recognize. You may be moved into ecstatic chanting.

Heightened Perceptions: You might know things before they happen, receive precise intuitive information, speak in tongues, have unusual healing abilities, hear sacred music, smell sandalwood or incense, or see what could be images from a past life. You might see in your mind's eye lights, Strands of Consciousness, geometric shapes, and letters or words in Hebrew, Arabic, Sanskrit or other languages. You might also receive messages from departed loved ones or guides.

Expanded experiences: Samadhi, satori, or periods of time in unitive awareness, hours of completely absorbing peace, tranquility or heightened no-self experiences, laughing and crying from the beauty of it all, overwhelming joy, or waves of bliss.

❧

You can study with an experienced spiritual teacher, or meditate on your own energy system, feeling into where there might be blocks. Thought is energy, so you can send your thoughts there, noticing any feelings, sensations, images, and thoughts arising. You can also move as you feel intuitively directed, allowing any unwinding process to take place, or choose from a variety of spiritually based physical practices to help you align and open, such as Qigong, Tai Chi, Tantra, Core Energetics, and others.

MEDITATION: OPENING TO KUNDALINI ENERGY (*SIRI GAITRI MANTRA*)

The following mantra is taught by Yogi Bhajan[6] and offered here to help you connect with the earth and your body. The sounds will activate your chakras, helping awaken the Kundalini energy. The first part of the mantra draws vibrational healing to the physical level of consciousness and the second part supports bringing the Infinite down into the physical.

Mantra: *RA MA DA SA SA SAY SO HUNG.*

Meaning of Mantra: *Ra = sun; Ma = moon; Da = earth; Sa = infinity, universal energy; Say = personal embodiment of Sa; So = personal sense of Unity with Sa; Hung = the Infinite.*

Sit comfortably and repeat the mantra for 5 to 10 minutes. Allow yourself to do any physical movement that presents itself.

Surrender

God had brought me to my knees and made me acknowledge my own nothingness, and out of that knowledge I had been reborn. I was no longer the centre of my life and therefore I could see God in everything.

—Bede Griffiths

From a psychological perspective, some people see surrender as resignation, admitting defeat, or giving over personal will. Spiritual surrender is different.

You ultimately come to a point in your personal journey when there's nothing to do but surrender. This spiritual surrender is not about giving up, or rolling over and playing dead. It's our next step, our next act of bravery. You aren't being a doormat, or giving up your power to heal yourself; on the contrary, you know from Emanation-Spiritual that you're surrendering to God and Wholeness itself. Opening to receive is surrendering. You surrender to the emptiness and silence that's always there. Touching the silence feeds your soul. The luminous darkness feeds you in ways you couldn't know otherwise. You've come to an attitude of acceptance and patience, knowing there's a bigger picture you might not be seeing in this moment. You're mature enough to accept the Universe on its terms, not always yours.

You can't help but relax, move from the truth of your heart, and open to compassion and love. Your body lets go and tensions melt away. You begin to let go of old ways, and feel the expansion of new ways that really are your essence reflecting the True Self. Surrender leads you to the next, right action for you. When you finally come from this internal cohesion, you have enough ego strength to stop the constant repetition and reaction. You have the space inside to step back, let go, and be. You can trust yourself and the Ground of Being. You can surrender the self to a larger Self that includes all of you.

In meditation, you can experience surrender with the rising and falling of your breath. You inhale, surrender, and exhale. In the moment-to-moment experience of emptiness, as it is with your inhale, everything arises out of the void, nothingness, and emptiness. Then, just as it arose from nothing, you exhale, surrendering back into the void, nothingness, and emptiness. You hear a sound and it disappears. You have a thought and it dissolves. The thought and the breath go back to the emptiness.

MEDITATION: SURRENDERING AND BREATHING

Deep breath. As best you can, allow your inhale to arise from the emptiness. Surrender to God, to Wholeness. Allow your exhale to go back to emptiness. Follow this rhythm to stillness.

Our Journey to Wholeness

Those who understand see themselves in all, and all, in themselves.
—Bhagavad-Gita

You first began this journey through the spectrum of consciousness by ascending from Action-Physical, exploring and discovering the many facets of you and the universe. You discovered you're more than you thought you were; not just your body or narrow ideas. You began holding and processing your feelings and emotions. You start seeing you aren't a victim or trapped by your circumstances, but can choose what you do or learn about life and yourself. You can even create your life, to a certain degree, from this searching, learning, and journeying.

You can empower yourself. Some longings start to be met, and you begin having spiritual experiences, providing the fuel to keep going. In your ascending through Formation-Emotional and Creation-Mental consciousness you learn mastery, recognizing the importance and value of your stories. You move from the densest dimensions of consciousness and experience to the pinnacle of subtlety and truth. This journey has been primarily that of discrimination, differentiation, and individuation.

Now, when anything in your life calls out to be seen, you gladly deal with it because you understand you'll become freer. Your life deepens as you grow; you become happier and more content. You come to the place where you've satisfied your search and your soul's longing, in certain ways. Then, you experience you're made of "God-stuff," are part of the One, have free will, and can choose to live from your heart. You've felt bathed in the light. You can tolerate and welcome levels of emptiness. You notice that from your strength, you naturally move toward a reality with greater subtlety and emptiness, more void of concepts and form.

This more subtle perception is transcendence itself, or Emanation-Spiritual consciousness, the enfolded Wholeness including both oneness and two-ness. You've expanded to the fullness of creation and manifestation, coming to emptiness, where emptiness and fullness are experienced separately and simultaneously. You've touched into the Source, and now you feel called to surrender. You could choose not to, but you know you must. You willingly go into the unknown, the unknowable. At some point in here, you realize your own unfolding naturally moves you from ascending into descending and you descend toward physical reality with a newly informed viewpoint.

In surrendering to the unknowable you continue your life's journey, but with a different perspective. You now know the luminous emptiness and see beauty in everything everywhere. You want to return to the preciousness of it all, including physical reality, bringing emptiness into manifestation. The journey of descent goes back through all the dimensions of consciousness carrying the viewpoint of Emanation-Spiritual. You bring the knowledge gained from your ascent as you descend. Emptiness is infused and recognized in all manifested form. You know that what the Buddhists call the Ground of Being is here, now. The Presence of God, the Absolute, Divinity, is here, now. A tree is still a tree, but it's not just a tree. When you see a flower, it's not separate from transcendence. Flowers are transcendence. Transcendence is inseparable from everything in your life. You now clearly see and experience that duality and oneness *are* One. The Real or Presence is in what you say and do here, now. You embody Wholeness, and then appear to lose your way for a moment—or sometimes days—then resume the journey. Your movement is one of repeatedly ascending and descending. In the Kabbalah this is called "running and returning."

As you're ascending, you assimilate new levels of self-realization and individuation, which you take with you as you descend into new levels of maturation, moving you into an even greater individuation. This developing individuation integrates in all the dimensions, along with the wisdom gained in each. Then, as you descend, all of the Wholeness you encountered in Emanation-Spiritual consciousness accompanies you, penetrating and integrating into all levels of your being, leading you to the understanding and experience of the wholeness of Reality. This ongoing learning to hold and experience the world from the unified state leads you to greater levels of transparency, embodying more of God's Presence.

Author Andrew Harvey says, "Even in the inner lives of the greatest saints and mystics, there is always still work to be done, for the demand and the power of divine love are infinite and endless. Christ himself, though one with God in love, never stopped growing to incarnate more of that love. All those who love and follow him submit to the same ruthless laws of continual transformation."[7]

You're always awakening and becoming more transparent. It's never completely finished. You never arrive, because you're already here. You become increasingly perceptive of the full spectrum of consciousness that's present, here and now. It's more visible to you. You awaken to awakening. Yet, if you think you'll arrive somewhere, or that self-improvement is the path to God's love, or that if you're good enough you'll never get sick and die, then you're on a path of perfectionism, a path that will always leave you feeling as though you're not enough. Although you remember that Grace is here, right where you are, if you think this means you don't have to notice what's arising within you, or don't need personal development work and a spiritual practice, you're in a fantasy about life, yourself, and the world, ultimately leading you to disappointment and living in illusion.

Some have said that transparency is the quality of letting the unencumbered light pass through, so that Reality may be seen for what it is. Isha Schwaller de Lubicz says, "Transparency becomes illumination within and radiance without. It does not prevent the selfish assaults of the Ego, but weakens them." She goes on to say, "Peace on Earth cannot mean the suppression of the opposing forces, but their reconciliation in working for a common aim, which is indestructible life."[8]

The River Runs Through Us

If you leave the pool you have dug for yourself and go out into
the river of life then life has an astonishing way of taking care
of you, because then there is no taking care on your part.

—Jiddu Krishnamurti

In speaking of the dimensions of consciousness, we've talked about degrees of fluidity. The ultimate fluidity is embodied in what some spiritual teachings refer to as the Great River of Life. We get so caught up in our self-concepts, we're not aware of the movement and dynamic nature of our ongoing experience. Our over-identification with our relatively stable body image can keep us from knowing how the river runs through us. The dynamic flow of life is always moving, and our inner events always changing. Understanding intellectually that life consists of flow and change isn't the same as directly experiencing your life as flow and change. To know your soul directly, you must experience the river as the foreground of awareness, while events recede into the background.

It's important to remember your soul isn't a state or condition; it's a medium and locus in which states arise. All the inner states and events you experience are forms within your psyche, and part of your soul. The soul is dynamic and constantly changing. If you allow yourself, you'll notice your experience consists of constant change and transformation. One thought, one feeling, follows another. Your inner space and body sensations are in continuous movement. Both the earth and your life are in constant expansion and contraction.

We're usually not attuned to the fluidity and flow of the river because we're absorbed in events. As you disengage from your self-concepts and the content of your day-to-day life, your awareness of the flow brings you closer to your soul. We're usually so focused on the many forms passing by, we're unaware of the medium in which they flow. That medium is God, or the Universe.

The highest truth is that life *is*. It flows of its own volition and timing. We can fight it, or flow with it, but we cannot control it. To surrender to the Great River of Life is not defeat, it's recognizing and embracing life's true nature, finally knowing we *are* the river.

Enlightenment is a gift of Grace, not a graduation present. It doesn't come from striving, and yet it's important to do whatever work the River of Life presents to you. The more you can relax into inner stillness and trust the inspiration that arises, the more fluidly you'll live in, and from, your multiple levels of consciousness.

MEDITATION: THE RIVER

Deep breaths. Sit quietly and feel yourself moving into relaxation. Focus on your breathing for a while. As best you can, allow yourself to drop beneath your stories. Beneath your thoughts and feelings. Experience yourself floating in an inner tube. Floating gently on this great river of life. Feel the peacefulness. Feel the calmness. Feel the stillness, as the river carries you. Feel the warmth of the sun on your skin like you're being kissed by Grace. Above you, like clouds floating by, you see your stories passing. Your feelings passing. Your thoughts, just moving by like clouds. Continue riding the gentle current of this great river of life, feeling held and carried by the flow you can count on. Knowing you can trust it.

Dark Night of the Soul

Your dark night is your own invitation to become a person of heart and soul. Every dark night is unique.

—Thomas Moore

We seek to understand the stories of our lives in order to deconstruct them, loosening the knots in our Strands of Consciousness and returning our tapestry to Wholeness. The Buddhists call this returning to your original face; where you're *in* Reality rather than looking at it.

We consciously travel into our own dark night of the soul, into the deepest, darkest crevices to mine the gold of our being. It's the compost that makes us rich. We willingly journey into our shadow self and all the parts we don't want to see or didn't know were there. Facing our shadow self helps us strengthen in some ways and let go in others. In the same way that Cranial Sacral work helps us unwind the body, our shadow work allows our body, feelings, and thoughts to unwind, relaxing us into wholeness. As long as we don't know what lies inside, it's hard to become who we truly are at the deepest levels of consciousness.

> **We come to understand that our sense of self, which we've so sweetly tied in a bow must come untied for us to have a greater Truth.**

As we swim in the waters of Emanation-Spiritual consciousness, we're faced with what arises as we go into the emptiness, silence, darkness, and union. The darkness is a metaphor for the difficulties that are necessary for us to confront on our journey to union with the Creator.

Christian mystic St. John of the Cross tells us, in *Dark Night of the Soul*, of his journey from Action-Physical to Emanation-Spiritual, and his union with God. "This dark night is an inflowing of God into the soul, which purges it from its ignorances and imperfections, habitual, natural, and spiritual, which is called by contemplatives infused contemplation, or mystical theology. Herein God secretly teaches the soul and instructs it in perfection of love...illumining it."[9]

Andrew Louth, in *The Origins of the Christian Mystical Tradition*, talks about the ascent of Moses up the holy mountain, and into what he calls divine darkness: "And then Moses is cut off from both things seen and those who see and enters into the darkness of unknowing, a truly hidden darkness, according to which he shuts his eyes to all apprehensions that convey knowledge, for he has passed into a realm quite beyond any feeling or seeing." He's talking about the unknowable nothingness here in Emanation-Spiritual. He goes on to say, "Now, belonging wholly to that which is beyond all, and yet to nothing at all, and being neither himself, nor another, and united in his highest part in passivity with Him who is completely unknowable, he knows by not knowing in a manner that transcends understanding."[10]

- *In what ways have you experienced a dark night of the soul?*
- *What shift in understanding, growing, healing, or connecting with God did you receive from it?*

Transcendence and Relaxing into Grace

Surrender your own poverty and acknowledge your nothingness to the Lord. Whether you understand it or not, God loves you, is present in you, lives in you, dwells in you, calls you, saves you, and offers you an understanding and compassion which are like nothing you have ever found in a book or heard in a sermon.

—Thomas Merton

Transcendence is going beyond our limited consciousness, moving into larger and larger contexts. Looking at this from matter we become clearer on our role as a reflection of greater Wholeness. When we're following our deepest longings and open to our potentials, we naturally move toward compassion and some sort of service to others. In the view from Wholeness we're one with everything, so serving one is serving all.

Following our longings connects us with our basic, human desire to unite, cleave to, or become one with something greater than ourselves. As we grow, integrate, and transform through our self-development, we naturally move toward something larger. For some, this might mean serving humanity without any thought of God or Spirit. It's common to begin the path, see results, and long for the "you" just beyond the next hill, and then the next. Rabbi Schneur Zalman, author of the ancient Kabbalistic text *The Tanya*, suggests this journey requires a lifelong devotion, with appropriate use of both intellect and emotion.[11]

We could say, then, that evolution is self-development, is self-realization, is transcendence. We progress in our evolution to know we're more than our ego structures, and learn we have much more control of our lives, oddly enough, when we let go and surrender. As we evolve, each higher or deeper level of transformation emerges in consciousness, and a deeper structure unfolds and begins to operate. People often talk of higher states, and the Kabbalah refers to deeper states, so I use both. A higher/deeper level then integrates, and as we work on ourselves, we move to the next higher/deeper realm. We struggle with this newer level and integrate that structure, then move on to the next level, and so on. As we progress, we continue unifying.

As your transformational evolution continues with each new level, your ego becomes increasingly differentiated, becoming your real self, and closer to your essence and the True Self. The ego eventually stops identifying with the present structure and begins identifying with the next, higher structure.

MEDITATION: RELAXING INTO GRACE

Breathe deeply. Feel yourself moving into relaxation. Notice your breath, and let it be as it is. Notice how or if you want to change it, and then let it be. Open to the possibility of your highest Source. Open to all that's necessary for you to brush up against or touch your highest Source. Just be with that for a while. Allow the connection to open even more. Feel yourself being nurtured and held by your highest Source or Grace. Let it hold you, be in you, be around you, be you. You're one with Source. You're one with Grace. Drop even more deeply into Source. Relax even more into Grace.

The Heart of Nothingness

At the heart of Emanation-Spiritual is the *nothingness* spoken about in many spiritual teachings. It's the realm of all potentials and unified consciousness. It's pure Being, before the creation of concepts. It's the infinite, hidden, ineffable, unknowable nothingness that is bound to somethingness at the continuously unfolding creation point in consciousness. Opening up to this spiritual nothingness allows you to create from your vast potentials.

Thinking of this velvety blackness, emptiness, and nothingness might bring up the experience of joy, fulfillment, or deep peace. We see from our practices and deep attention that nothingness and emptiness is everywhere. When we carefully focus on a sensation, feeling, or thought we experience spaciousness within them and around them. Our ideas of solidity disperse and dissolve into the moment and the experience of emptiness is rich and precious.

For many of us, nothingness and emptiness can produce a fear of obliteration and annihilation. This relates to a rite of passage that takes us from an existential angst and despair into our spiritual nature, which is a dark-night-of-the-soul experience. It also relates to the primitive woundings from our childhood programming. The fear of eradication can feel like an overwhelming, unspeakable anxiety, as if you're falling into an abyss, completely isolated, falling to pieces, or disconnecting from your body. It takes us back to the pre-personal, pre-verbal Slivers that need reclaiming to tolerate the opposites of life, and awaken to our transpersonal Reality.

In her book, *When Things Fall Apart*, Pema Chödrön states, "When things fall apart and we're on the verge of we know not what, the test of each of us is to stay on that brink and not concretize. The spiritual journey is not about heaven and finally getting to a place that's really swell."[12] It's about staying with our process, what is, and living in the transpersonal that holds everything. She goes on to say, "...only to the extent that we expose ourselves over and over again to annihilation can that which is indestructible be found in us."[13] True awakening is the unraveling of everything.

When you process your personal woundings enough, you can sit in this profound level of empty nothingness or Presence and experience it as light, empty, and boundless. You'll feel open to yourself and others, and feel a sense of freedom releasing you into all possibilities. You'll experience yourself and the entire manifest world as fullness, and at the same time, a deep, restful nothingness.

> ❧
>
> **When you can allow your distracting mind, painful shame, and deficient, frightening emptiness to be there with all your feelings, transformation happens.**
>
> ❧

A.H. Almaas says, "When a student finally settles into the experience of deficient emptiness, allowing it without judgment, or reaction...it transforms naturally and spontaneously into a luminous vastness, deep spaciousness, a peaceful emptiness."[14] This deficient, black emptiness turns into luminous freedom, lightening your burdens, and it becomes an emptiness that's rich and satisfying, because it's empty.

Emanation-Spiritual is the synthesis of empty nothingness and the fullness of being. Mahayana Buddhism's Heart Sutra expressed it well. The Prajnaparamita (Perfection of Wisdom) says, "Form is emptiness and emptiness is form."[15] This emptiness and nothingness is an empty womb or Great Mother that's filled with potential. Physicist Stephen Hawking said, "What we think of as empty space is not really empty, but it is filled with pairs of particles and anti-particles."[16]

Physicist Franco Nori, PhD, observed light particles flickering in and out of existence in a vacuum, once thought to be empty. Nori said, "One of the profound consequences of quantum mechanics is that we know that something can come from nothing."[17]

The exploration of the infinite, unfolding into the finite in Emanation-Spiritual, is diving into what the Kabbalah says "binds the thinker to the thought." It moves into the state between potential and actualization.

Binding ourselves to this knowable nothingness allows us to know the other side of something, called Wholeness. Rabbi Aryeh Kaplan teaches, "When a person wants to bring new sustenance to all universes, he must first attach himself to the level of nothingness."[18] According to *The Zohar*, both the Commandments and *The Torah* are hidden nothingness and revealed somethingness. We might say the same about the sacred scriptures from other religious traditions. To understand the Creation-Mental Dimension, it helps to know that it emanates from nothingness and Emanation-Spiritual. Cleaving or binding to this luminous blackness, emptiness, and nothingness is an important exploration for committed seekers.

This mystery, or the unknowable level of consciousness, is referred to in many other spiritual traditions. Christian mystic Meister Eckhart says the Godhead (unknowable aspect of God) gives birth to the trinity: "Truly you are the hidden God in the ground of the soul, where God's ground and the soul's ground are one ground." He goes on to say, "If my life is God's being, then God's existence must be my existence, and God's is-ness is my is-ness, neither less nor more."[19]

MEDITATION: BOUNDLESS SPACIOUSNESS AND EMPTINESS

Deep breath. As you breathe, feel your body moving into relaxation. Deeper and deeper, even further into relaxation. As best you can, allow yourself to move into the spaciousness and emptiness that's in your body, everywhere. Feel the boundless space inside of you. Even the space between your cells. The spaciousness between each breath. Continue further into inner spaciousness. Sit with this for a while. Now, turn your attention to the boundless spaciousness and emptiness outside of you. Between you and everything around you. Even in-between the molecules of air. Continue further into outer spaciousness. Sit with this for a while. Now, allow yourself to experience outer spaciousness connecting with inner spaciousness. As best you can, sit with this for a while. And notice what happens.

The Emanation-Spiritual Dimension Profile

Reminder: You can download the Emanation-Spiritual Dimension Profile (along with the other four profiles) at my Website, *www.YourUltimateLifePlan.com*.

PART III

YOUR ULTIMATE LIFE PLAN

CHAPTER 11

The Multidimensional Awareness Practice

*We are all multidimensional beings—simultaneously expressions of
the God-impulse and embodied, living, breathing humans.*
—Andrew Cohen

The *Multidimensional Awareness Practice*, or *M.A.P.*, is a dynamic healing tool. More than a mindfulness practice, it guides you on your transformational journey. First, it brings you powerfully into the present moment through your awareness of the Four Dimensions of Consciousness, more comprehensive than the Presencing meditation; then, it helps you identify and work with your sensations, feelings, thoughts, and Strands of Consciousness showing up.

There are three distinct types of *M.A.P.s*: a *Basic M.A.P.* is used to follow anything uncomfortable arising in the moment; an *Exploring M.A.P.* is used when exploring a specific issue, relationship, or habitual pattern that's been a problem in the past; a *Deep M.A.P.* includes the mindsets of each dimension, and guides you with insight-provoking questions specifically designed to further your exploration and increase your self-awareness. Beginning with the *Basic M.A.P.*, each is more complex than the *M.A.P.* before, and provides you with a great deal of flexibility in applying them.

Regardless of which *M.A.P.* you're working with, you're invited to be with what comes up. By following whatever's arising in the moment to its source, you're led to a greater awareness of the motivations, historical connections, and unconscious programming affecting your life. You'll resolve difficult or painful feelings and thoughts, uncovering more of who you really are.

Multidimensional Awareness Is an Essential Element for Creating Lasting Change

The *Multidimensional Awareness Practice* isn't a magic wand, it's a map for healing, a powerful tool that supports you in focusing long enough and deeply enough to create the transformation and lasting change you've been wanting. When you follow a Strand of Consciousness as far as it will take you, your journey of healing continues until you come to a resolution. It's like when you hear the four opening bars of Beethoven's Fifth Symphony—short-short-short long—that longer chord provides a release, a momentary relaxation in the body. Whether a resolution provides a sense of release, a settled feeling, inner spaciousness, clarity, or another potential—such as truth, strength, or peace—you'll have greater access to expressing your deepest Self. When you stay with a Strand to its resolution, two things happen: first, whatever has just healed returns and integrates into the bigger being that you are, and second, what's still unresolved begins to loosen and unravel, which allows the emerging of the next Strand, or layer, or piece of your woundedness that's calling to be healed.

It's important to see the dimensionality of life. Without looking at the different layers and dimensions, you might feel overwhelmed by seeing everything at once, or miss something that unlocks the door to exactly what you've been trying to heal. You might not be able to see beyond the piece right in front of you to the greater whole, and without the big picture, this piece looks like the answer. You're likely to believe all of life is just this tiny part you're living. The issue then becomes difficult, if not impossible, to resolve. That's why working with the four dimensions in the *Multidimensional Awareness Practice* is key to your healing. It's easy to stop halfway, and think you're done—to mistake the Band-Aid for healing. So much more is possible. Real healing and transformation can happen right now.

The Basic M.A.P.

One way to work with the *Multidimensional Awareness Practice* in your day-to-day life is to apply it to what feels uncomfortable or difficult as it's arising in this moment. If, as you breathe into the discomfort, it disappears, and you naturally move into a release—inner spaciousness, clarity, or another potential—then nothing more is needed. That's the holographic perspective in action, having access to all of consciousness in every moment. The experience of inner spaciousness begins to take you into the embodiment of Wholeness, the Absolute, or God, that's inherent in every moment and always available.

However, if something difficult arises and doesn't shift, use this process to work with it. If you stay with it and breathe into it without a release or a shift, that's when you need to follow the Strand of Consciousness that's arising back to its origin.

You can apply the *Basic M.A.P.* when something suddenly pops up, like a thought, feeling, sensation, image, issue, or problem, and you get caught in it. You weren't deliberately looking for something to work on, nor had you set an intention, but here it is anyway. Do your best to stay open and curious. If more than one emotion, thought, or sensation arises at the same time, choose the one you're most drawn to and follow it, because they're all connected anyway. Be willing to follow wherever the Strand leads, and stay open to wherever it takes you. Although at first you might travel through familiar territory, let this journey take you beyond the everyday facts you think of as your life—present and past—and lead you deeply into the mystery of you.

Here's an example of this process that can serve as an instructional guide:

Start by being present to what's arising in this moment, and breathe into it. If it doesn't seem to shift...

Follow the emotion, thought, or physical sensation by noticing where this Strand of Consciousness takes you. The Strand may begin in one dimension, then lead you into other dimensions. For instance, if you have a pain in your neck, and you breathe into the physical pain, you might notice an emotion with it. Try to name the emotion. Let's say it's discouragement or hopelessness. Breathe into the emotion. Notice what happens. If you haven't moved into inner spaciousness, clarity, or relaxation, continue the process by noticing the physical pain again, and see how it may have moved or changed. Then, go back to the emotion of discouragement or hopelessness and notice ways it may have changed.

If there isn't a significant change, ask yourself, "If this emotion had a voice, what would it say?" You might hear or feel the response, "Life is hard." Then, sit with or breathe into the thought, "Life is hard." If you don't feel movement into spaciousness or clarity, be with what arises from this thought. It could be another emotion or thought, or a deeper level of discouragement or hopelessness.

You might sense something underneath these feelings. Open and breathe into this sense of something deeper. Maybe a more primary feeling shows itself, such as sadness. Just sit for a moment in this pervasive feeling of sadness, as best you can, and do whatever's needed to be with it more deeply. If, after a while of being with it, you notice the pain and emotion hasn't shifted, breathe

ॐ

We heal in layers. You may need to pass through a particular issue many times before it completely loses its problematic charge and power.

ॐ

and feel a little deeper into all that's there. Notice if anything else arises from under those emotions, thoughts, and sensations. If nothing changes, you can still play with this further.

You can continue to work with this by tracing the Strand back to the earliest memory you have of this emotion or thought. Follow the energy. Don't worry if it's "the" earliest memory or not. Trust that any memory coming to mind is here to be seen and felt, and is part of the process. Simply be with it. See what other images, emotions, and thoughts want to come up. Now, notice if the issue has lightened or released, and if you're opening to spaciousness, clarity, or another potential.

As you open into deeper levels of emotion, thought, or sensation, you may find it a helpful release to cry, pound a pillow, write, or sit quietly and be with all of this for a while before it shifts noticeably. You might notice some resistance coming up, which could be deeper fear or a very painful emotion. Please be gentle with yourself, and understand you might need more time if an unusually difficult memory arises.

Your job is to keep following the Strand until you feel a sense of relaxation and spaciousness inside. When you do, you'll likely sink into a sense of the poignancy and preciousness of life, and a deeper compassion toward yourself, and all of existence.

When you've followed a Strand of Consciousness to its source, you relax into an inner stillness that allows you to just be. But if you try to circumvent, bypass, ignore, or rush through the layers that need to be seen, heard, and felt, you end up with a pseudo-emptiness, not the real peace that passes all understanding. If you instantly go into bliss every time you sit to be with yourself, I would ask you if some fear, or another uncomfortable emotion, is actually present that you're avoiding. I've seen many spiritual seekers get caught in this kind of spiritual bypass. In my experience, most of us still have personal work to do.

There's good news and bad news. If for any reason you can't stay with the cycle long enough to feel an inner relaxation, life will offer you other opportunities, down the road, to further your healing. Again, healing happens in layers, and you might pass through an issue many times before it completely loses its power and problematic charge.

Be kind to yourself as you do this work. I invite you to relax into the process, and trust that your essence is showing you what you need to see. There's no right or wrong way to do this; there's only being present to what arises, and following where it leads. If you get stuck, or caught up in trying to do this perfectly, simply take a breath, relax, and allow whatever comes up to be there.

The Exploring M.A.P.

Another type of the *Multidimensional Awareness Practice*, called the *Exploring M.A.P.*, is used when returning to a difficulty that isn't currently triggered, such as an issue you've struggled with in the past, a relationship problem, or your reaction to something happening in your life or the world. It's also valuable when, in following a Strand of Consciousness, you see a habitual emotion, thought, or reaction—a longtime issue—you'd like to explore.

Some issues seem as though they've been with us forever. If we go there often enough, these issues become the lens through which we view our lives. As you successfully work through the layers of an issue, it will lighten over time. If it's persistent or stubborn and doesn't shift, there may be an unconscious, secondary gain keeping it in place.

For example, if someone is asked why he is or isn't doing something, and he answers quickly, "I don't know," his secondary gain could be keeping people at bay, and avoiding a feeling or responsibility. As with our personal programming, our long-held issues often color our worldview and become our automatic, knee-jerk reactions.

Here are two short examples of this practice. Each student began in a similar place, but had their own poignant outcome.

Sheila came to a session and shared she'd been antsy and anxious all week. She couldn't figure out what to do with herself, and paced around the house. After following this Strand, and processing several different sensations and emotions, she uncovered a great deal of fear and sadness. As we sat and explored the fear and sadness, it opened into terror, and then released with the thought, "I can't be more than I am, right now." A calmness came over her and she wept briefly, feeling relief and a sense of peace.

Tom came to a session feeling anxious, unable to sit or figure out what to do with himself. He breathed into what was there, going through many blocked and stuck places he'd avoided in the past. By staying with the sensations, thoughts, and feelings, and following where they led, he finally arrived at a place where he could experience deep satisfaction and happiness. As a child, he wasn't allowed to feel happy and giddy. Through this process, he opened to his potential for giggly happiness. We sat a few moments and laughed, enjoying life's possibilities.

Using the Exploring M.A.P.

Begin this process by setting your intention, and bring to mind what you're choosing to explore. Perhaps it's your relationship with your father, spouse, or boss, and maybe they're connected. Or, you could choose a fear of intimacy, flying, or success.

Focus on this issue, and ask:

- *What physical sensations do I feel when I think about this issue?*

  Deep breath. As you think of this issue, tune in to your body. What physical sensations do you notice? Where are they in your body? What exactly are you experiencing? Tightness? Headache? Tiredness? As you experience and follow them, do they change? Once you recognize and name what's happening with this issue in your body, breathe into it, and ask, *What's under this physical sensation?* You might feel another sensation, an emotion, or a thought. Follow it until it releases, or moves into something else. Continue following the next sensation, thought, or emotion until it releases or opens into something greater.

- *What am I feeling emotionally, right now, as I think about this issue?*

  Deep breath. As you think of this issue, tune in to your emotions. What feelings are you experiencing? Anger? Sadness? Frustration? Fear? More than one? Pick one and follow it. What name would you give it? Notice if you'd like to run away, or avoid that emotion. Once you name it, breathe into it, and ask, *What's under this emotion?* It might be another emotion, thought, or sensation. Follow it until it releases, or moves into something else. Continue following the next sensation, thought, or emotion until it releases or opens into something greater.

- *What are my thoughts and beliefs about this?*

  Deep breath. As you think of this issue, tune in to your thoughts. What thought do you notice first? What thought comes next? Do you see a story or theme? As you sit with it, notice what happens. What beliefs come up around this issue? Do you find your mind wandering? What thoughts are in the wandering? Notice the gaps between thoughts, as best you can. What's beneath the first level of thoughts? Do you open to inner spaciousness? Breathe into your thoughts. Notice if something else more essential is under them, and ask, *What's beneath these thoughts?* Follow it until it releases, or moves into something else. Continue following the next sensation, thought, or emotion until it releases or opens into something greater.

- *What happens when you connect to your deeper self, essence, or spirituality about this?*

  Deep breath. Feel yourself moving into relaxation. Deeper and deeper, even more relaxed. As you think of this issue, tune in to your deeper self, your essence or spirituality. Moving into calmness and quietness, sense your connection. What do you notice? What information is available from this aspect of you? From this larger view, does your issue have a deeper theme or a specific meaning? What insights are you receiving from the higher sources of wisdom? When you sink into emptiness, what happens around this issue? Which potentials are arising from your essence as a result of your journey with this issue? Follow what's there until it releases, or moves into something else. Continue following the next sensation, thought, or emotion until it releases or opens into something greater.

The Deep M.A.P.

By cultivating the habit of asking powerful, mind-altering questions, you are training your right brain to respond to the signals from your subconscious.
—Richard Bartlett

Deep M.A.P.s give you the opportunity to pursue anything you might be working on in your life, in greater depth. It could be a painful relationship, lack of success, or another Sliver you're ready to dive into and unravel even further, integrating the many Strands of Consciousness it contains.

The *Deep M.A.P.s* synthesize many of the *Conscious Living 2.0* principles and practices. *Deep M.A.P.s* pick up where the *Exploring M.A.P.* leaves off, and includes: guiding questions; the dimensional mindsets; uncovering your personal programming; discerning your wise, inner voice from the voice of your woundedness.

Deep M.A.P.s help you work with your "six" issues more deeply. Sometimes our story of long-held issues is so familiar, we easily get stuck in believing we know the whole story. Some of the questions in a *Deep M.A.P.* may sound familiar, eliciting your practiced responses. Whenever you hear yourself telling a familiar story, dive deeper. Other questions here ask you to look at your issues from angles you may not have considered before. Be adventurous; let yourself embrace the unknown.

How to consciously approach the *Deep M.A.P.* and meet what arises:

• Set aside a block of time, at least 45 minutes to an hour each session, to give yourself the space to look deeply into yourself. This exploration will probably take several sessions to complete, and can be repeated as often as you wish with new issues, or you can go deeper on an issue you've worked with before.

- Presence yourself first. You can also invite your guides or angels to help and support you, surround yourself with healing light, pray, or do any other sacred blessing practice you feel inspired to do.

- Let conscious awareness, truth, and healing be your companions on this journey. Be open and willing to face whatever comes.

- Know that you're safe, you're choosing to explore this, and you can stop at any time if something feels too intense, and come back to it later. At the same time, as best you can, cultivate a willingness to experience the discomfort of truth-telling, change, and growth.

- As you explore an issue, notice your level of comfort or discomfort, and any desire you have to escape or avoid feelings, thoughts, physical sensations, memories, or mental images that arise.

- Throughout this process, notice what arises in all Four Dimensions of Consciousness. Consider your answers in the light of all four dimensions, even if the question focuses on only one of the dimensions. For example, when you're looking at how an issue manifests physically, look at what feelings, thoughts, intuitive knowing, and physical sensations arise in response to your answer, as well as what elements of the dimensional mindsets may be present.

- Be aware of whose "voice" you're hearing as you respond and answer these questions: Is this the voice of your inner wisdom, your woundedness, or your childhood programming?

- Meditate, or simply take a few deep breaths and quiet your mind, both before and after doing this process.

- Journal your answers and insights, as well as your experience of this process as a whole.

- Know that healing takes time, and this deeper work will gradually unravel, dissipate, and integrate the Slivers of Consciousness giving you pain. At the same time, Grace, readiness, and openness might lead to a sudden, profound healing of your issue, or an aspect of it.

- This is more than an awareness practice. As we began this conscious journey together, I told you that how you are when you're with your stuck issues is key to moving, changing, or shifting them. Take your time with this. When a sensation, feeling, or thought comes up, sit with it and really take it in

- If you find yourself drawing a blank with a question, take a deep breath, relax, and know that the answer will come when you're ready.

Using a Deep M.A.P. to Explore an Issue

Begin the process by choosing an issue you'd like to work on. First, the questions will ask you to step back and look at it as a whole. It can be a general issue, such as "intimate relationships," or it can be a specific aspect of that issue, such as "why I get so angry when this happens..." or "why I feel so much fear in this aspect of relationships." Either way, you'll be led toward becoming more specific.

As you make your way through the questions, you're going to explore the myriad details of your issue from a number of different perspectives. By asking questions from so many directions, answers will shed light on Strands you'll want to pursue in the future.

As you move from the larger view, winding further into the issue, more is revealed, and you'll open to deeper levels of being. When you've worked through the entire *Deep M.A.P.*, your journaled responses will provide valuable insight about your relationship to these stuck and painful places in your life, including ways you hide or avoid feelings, memories, or truths.

Looking at the issue you've chosen as a whole, answer the following:

- *Give a general description of the issue.*
- *What are the primary ways it manifests in your life?*
- *What emotions are held around it?*
- *What thoughts arise as you sit with it?*
- *If this is one of your "six issues," or has been around for a while, what's your best theory about why it's so stubborn and slow to change?*
- *What does it keep you from doing, being, or having in your life?*

Exploring your issue from the Action-Physical Dimension:

- *What physical sensations do you notice when you think about this issue?*
- *What physical events or sensations might "trigger" the issue?*
- *When you get triggered, what's your habitual or knee-jerk reaction?*
- *How does this issue manifest physically in your life?*
- *What actions do you take, or avoid, when caught in this issue?*
- *Where do you see black-and-white, right-or-wrong thinking with this issue?*
- *If this issue had a color or shape, what might it be?*
- *What aspects of this issue do you rarely or never question, thinking, "That's just the way it is," or "This is simply who I am"?*

- *What other aspects of the Action-Physical Dimension mindset (Chapter 7) do you see in your relationship to this issue?*

Exploring your issue from the Formation-Emotional Dimension:

- *As you're exploring this issue, what emotions arise?*
- *Which of the 12 primary emotions do you most strongly associate with this issue?*
- *Where do they take you?*
- *What is your wounded, child-self saying or feeling about this issue?*
- *In what ways have you embraced your suffering around this? Or not?*
- *How might you feel more compassion for yourself, and others involved with this issue?*
- *What are some of the familiar stories you tell yourself about this issue? The negative ones? The positive ones?*
- *In what ways does this issue now seem different from what you originally imagined?*
- *What other aspects of the Formation-Emotional Dimension mindset (Chapter 8) do you see in your relationship to this issue?*

Exploring your issue from the Creation-Mental Dimension:

- *As you're exploring this issue, what thoughts arise?*
- *What thoughts do you notice when you're caught up in this issue?*
- *What beliefs are underneath this issue? What beliefs about yourself, others, and the world? What limiting beliefs? What life-enhancing beliefs?*
- *In what ways have you tried to spiritually bypass—deny or jump over— your feelings, thoughts, or the work you need to do to face and heal this issue?*
- *In what ways have you been able to hold paradox (opposite or contradictory feelings, thoughts, or viewpoints) around this issue?*
- *In what ways has this "problem" been a "gift" in your life? What have you learned about yourself and life, and how have you grown because of it?*
- *How have you used metaphor to describe this issue or its impact on you?*
- *What other aspects of the Creation-Mental Dimension mindset (Chapter 9) do you see in your relationship to this issue?*

Looking at your issue with discernment:

- *Looking at some of the repeating thoughts you have when caught up in this issue (from your list made in the Creation-Mental section), ask yourself, for each thought—both positive and negative—Whose voice is this? Is it the voice of your inner wisdom, your wounded child-self, or someone from your past? Or does it reflect your family's belief structures, the tenets of your spiritual path, or the generally accepted view of society?*

- *In what ways do you allow yourself to be distracted from doing this deep healing work?*
- *In what ways have you reached for a quick fix to try to heal this issue?*
- *What are some hidden payoffs or secondary gains you might be getting by holding on to this issue?*
- *When you've worked on this issue in the past, what helped you move forward, and what didn't?*

Exploring your programming around this issue and the effect it has on your ego:

Your personal programming includes sensations, emotions, and thoughts, and we've covered these with the preceding dimensional questions. So this section will focus on childhood experiences that helped to create the habitual patterns and responses at the heart of this issue.

- *Where might this issue have come from in your childhood or youth?*
- *What's the earliest memory you have relating to this issue?*
- *If there's a specific experience you know of that triggered this, what happened, and when?*
- *In what ways might this issue have started as a positive coping strategy based on a desire for self-protection or self-defense?*
- *In what ways might your real self peek through when you experience this?*
- *What messages related to this issue, both positive and negative, did you get from your parents, caregivers, etc.? What were you told?*
- *What elements of this issue did you see modeled in your home and family? By whom? How did they feel about it, and how did you feel about them?*
- *What positive experiences did you have, if any, around your issue: at home, at school, in some other environment, or with other family members?*
- *How does this issue affect your sense of identity? How do you define yourself in light of this issue? "I am _____." How has your definition of yourself changed through this exploration?*

Exploring Your Issue from the Emanation-Spiritual Dimension:

- *In what ways has this issue closed you down to Spirit, God, or Oneness?*
- *In what ways has it helped you open to Spirit, God, or Oneness?*

- *In what ways can you engage your wise inner voice with this issue?*
- *How has this issue contributed to your awakening?*
- *In what ways has this issue contributed to you experiencing a "dark night of the soul"?*
- *In what ways has this issue inspired spiritual surrender and letting go?*
- *When you connect with your essence, how does this issue look and feel?*
- *When you're seated in Wholeness, Oneness, or Emptiness, what's your experience of this issue?*

Practicing Kindness

The *Multidimensional Awareness Practice* is not about perfectionism or hypervigilance. It's not necessary to explore every feeling and thought, every moment of the day. However, it's helpful to explore where you get stuck, or feel pain or resistance that holds you back from experiencing the fullness of who you are. Pain can be a great teacher.

Even though exploring the meaning of your pain is an important practice, bringing insight and ultimately freedom, some communities take this too literally. At times it seems they get mired in an overly simplified, surface interpretation about the meaning of certain problems and difficulties. For example, a woman with a stiff neck might be told she's being inflexible and needs to clean that up in order to heal. However, she could have simply slept the wrong way, or might be dealing with stress causing physical tension.

Yes, we're responsible and accountable for our own lives, and have great power in creating them, but sometimes a simplistic view implies people are to blame for a tragedy or life-threatening illness. There's a difference between accountability and blame. Although we have a lot in common, each person is a unique universe. Kindness toward ourselves, as well as others, can go a long way toward healing our pain.

Conscious Living 2.0 is a fierce, but not cruel practice. Not every hangnail contains deep meaning that will aid your spiritual development. Even Freud is rumored to have said, "Sometimes a cigar is just a cigar." However, if you continually dream of cigars, or find yourself worrying about them, it's worth your time to explore it. This tool will take you into your humanity with all its beauty and foibles. So as you're diving into your psyche I invite you to treat yourself with the utmost care, patience, and respect.

Using This Practice to Expand Your Gifts

The *Multidimensional Awareness Practice* can also be used to expand your gifts. Take dance, for instance. When you move, are you present with your body? Do you feel emotionally connected to the music and movement? Are you concentrating, worried, or in spaciousness with your thoughts simply coming and going?

You have the potential to be more deeply connected to whatever you're doing, whether it's walking down the street, cooking dinner, or gardening. Although you can't always jump into something you'd like to work on the moment it comes up, you can make a mental note to go back to it later, taking it into your practice.

As you explore the Four Dimensions of Consciousness more deeply, your experience of the *Multidimensional Awareness Practice* will deepen, and become broader and richer. You'll be able to flow among the levels easily, yet notice their differences.

Embodying Reality is sinking into the largest context, and at the same time, seamlessly feeling all dimensions at once. It's like being the largest Russian nesting doll, while fully aware of all the others you contain. You would notice your body with all of its organs, bones, systems, and sensations, and everything else contained in the Action-Physical Dimension's perspective. You would feel whatever emotion is present in the moment and the layers of feelings clustered around it, along with all the layers of the Formation-Emotional Dimension's perspective. You would sense your thoughts and beliefs and their connection to everything in the Creation-Mental Dimension's perspective. And you'd know that all of this is held in the relaxed, spacious awareness within the Emanation-Spiritual Dimension. You're not usually aware of all this in your ordinary everyday consciousness, but as you follow a Strand in any given moment, you have the opportunity to wake up to the awareness that all of this is present. Multidimensional awareness brings you to the wholeness and aliveness of who you really are.

CHAPTER 12

Meeting Every Moment Awake, Aware, and Alive

To be awake is to be alive.
—Henry David Thoreau

Living consciously is like being a jazz musician, spontaneously interpreting a tune, never playing a song the same way twice by staying awake, aware, and alive. Akin to being with life as it is, the music depends on the musician's state of mind and experience, as well as interactions with fellow musicians and audience members. When you're an improvisational musician, there's no score to follow. Instead, often jamming with whomever shows up in the moment, you flow with your own vitality and inspiration. To respond and blend, as jazz calls for, you need the knowledge, skills, and ability of a trained musician.

Similarly, to be present in the moment, flowing with whatever life throws you, you need the deep self-knowledge, skills, and tools necessary to create the life you desire and meet any upset along the way. You're being guided here to play the music of your soul, with the individuation, interaction, and collaboration of a great jazz musician. As you apply the principles and practices of *Conscious Living 2.0* and *Your Ultimate Life Plan*, you're learning to play your instrument, creating music that's the truth of who you are so well that you can jam with life however it shows up for you.

Creating Changes that Last

No one is in control of your happiness but you; therefore, you have the power
to change anything about yourself or your life that you want to change.

—Barbara De Angelis

How do we change...really change?

When we feel stuck or want to change something, it usually comes from the desire to improve or rid ourselves of something we don't like, or that's painful. When something feels out of sorts, not quite right, or you have a negative feeling or judgment about something, it's an opportunity to investigate and learn from it.

Perhaps you're inspired to change because you see others having or doing something, or being a particular way that sparks yearning in you. The world around us can motivate us to question ourselves and connect with our dissatisfaction.

You might be motivated by an inner stirring or unfulfilled longing. Actualizing a deep longing gives a sense of achievement and fulfillment. It's important to feel what you do in life is meaningful, of use in the world. We might say that finding what we're meant to do is part of incarnation, being here in the body.

You might be looking for a result, or something to be fundamentally different, requiring change to alter or transform it. From Action-Physical, we look at changing behavior. In Formation-Emotional, we want our life to feel better. In Creation-Mental, we might transform our belief systems to change aspects of our lives. In Emanation-Spiritual, we add the idea of transmutation, an alchemical change that elevates the value of something. Your practices help transmute painful issues, revealing the hidden jewels within them. Your potentials emerge, such as wisdom, maturity, compassion, courage, inspiration, authenticity, gratitude, and others. This is why our practices eventually become our greatest pleasure, our soul's nourishment, because we know it results in changes that last.

Sometimes changing, or creating what we want, is more difficult than we expect. Change happens bit by bit. Personal development is measured in degrees; you become *freer*, have *more* happiness, and embody *more* of your essence. Unfortunately, many people rarely get the full picture of what's needed to heal and grow, and then wonder why they don't change. You've probably heard yourself or someone say, "I want to move forward," or, "I've tried to change but couldn't."

Paradoxically, lasting change comes faster when we embrace slowing down, going deeper, and being mindful. It is possible to move beyond "Been there, done that," and change. We know from working with our wounded egos and personal programming that when we do the same old thing, the same old way, we get the same old results.

When you're aware, you feel the subtle, inner stirrings that either inspire or direct you to change aspects of your life, guiding you to the True Self. You courageously engage in self-inquiry and start to recognize you do affect the course of your life. You grow more willing to take risks, empowering yourself toward creating desired changes.

Using your new knowledge, and examining and engaging the four dimensions, helps frame lasting change into degrees of workability. You know from earlier chapters that everything is consciousness. From the nondual state, everything is One. As you learned in Part II, if you can understand and feel the nature of change, from the deepest levels of creation, it's easier to create the life you want.

Oddly enough, even though we wish a number of things were different, we often resist change. For most of us, fear prevents us from being fully ourselves and in the constant flow of movement. There are many known and unknown fears, as well as shame, grief, or sadness impeding the current of the Universe from flowing in our lives. We might fear what change will bring, or mean. Maybe you won't like it, or you'll need to leave someone, or physically move somewhere.

Because we live in bodies and the physical dimension, we tend to see and experience everything as solid, and therefore unchangeable. Remember, from Action-Physical *only*, life seems impossible to understand or change. Your personality equates the solidness with safety, believing if you can predict life, then you won't have to face your fear of the unknown. But predictability is an illusion, based upon unconsciously expecting or repeating past responses in the present moment. This narrow understanding of life often leaves you feeling powerless, with a false sense of ego strength that will surely be challenged at some point in your lifetime.

Out of our misconceptions about consciousness and God, we try to create a solid, seemingly secure and stable life. We resist the underlying and constant process of change. We think, "If I can keep things the way they are, even though I hate it, I'll be safe." Living in the ever-changing flow is embracing what Alan Watts called "the wisdom of insecurity."[1] W.H. Auden said, "We would rather be ruined than change. We would rather die in our dread than climb the cross of the moment and let our illusions die."[2] So as much as we say we want to change, part of us may not.

Our unhealed egos have trouble letting go of the illusion that we can control everything. We remain lost in our stories, and think change, and ultimately happiness, is beyond us. We keep chasing our tails, jumping from shiny object to shiny object, seeking fulfillment outside ourselves—rooted in misunderstanding, unprocessed emotions, and old programming.

Lasting change occurs when we integrate these distorted ideas and historical knots, loosening our tight feelings and views. With courage, tenacity, commitment, and skillful means, the disentangled Strands of Consciousness shift, returning our soul and psyche to wholeness, and fulfilling the change we desire.

As you deepen through this work and your desired changes unfold, you move past the "ah ha" moments, into an inner knowing. You travel inward to the hidden crevices that help make you strong. You name and understand your feelings, deconstruct your stories, and embrace your imperfections. Inner softening and compassion grow into self-acceptance, encouraging change.

You may see change as it happens or notice it later, realizing you no longer do "that thing" you wanted to stop doing, or you are doing what you've been wanting to do. Change happens with persistence. How long depends upon the depth of the issue and the time you've spent working on it. Or you might be ripe and ready, and things will change quickly. It takes a certain amount of psychological and spiritual work to get beyond thinking our ego structures can run the entire show. At this turning point of growth and maturity, we surrender, which is essential in creating what we came here to be.

This journey of change helps us mature into wisdom, knowing the impermanent, transitory nature of all phenomena. A healthy sense of "I" helps us not hold so tightly to this impermanent self. With this wisdom we can relax, release, and surrender into the pulsation of all things. Living in the flow of impermanence brings waves of deeper realizations, and we embrace our humanity and the suffering that goes with it.

To deeply change requires sinking through the layers of self into your core, your deepest connection with creation. You feel the ever-present Wholeness, and experience a quality of fluidity from which you can more easily see and create your life. You drop into Oneness and unitive consciousness at times, feeling your soul connecting to the All-That-Is, or the Plenum. As you sink through these layers, you move through the chaos, discomfort, and delight to get to the origin of your thoughts and the metaphors that create your life, and then beyond into more healed states.

What does it mean to be in the flow of the universe? Change is constant. From a larger spiritual perspective, the universe is nothing but movement and constant change. I hear a sound and it's gone; I had a thought and it's gone. Being aware that change is constant takes you to the next, deeper level.

Change takes place in the now. Your willingness to face whatever arises and meet life without assumptions allows you to see every moment as new. You can examine your past, but your insight loosens knots in this moment. However long you've searched, something alchemical happens and a piece of your own mosaic returns. You shift. You change.

Finally, you come to see that change flows from being with the emptiness. Lasting change is the soul and spirit becoming conscious of each other; conscious and unconscious becoming one. You become who you truly are. As you see you're the emptiness and the silence, you realize you're both the observer and the observed. You're not separate. From here, you observe all Reality as the totality of Consciousness, or God.

Going Deeper With Exercises and Meditations

This book contains many exercises and meditations. You can also download exercises and meditations at my Website, *www.YourUltimateLifePlan.com*. Please find the ones that work best for you. Whatever you choose, I would suggest a regular practice. A daily practice has powerful transformative capability. If your primary practice involves movement, like yoga, it's very helpful to add a sitting practice.

Here are a few extra core exercises and meditations to help you connect with your essence and move into the embodiment of the True Self.

Grounding Exercises

Being grounded means having your feet firmly planted on the earth and fully inhabiting your body and being. Learning to navigate the deepest/highest consciousness requires a certain groundedness. When we're ungrounded, we're scattered, can't think as clearly, and have difficulty focusing. It's harder to be calm and relaxed, our decision-making is compromised, and our judgment can be skewed, making it harder to read situations. So, to achieve the improvements and goals you'd like for your life, it's important to make grounding yourself a regular practice.

Here are three grounding techniques. The first can be done any time, and almost anywhere. The second is done outdoors, and the third requires some time. You can use any of these before doing something you consider difficult, challenging, or stressful, or whenever you feel anxious or out of sorts. It's also helpful to ground yourself before meditating or doing other *Conscious Living 2.0* practices.

QUICK GROUNDING

Feel your feet connected to the earth, as if your energy extends beyond your feet and into the earth. Notice any difficult sensations, emotions, or thoughts that come up while continuing to feel your connection with the earth. Allow mother earth to support you.

TOUCH THE EARTH

Go outside and touch the earth, sit on the ground, or walk. Feel the earth's energy flowing into your body through every part of you that's touching the ground.

TAN TIEN

In a standing position with knees flexed, start by feeling energy in your tan tien, a point located about two inches below the belly button inside your body. Setting your intention, connect your tan tien with an energy cord that travels down the midline of your body and into the earth. From your tan tien imagine sending your energy cord down through your perineum all the way to the center of the earth. Connect your energy cord into the power and strength of the earth's molten core. Really feel that connection. Now allow this earth energy, which is touching your energy, to move back up into your body to your tan tien. Feel the grounding warmth solidly anchoring your physical body, moving through the layers of your being. Feel it getting stronger. Stay here for a while.

You can stop here, but if you'd like to take this further, when you have time you can include the following:

Now, allow that strong grounding warmth to continue traveling from your tan tien up through the midline of your body to the hollow, or base, of your throat. Sense into the connection with your inner longings, leading you to the next right step in life. Sense into your connection to who you are and what you know about yourself, as best you can. Feel it getting stronger. Stay here for a while.

Now allow this strong grounded energy to travel from your throat up your energy cord through the midline of your body through the top of your head to about 3 1/2 feet above your head. Here you connect with your essence and the part of you that emanates from the True Self. Feel it getting stronger. Stay here for a while.

Now, bring all this back down your energy cord through your head, back through the hollow of your throat, back to your tan tien. Feel your strength and groundedness physically, emotionally, mentally, and spiritually. Feel it getting stronger and re-energized. Stay here for a while.

Stopping Meditation

Many traditions have some version of a stopping meditation. Here are three that produce slightly different results.

QUICK STOP

A few times a day, wherever you are, stop completely for 10 seconds. Stop and be very still; be present to what's happening in whatever way feels right to you. You can focus on what you notice as you stop, or on the stopping itself, and see what happens.

SIX STOP

Six times a day, whether scheduled or spontaneously, stop everything you're doing for a moment, and be present to what's there. Be still. Notice whatever's around you: noise, movement, colors, people, animals, shapes, smells, sensations on your skin. Feel the surface under your feet, and any other details of your experience. Now feel your breath, heartbeat, and any other bodily sensations. Now, notice your emotions, thoughts, and your connection to Source. Be present to the Four Dimensions of Consciousness just for a moment. Invite yourself to experience everything in a different way.

NO AGENDA

In a sitting position, relax your eyes into a soft focus downward. Gently stop any agenda that presents itself. If you notice you want to focus on your breath, stop. If your mind wanders, stop. If you're trying to find stillness, stop. If you get caught in a story, stop. If you follow a body sensation, stop. This is a deep practice, so begin with a few minutes a day. The peace you feel may surprise you.

Divine Breath

Using your breath as a meditation tool can be powerful because the breath is a great teacher. You have it everywhere you go and you can choose to change your breathing or let it be. Our breathing can help us heal in many ways, and open us up to new information and new possibilities.

In the Kabbalistic text the *Likutei Moharan* (I, 8:1), Rabbi Nachman of Breslov said, "The world was created with breath—the breath of God. Divine breath is the sustainer of life. If breath is lacking, life is lacking."[3] The Hebrew word *Ruach* means breath, wind, or spirit. So as you breathe, feel the breath of life filling you with spirit.

According to the Bible, "...the Lord God formed man of the dust of the ground, and breathed into his nostrils the breath of life; and man became a living soul."[4] (Genesis 2:7) The great Sufi poet Rumi said, in *Give Me Ecstasy*, "How can a being made of water and clay find life, If Divine Breath does not Itself kindle it?"[5]

BREATHING EXERCISES AND MEDITATIONS

INTENSIVE BREATHING

Lying on your back with your mouth open, breathe continuously through both your nose and mouth at the same time. Don't pause at the end of the exhale or inhale, keep the flow going. Start by doing this for a few minutes, and work your way up to 20 minutes. Bodily sensations might arise, as well as emotions, memories, or spiritual experiences. Intensive Breathing loosens your usual fixed internal ways of holding feelings, thoughts, and memories, creating space inside for shifts toward a new and different flow of information.

ALTERNATE NOSTRIL BREATHING

Using your thumb and index finger, breathe in through the right nostril and out through the left for 5 minutes. Now reverse and breathe in through the left nostril and out through the right for 5 minutes. You can use long, deep breaths, your natural rhythm, or faster breaths.

FIRE BREATH

Start by filling the lower portion of your lungs first, expanding the diaphragm downward. Then, with your mouth closed, breathe through the nose only, and begin rapidly forcing the exhale using your diaphragm, as if you're panting like a dog but have your mouth closed. This has energizing and cleansing effects. Start with a few minutes, working up to 15 minutes.

ENTIRE BODY BREATH

Start by noticing your breath. Notice the air outside of you. Now notice the breath in your lungs and inside your entire body. As you breathe in, imagine you could breathe in through your entire body, as if your skin, bones, and organs can take in the breath. Now exhale with your entire body, as if the breath can leave through every part of your body. Spend a few minutes breathing in and out through your entire body.

BREATHE INSIDE AND OUTSIDE

Deep breath. Notice your breathing just as it is for a while. Now become conscious of the air around you. Feel it touch your skin, your hair, your head, your arms, your legs; feel the air touching your entire body. Now feel the breath inside you all the way to the deepest part of your lungs. Feel it deep in your belly, and in and around every cell in your body. Now feel the air outside and the breath inside touching. Continue feeling the air outside and your breath inside joining, becoming one.

Names of God

Words have great power. They carry meaning for us along with vibrations and energy. Like brain entrainment in neuroscience and transmissions from advanced spiritual individuals, invoking Names of God carries vibration and the morphic resonance of the name, which holds the charge and reverberating impact from hundreds if not thousands of years. Using a specific name of the Divine can open you to new avenues of being, helping you deepen in ways beyond words.

The mystical traditions of many religions have practices associated with sacred names, whether it's the Sufi practice of repeating the names of God in Arabic, the Kabbalistic prayers reciting the names in Hebrew, or the Hindu chanting of names in Sanskrit. When you chant, say the name (or names) silently to yourself, move, dance, or rhythmically breathe the different names of God, you are embracing and embodying new possibilities.

Following are a few names of God from the different traditions to get you started. You might try spending a week with the names in one tradition and then go on to another, or mix them together in whatever way feels right to you. As you practice these, see if you can experience them in your body, and then notice your thoughts and emotions. You might experience the urge to move as you do this, or experience great stillness and silence. You can begin your practice with these names and then add to your list as you'd like to. You can do this in several ways:

1. **Name on the Breath:** *Following your breath, say one of the names of God on the inhale and repeat it on the exhale, either silently or out loud.*

2. **Breathing God In and Out**: *You can combine more than one name, using one as you inhale and another as you exhale, either silently or out loud.*

3. **Chanting:** *Start chanting any vowel sound, or use "om," and then move into one or more of the names. You can use any pitch or notes that come to you.*

4. **Drawing:** *If the names are in another language, you can draw the letters on paper or in the air while chanting them at the same time.*

Sufis, the mystics of Islam, often speak of the 99 Names of God, which are described in the Qur'an. Some of the names include Allah (The All-Powerful and All-Knowing Creator); Al-Malik (The King or Absolute Ruler); Ar-Rahman (The All-Merciful); and Ar-Rahim (The All-Beneficent).

In Judaism, the four-letter name of God, YHVH, known as the Tetragrammaton, is the ineffable Name, the name beyond words. In *Gates of Light* Joseph Gikatilla says that like the "trunk of a tree that nurtures the branches which are the other Names of God, each of these branches bears a different fruit."[6] YHVH, pronounced or whispered Y (yod), H (hey), V (vav), H (hey), for many Jewish people is considered forbidden to be uttered except by the highest Rabbi in the Holy Temple on Yom Kipper. Instead, they read it as Adonai (My Lord). It can also be called Yahweh.

In the Bible (Exodus 3:13–15), Moses asked God for his name, and God replies, "Ehyeh-Asher-Ehyeh" (I Am That I Am).[7] Other names are Elohim, the first name of God in the scripture; El (God); El Shaddai (God Almighty), pronounced (shah-'dah-yy); and El Gibbor (God of Strength). The Shekhinah is the manifestation or presence of the descended "indwelling God." In the Qur'an, the Arabic word for the Sophia, or Wisdom, is Sakina.

"Om" is the primordial sound and sacred symbol of Brahman in Hinduism. According to Siddha Yoga, chanting the Hindu Sanskrit phrase, Om Namah Shivaya, is a redeeming mantra meaning "the Lord who dwells within you as you." There are many names of God, and Para Brahman (The Absolute Truth) is considered the ineffable name, along with Brahma (The Creator) and Bhagwan (God). Within the different Hindu traditions we have Vishnu (Preserver of the Universe), who has many other names corresponding to a variety of attributes. Other sacred names in the Hindu tradition are Krishna (Love and Divine Joy), Rama (Supreme Personality of the Godhead or Supreme Essence), Lakshmi (Goddess of Light, Beauty, and Wealth), Kali (Goddess of Transformation, Fierce Divine Mother, Kundalini Energy), Durga (Mother Goddess, Unification of all Divine Forces), and Shiva (The Destroyer of False Identifications, Habitual Reactions, Attachments), supporting the True Self to flourish.

In the Native American traditions Great Spirit is called by many names depending on the tribe. To the Sioux, it's Wakan Tanka. Russell Means, a Lakotah activist, says a better translation of Wakan Tanka is "the Great Mystery." The Chickasaw call God, Ababinili; the Cheyenne, Maheo; and the Cherokee, Yehowah.

Most of Buddhism doesn't think in terms of the names of God, but there are some variations in the words they use in the different traditions. In Mahayana

Buddhism, Samantabhadra Buddha is considered "the essence of the heart of all Buddhas." In Shin Buddhism, the eternal Buddha is Amida Buddha. Amitabha is the Buddha of Infinite Light and Amitayus is Infinite Life. There are also ceremonies invoking the Bodhisattvas' names. According to His Holiness the Dalai Lama, by chanting the Buddhist phrase, Om mani padme hum, pronounced Om (ohm) Ma (mah) Ni (nee) Pad (pahd) Me (may) Hum (hum), "you can transform your impure body, speech, and mind into the pure exalted body, speech, and mind of a Buddha."[8]

Christians use Jesus, Father, Abba, Yahweh, Jehovah, Lord, Holy Spirit, Holy Mother, Mother Mary, and many of the Jewish names that came before.

Embracing the Mystery

Books, workshops, prayer, meditation, personal work, and spiritual practice all help us participate in creating our lives, but there's still deeper ground beneath holding the Mystery.

How do we uncover the Mystery? Besides facing your personal programming, difficult feelings, and beliefs, you follow the inner calling to something greater. Whether we're in touch with it or not, people encompass all aspects of the Four Dimensions of Consciousness. As we become familiar with our inner life, we're naturally drawn to the spiritual realm and higher aspects of our humanity.

To embrace the Mystery, we have to acknowledge that we don't have all the answers; we don't know it all, and probably never will. Part of becoming happier is facing the unknown. If we don't face it, and instead stay in our fear, then we'll cling to the unhappiness we know and miss out on all the "goodies" the Mystery brings.

Experimenting with and experiencing connections in deeper spiritual territories inspires us to continue growing toward transformation. Most of us long to feel deeply connected. Taking the time to find the right spiritual practice, or combining modalities, facilitates the stillness and experiences the spiritual realm brings. These spiritual experiences give us a taste of something outside our everyday existence, which can have such a soul-stirring impact; it grows into the possibility of living the Ground of Being, and experiencing Grace that profoundly nourishes us.

Your spiritual practices open you to the Grace that's always there. Grace is ultimately how we heal and embody God, the Universe, or the All-That-Is. Quantum leaps happen. Sometimes this Divine opening can last days, months, or a lifetime. Besides the personal work, part of living consciously is doing your spiritual practices so you can embody the deepest, widest connection you can, which leads to lasting changes, improved relationships, a fulfilling livelihood, and a rich, humble life.

CHAPTER 13

Creating a Life (and World) That You Love

Warriorship here refers to realizing the power, dignity and wakefulness that is inherent in all of us as human beings. It is awakening our basic human confidence, which allows us to cheer up, develop a sense of vision and succeed in what we are doing.

—Chogyam Trungpa

Spiritual Warrior

It takes courage to face life as it arises; it takes becoming a spiritual warrior. To be a spiritual warrior is to stand for *what is*, and tolerate choosing, again and again, to be here in this moment. Committing to wrestle with awakening and walk the path of rigorous self-discovery is holy work. The mark of a spiritual warrior is moving toward sacred awakening with determination, persistence, and tenacity. We mature psychologically and spiritually when we face darkness, personal challenges, spiritual impediments, and groundlessness one moment at a time. Your willingness to confront your stuck places, and work through the layers of false self, uncovers your authentic self, allowing you to create a life that you love.

The warrior strips away layer after layer to live in greater Truth and Presence, no matter how weary and battered they become. When you have true compassion for yourself and the world, you love the Truth more than your momentary comfort.

The spiritual warrior ("Tzaddik" in the Kabbalah) lives with honesty and integrity, high morals and ethics, and responds with right words and actions. According to Rabbi Joseph Gikatilla's book *Gates of Light*, the Tzaddik or "righteous one" infuses his/her blessing and goodness on everyone, sustaining all of creation, holding the pleasure and delight of God, as well as human suffering.[1]

To be a Tzaddik, you live with a compassionate, humble heart. You're self-contained and personally differentiated. Humility is knowing what and who you are and are not, not just in the ego sense of personal limitations, but in the vastness and awe of an infinite Universe and God.

The Buddhists call it the Bodhisattva Vow, to stay with the world as it is—the good, the bad, the beautiful, and the ugly. At the same time, you see the larger goodness, and help others see it too. You also notice when you're living in fear and grasping, and are willing to work through it. Then you soothe yourself, sinking back and settling into who you really are, and the pulsatory movements of the world.

> As you do the exercises and meditations in this book, you'll become more malleable and have greater symmetry.

Being with the pulsatory movements of life allows you to sink further into the Strands of Consciousness, and what makes up the fabric of the universe. Your commitment to self-examination and rigorous personal work allows you to live more fully in all dimensions of consciousness. You're flexible. Your malleability helps connect you to reality outside your concrete, 3-D world, and to Emanation-Spiritual.

You made the commitment and entered the gateway to change yourself and the world. You have preferences, yet receive everything as it is. You've taken the vow to be present, and to see when you're not; to gently remind yourself, and others, to live in and from Truth, returning to the ever-present Wholeness and Grace awaiting you. These are the tasks and pleasures of being Spiritual Warriors, Tzaddiks, and Bodhisattvas.

- *What does the phrase "spiritual warrior" mean to you?*
- *In what ways do you see yourself as a spiritual warrior?*
- *In what ways do you wrestle with awakening?*
- *Where in your life does your grasping show up?*
- *What do you give the world in your own special way?*

MEDITATION: SPIRITUAL WARRIOR

Deep breath. Relax your body, beginning with your feet and moving upward to your legs, buttocks, stomach, back, chest, organs, shoulders, neck, head, jaw, eyes, and scalp. Starting at the top of the head, allow your crown chakra to open. Allow whichever color of light seems most nurturing to you to enter. Allow this healing light to move down through your entire body. Let it bathe you, soothe you, support every cell, every part of your body-emotion-thought-spirit. Let it support you as a spiritual warrior, a Tzaddik, a Bodhisattva. Feel the light bathing you inside from head to toe. It's supporting you, healing you. Now, notice a bubble of light surrounding you. It's holding you and all your energy. Let this bubble of light strengthen you. Now, let this bubble fill up with even greater light. Very slowly, ever so gently, open to the idea of other people and their bubbles of light. Imagine your bubble and your body connecting to others with their bubbles and their bodies. Take that in. You have your energy, you're a spiritual warrior, and you can still connect with others. Sit with this for a while. Now, come back to yourself. Take a few deep breaths.

Body as Temple

Having touched the expanded heights of consciousness, as we move back down the ladder from our journey in Emanation-Spiritual, Action-Physical is experienced as the marriage of Heaven and earth. It's God's creation fully realized. It's all that's here and now. It's this moment, breath, and Reality. We can rest in our home, our temple, our body.

MEDITATION: THE BODY AS A TEMPLE

Deep breath. Notice your breathing and be with it. Notice the rising and falling of your chest. As the air moves into your lungs, sense the air nourishing your body and everything about you. As you exhale, let go. Remembering that the Sacred is everywhere, inhale the Sacred, the Divine. Notice the Sacred bathing you everywhere inside. Feel your breath as Sacred. Your body is sacred as it houses the Sacred. Your body is a temple. A temple for the Sacred. In this moment you're a temple, the embodiment of all that ever was and ever will be. Breathe into all of that. Be with this for a while.

Now, answer the following questions:

- *What are you seeing in your mind's eye from this meditation?*
- *What about you as a temple are you noticing? Physically? Emotionally? Mentally? Spiritually?*
- *In what ways could you honor your body as a temple even more?*

Authenticity and Integrity

*When we discover that the truth is already in us,
we are all at once our original selves.*

—Dogen Zenji

As you commit to yourself, saying yes to all you are, you feel called to the sacred purpose of knowing yourself. As you sink more deeply into you, you drop into the depths of the Universe.

This dedication brings a desire for authenticity and integrity. Author Lance Secretan describes authenticity from the personal perspective as "the alignment of head, mouth, heart and feet—thinking, saying, feeling and doing the same thing—consistently."[2] Authenticity is often equated with being congruent and true to one's personality, spirit, or character. This is certainly true. Yet there's a larger way to view authenticity that connects us with our impersonal nature, described as "conforming to an original in order to reproduce its essential features."[3] In other words, authenticity isn't only about alignment and consistency, but also captures essence, spirit, inherent nature, and truth.

These original features are our "original nature," or "original face." Relaxing into our authenticity takes us to our essence, opening us to our potentials. Composer Meredith Monk said, "That inner voice has both gentleness and clarity. So to get to authenticity, you really keep going down to the bone, to the honesty, and the inevitability of something."[4]

Being authentic we embrace honesty, strong moral principles, and uprightness, which point to integrity. Buckminster Fuller said, "Integrity is the essence of everything successful," and "Human integrity is the uncompromising courage of self determination."[5]

As with many of our potentials, integrity is subjective. Our personal definition depends upon our emotional history, childhood experience, and the culture we were raised in. Some people feel they have integrity even though they're not being *fully* truthful. Even the idea of moral uprightness occurs differently to different people. Some people "fudge the truth," taking actions others might see as devious, and possibly causing harm. They might rationalize their fudging as taking care of their family or teaching someone a lesson, and they think they're right.

Some people go in the other direction, telling the "unvarnished" truth in hurtful and cruel ways. They'll say they're just "telling the truth" as they use their opinion to zing someone with words. When a woman asks if she looks fat in what she's wearing, there's a kind and tactful way to say it might not be her best choice. It doesn't have to be humiliating to her.

To create the life you long for, you're guided by authenticity and integrity and your task is to continue going deeply within, questioning yourself, and growing in your sense of truth and wisdom. You'll discern and cut through the habits, beliefs, feelings, and unconscious programming that often run the show and don't serve you well.

A larger view of integrity could be defined as "the state of being whole and undivided," and would be acting from, speaking from, living from, and working from the wholeness of your being, your deeper self, your essence.

Please nurture your inner life, and take an interest in what motivates and drives you. Take time to sit down, get quiet, and listen, allowing you to question deeply. Learn to live from your essential self, embracing and embodying aspects of your essence still unexpressed.

Passion and Purpose

Passion is energy. Feel the power that comes from focusing on what excites you.
—Oprah Winfrey

With authenticity and integrity, you sink more deeply into who you truly are, which naturally leads to living with greater passion. Yet the word *passion* has been bandied about so much it feels watered down and has lost its deeper meaning. Passion runs the gamut from a strong liking or deep interest to intense, boundless enthusiasm; or it could be a conviction that drives you to have, do, or be something, or contribute your gifts to the world. People talk about their passion for hobbies and entertainment, such as sports, collecting shoes, gaming, gardening, or a favorite TV program. Some of these supposed passions are external hungers and addictions used to avoid difficult or painful feelings, taking you away from your essence and deeper self.

Being conscious helps us discern the difference between addictive thinking and our deepest sense of passion. The voice of addictions, even the softer ones, tell us it's a good idea to do, think, imbibe, or say something that's ultimately destructive. That's not true passion.

Yes, passion comes from desires, but where are they coming from inside of you, and where are they leading you? Are they leading you to discerning awareness, openness, and fulfillment, or to more impossible-to-fill hungers?

True passion flows from our very deepest source, our highest level of existence, our essence. It's a calling, an ache inside that's summoning you to be the person you were meant to be, so you can make the contribution to this world only you can make. It's this passion that's moving you closer to your "purpose."

Your purpose is your raison d'être, your reason to be, to exist here and now. It's not just about action and what you create; it applies to who you are. Coming from your purpose helps create a life and lifework rooted in your passion, smoothing out the effort it takes to be successful. Purpose and passion generate the inspiration needed to pursue your personal and professional goals. When rooted in your purpose, you can more easily tap into your true passion.

Authors Chris Attwood and Janet Bray Attwood, of *The Passion Test*, have seen that "Passions change and morph over time as one comes to know and understand oneself more deeply."[6] As we grow and change we become clearer about who we are, and what we truly want and need, and find ways to make our lives, relationships, and careers better. We develop healthier and more conscious relationships based on mutual respect, sharing, and trust. We communicate openly and honestly, admitting our mistakes and accepting responsibility for ourselves. In our intimate relationships, both partners are equal, sharing power and control. We listen to each other with respect, valuing the other's opinions. We support each other's goals and life's purpose, and the right to have different points of view, activities, friends, and interests.

As you follow your inner longings, you might have the desire to find work you feel more passionate about, looking to be a more conscious businessperson. If you haven't found, or created, the job of your dreams yet, you can probably find an aspect of your current work that taps into your passion. Motivated by purpose and passion, you're led to approach all facets of business more consciously. Finding where your particular skills fit best allows you to contribute your unique gifts. This leads to inner fulfillment and a life that feels so rich you're naturally inspired to serve and make a positive difference in the world.

What is your vision for your greatest life?

Success is relative, and each person has his or her own vision of happiness, fulfillment, and realized goals. Yet we've integrated enough to confidently know that whatever happens, we'll figure it out, because our mature, adult self will take care of it. If something seems too big to handle, we trust our inner resources to embrace the uncertainty. We know we'll find the external resources needed to grow and change.

MEDITATION: THE GIFTS OF ESSENCE

Breathe deeply. Let go of all the internal chatter, even if only for a moment. Now feel the letting go in your belly. Bring yourself back to your breath. As best you can, allow yourself to sink into the silence and stillness that's always available. Allow your whole body to experience the silence as you breathe. Even if you hear noise, feel the presence of silence, of stillness. Go into the silence, the quiet, the stillness, breathing. Simply allow yourself to deeply rest for a moment. The ever-present stillness surrounds you and feeds you as you breathe. It's in perfect harmony with you. Stillness breathes you. Allow whatever's coming up to just be as it is. Imagine for a moment that you're offering the gifts of your essence to the world. Your gifts spring forth from the depths of your essence, from the depths of your heart and soul. Feel what that's like. You know your essence and you can share it with others. Now, see if you can allow the world to receive your gifts. Just breathe and notice what you're feeling in your body. What emotions might be coming up, what thoughts? Notice what you see. You're giving from your essence. Notice anything else about this experience. Sit with this for a while.

The Attitude of Gratitude

Gratitude is not only the greatest of virtues, but the parent of all the others.
—Cicero

In creating a life and world you love, you'll not only meet life with a compassionate and humble heart, but a grateful heart as well. We experience gratitude for the *things* in our lives: a favorite rocking chair, our morning cup of coffee, or other creature comforts, such as healthy food and a cozy home, surrounded by objects that mean something to us. Yet we're also grateful for *people* who have been good to us in some way, whether they know it or not, such as mentors, teachers, family, friends, or even the checkout lady or the friendly bus driver.

Daily interactions can warm our hearts, and they're a great way to generate and energize gratitude. From a psychological perspective, our hearts open when we appreciate someone or something. This is a starting point as we work to embody gratitude.

We can feel grateful when gazing at nature's beauty; a mountain or sunset, a full moon, gorgeous flowers, an azure sky, a starry night. We're awed and open-hearted when we encounter this expansiveness, something much larger than ourselves.

Yet in tough times, when it seems our life rivals the biblical Job's, it seems hard, nearly impossible, to feel grateful. This is when you breathe and engage in one of your practices or call a good friend, your coach, or your therapist, or get an energy healing, and be gentle with yourself.

Research tells us you can increase your physical and emotional well-being, creating positive social effects, by giving thanks. Dr. Michael McCollough of

Southern Methodist University and Dr. Robert Emmons of the University of California at Davis conducted a Research Project on Gratitude and Thanksgiving.[7] Groups of people were asked to keep diaries; one group simply wrote what they did that day, while the other group kept a gratitude list.

This study indicated that regardless of faith or religion, daily gratitude exercises resulted in higher reported levels of alertness, enthusiasm, determination, optimism, and energy. Subjects described experiencing less depression and stress, were more likely to help others, exercised more regularly, and made more progress toward personal goals. According to the findings, people who feel grateful are also more likely to feel loved, and gratitude encouraged a positive cycle of reciprocal kindness, as one act of gratitude encourages another.

Not only can you choose to investigate your life, seeing events or states you're grateful for, but also, from a spiritual perspective, you can embrace and embody the potential of gratitude whether or not something feels good.

As we live more consciously, we eventually heal enough to see the larger picture, allowing us to appreciate this journey as a gift. Profound gratitude for our life experiences brings genuine humility, taking us closer and closer to God, Divinity, or Presence, the answer to our deep desires and longings.

Most spiritual traditions emphasize gratitude. From Cicero to Buddha, many philosophers and spiritual teachers spoke of the power of gratitude. Some Christian church liturgies have gratitude written right into them. For different traditions' perspectives on gratitude, go to *www.yYourUltimateLifePlan.com* for a download of inspirational gratitude quotes.

Rabbi Rami Shapiro says, "Gratitude is one of the most satisfying spiritual practices I know."[8] As with other potentials, gratitude can be cultivated. We can develop gratitude by reflecting on the gifts we already have. These reflections can be done for a minute, a day, or throughout a lifetime. We can be grateful because we're happy, but we can also be happy because we're grateful.

As we sink into the deepest waters, gratitude arises and permeates us. We can't help but feel grateful, and happiness becomes our companion. Not that bad moments don't occur—they do, but we hold them differently, more tenderly and wisely. Your heart begins to open, your belly relaxes, and gratitude appears. You begin to see and activate your connection to this Ground on which you stand, and from which everything springs. You may not feel grateful each moment, but you're standing on gratitude itself, which is ever-present Grace.

We then discover gratitude's healing power, see opportunity for growth in the midst of troubles, embrace the wisdom of beginnings and endings, and tolerate limitations. In these and a thousand other ways we see the unity of life articulating its sacredness in innumerable dynamics of relationships. We begin to breathe with the Universe.

According to Brother David Steindl-Rast, "When you are grateful, your heart is open—open towards others, open for surprise." He also states, "From there it is only a small step to seeing the whole universe and every smallest part of it as surprising. From the humble starting point of daily surprises, the practice of gratefulness leads to these transcendent heights."[9]

Meditation: Gratitude

Deep Breath. Notice the rising and falling of your breath. Do this for a while. Allow yourself to be breathed by All-That-Is, effortless breath. Feel the support of being breathed. Now breathe into your heart. Allow your heart to open to all the love that's available. Take it in. Send yourself love. Now send love into any situation that calls to you. Send love to anyone who calls to you, past or present. Feel the abundance of love available. Let yourself fill up. Now allow the gratitude to well up out of this fullness. Breathe infinite love. Infinite abundance. Infinite emptiness and fullness. In your breathing, send and receive gratitude. Rest in Grace and gratitude. Stay here for a while.

Into the World

As the mind goes beyond the ordinary, beyond its conditioning and small knowing, it overflows its banks and becomes the heart.

—Stephen Levine

Are you living the life you've always dreamed of? You *can* do it! You're *already* doing it! You're on your way, right now! You know from what you've read and experienced in this book, lasting change doesn't come from magical thinking, but from awareness that takes committed work and resolve.

This is *Your* Ultimate Life Plan, and now you can meet life tuned in to your wisdom, and present to everything around you. You recognize that holding the longer view of life helps you move beyond your "six issues," making life richer and more fulfilling. You understand happiness is an inside job, and that quick fixes and bypassing problems makes things harder, prolonging your suffering. You see that in the process of learning, growing, and changing, you move four steps forward and two steps back, while progressing along the path of self-improvement. You know from your work with the four dimensions, you can deeply explore your Slivers, as well as reach heights of subtle transcendence.

Even though it requires fortitude, as you deepen your practices, they naturally integrate into daily life. Life flows more easily. The longer you walk this path, the more energy, clarity, and insight you gain, uncovering and connecting with deeper, powerful, and more peaceful levels of being.

As you've done the exercises in this "workshop in a book," you've had a taste of the healing, Wholeness, and Grace always available to you. You've gone deeper, and now you can go wider. Allow all you've learned here to inform your life, using feelings as teachers, and reactions as doorways to greater awareness and healing. Lasting change is always possible here and now, but it's also a process. Give it time.

You accomplish goals for your fulfillment, but see that your work doesn't stop with your own sense of well-being. You extend yourself into the world in your own way. Serving others doesn't require a grand gesture; the smallest kindness creates a profound ripple effect. As you connect with others, you also connect with your authentic self. Instead of feeling isolated, you're awake, aware, and alive.

As Thomas Merton said, "The whole idea of compassion is based on a keen awareness of the interdependence of all these living beings, which are all part of one another, and all involved in one another."[10] Our awareness of interconnectedness brings a new level of compassion.

You've become illuminated from within and radiate outward. You've matured. As an openhearted spiritual warrior, you express your unique, inherent gifts in the world. You are an important, integral part of the universe, and are innately worthy, simply because you exist.

In this book, you've learned you can surpass your dreams and move beyond what you've imagined, creating the life you desire. Everyone has their song to sing. The world needs our chorus of voices, today more than ever. You're empowered to share your voice, your message, and ultimately your great joy with the world.

It's been my profound pleasure to guide you. This book has been my song. Now, it's your turn. My wish for you is that you live deeply from your essence, reaching your greatest heights, your deepest fulfillment. May you live a more conscious life, embracing delight, surprise, and greater happiness. May your striving move you beyond surviving, into thriving, and ultimately living the life of your dreams.

Recommended Reading

Almaas, A.H., *The Inner Journey Home: The Soul's Realization of the Unity of Reality*

Armstrong, Karen, *A History of God: The 4000-Year Quest of Judaism, Christianity and Islam*

Baier Stein, Donna, *Sometimes You Sense the Difference*

Bailey, Alice A., *Esoteric Psychology: Volume I, A Treatise on the Seven Rays*

Beattie, Melody, *The New Codependency: Help and Guidance for Today's Generation*

Beckwith, Michael Bernard, *Life Visioning*

Besserman, Perle, *The Shambhala Guide to Kabbalah and Jewish Mysticism*

Bly, Robert, *A Little Book on the Human Shadow*

Boorstein, Sylvia, *Happiness Is an Inside Job: Practicing for a Joyful Life*

Borysenko, Joan, *A Woman's Book of Life: The Biology, Psychology, and Spirituality of the Feminine Life Cycle*

Brach, Tara, *Radical Acceptance: Embracing Your Life with the Heart of a Buddha*

———. *True Refuge: Finding Peace and Freedom in Your Own Awakened Heart*

Braden, Gregg, *Deep Truth: Igniting the Memory of Our Origin, History, Destiny, and Fate*

———. *Fractal Time*

Bradshaw, John, *Reclaiming Virtue: How We Can Develop the Moral Intelligence to Do the Right Thing, at the Right Time, for the Right Reason*

Chödrön, Pema, *Taking the Leap: Freeing Ourselves from Old Habits and Fears*

Chopra, Deepak, *The Path to Love: Spiritual Strategies for Healing*

Das, Lama Surya, *Awakening the Buddha Within: Eight Steps to Enlightenment*

———, *Buddha Is As Buddha Does: The Ten Original Practices For Enlightened Living*

———, *Buddha Standard Time: Awakening to the Infinite Possibilities of Now*

Epstein, Mark, *Psychotherapy Without the Self*

Finley, Guy, *The Seeker, the Search, the Sacred: Journey to the Greatness Within*

Fox, Matthew, *Breakthrough: Meister Eckhart's Creation Spirituality in New Translation*

Frankel, Estelle, *Sacred Therapy: Jewish Spiritual Teachings on Emotional Healing and Inner Wholeness*

Godman, David, *Nothing Ever Happened: Volume One*

Goldstein, Elisha, *The Now Effect: How This Moment Can Change the Rest of Your Life*

Grayson, Henry, *Use Your Body to Heal Your Mind: Revolutionary Methods to Release all Barriers to Health, Healing and Happiness*

Greene, Brian, *The Fabric of the Cosmos: Space, Time, and the Texture of Reality*

Halevi, Z'ev ben Shimon, *A Kabbalistic Universe*

Hammeroff, Stuart R., Alfred W. Kaszniak, and David J. Chalmers, eds, *Toward a Science of Consciousness III: The Third Tucson Discussions and Debates*

Hanh, Thich Nhat, *Living Buddha, Living Christ*

Harvey, Andrew, *The Hope: A Guide to Sacred Activism*

———, *Radical Passion: Sacred Love and Wisdom in Action*

Hawking, Stephen, and Leonard Mlodinow, *The Grand Design*

Kaplan, Aryeh, *Innerspace: Introduction to Kabbalah, Meditation and Prophecy*

Keating, Thomas, *Manifesting God*

Kornfield, Jack, *The Wise Heart: A Guide to the Universal Teachings of Buddhist Psychology*

Lawrence, Brother, *The Practice of the Presence of God with Spiritual Maxims*

Lee, John, *The Flying Boy: Healing the Wounded Man*

———, *The Half-Lived Life: Overcoming Passivity and Rediscovering Your Authentic Self*

Lesser, Elizabeth, *Broken Open: How Difficult Times Can Help Us Grow*

———, *The Seeker's Guide: Making Your Life a Spiritual Adventure*

Lipton, Bruce H., and Steve Bhaerman, *Spontaneous Evolution: Our Positive Future (and a Way to Get There From Here)*

Look, Carol, *Attracting Abundance with EFT: Emotional Freedom Techniques*

Louden, Jennifer, *The Woman's Comfort Book: A Self-Nurturing Guide for Restoring Balance in Your Life*

Merton, Thomas, *The Inner Experience: Notes on Contemplation*

Michaelson, Jay, *God in Your Body: Kabbalah, Mindfulness and Embodied Spiritual Practice*

Moeller, Kristen, *Waiting for Jack: Confessions of a Self-Help Junkie - How to Stop Waiting and Start Living Your Life*

Nichol, Lee, ed., *The Essential David Bohm*

Pearce, Joseph Chilton, *The Biology of Transcendence: A Blueprint of the Human Spirit*

Prendergast, John J., and G. Kenneth Bradford, eds., *Listening From the Heart of Silence: Nondual Wisdom & Psychotherapy, Volume 2*

Rohr, Richard, *Falling Upward: A Spirituality for the Two Halves of Life*

———, *The Naked Now: Learning to See as the Mystics See*

Salzberg, Sharon, *Force of Kindness: Change Your Life with Love & Compassion*

———, *Real Happiness: The Power of Meditation—A 28-Day Program*

Shapiro, Rabbi Rami, *Rabbi Rami's Guide to God: Roadside Assistance for the Spiritual Traveler*

———, *Tanya, the Masterpiece of Hasidic Wisdom: Selections Annotated & Explained*

———, *The Sacred Art of Lovingkindness: Preparing to Practice*

Sheldrake, Rupert, *Morphic Resonance: The Nature of Formative Causation*

Siegel, Bernie S., *A Book of Miracles: Inspiring True Stories of Healing, Gratitude, and Love*

Stern, Daniel N., *The Present Moment in Psychotherapy and Everyday Life*

Taegel, Will, *The Mother Tongue: Intimacy in the Eco-field*

Tarrant, John, *Bring Me the Rhinoceros: And Other Zen Koans That Will Save Your Life*

Tiferet: A Journal of Multi-Faith Spiritual Literature, published by Donna Baier Stein, *http://tiferetjournal.com*

Warner, Priscilla, *Learning to Breathe: My Yearlong Quest to Bring Calm to My Life*

Welwood, John, *Toward a Psychology of Awakening: Buddhism, Psychotherapy, and the Path of Personal and Spiritual Transformation*

Wilber, Ken, *Integral Psychology: Consciousness, Spirit, Psychology, Therapy*

Young-Eisendrath, Polly, *The Self-Esteem Trap: Raising Confident and Compassionate Kids in an Age of Self-Importance*

———, and Melvin E. Miller, eds., *The Psychology of Mature Spirituality: Integrity, Wisdom, Transcendence*

Walsch, Neale Donald, *Conversations with God*

Zukav, Gary, *The Seat of the Soul*

Notes

Introduction

1. Keating, Thomas, *Intimacy With God*.

Chapter 1

1. Whitman, Walt, *The Complete Poems*, p. 123.
2. Lesser, Elizabeth, *The Seeker's Guide*, p. 60.
3. Fowler and Christakis, "Dynamic Spread of Happiness."
4. Shimoff and Kline, *Happy For No Reason*, p. 21.

Chapter 2

1. Keating, Thomas, *Invitation to Love*, p. 90.
2. Das, Lama Surya, *Buddha Standard Time*, p. 7.
3. University of Manchester, "Meditation Reduces the Emotional Impact of Pain."
4. Lipton and Bhaerman, *Spontaneous Evolution*, p. xxii.
5. Kabat-Zinn, Jon, *Mindfulness for Beginners*, p. 1.
6. Kornfield and Miller, "Finding My Religion."
7. Bhanoo, Sindyan, "How Meditation May Change the Brain."

Chapter 3

1. "Programming," *Merriam-Webster's Collegiate Dictionary*, p. 992.

2. Sheldrake, Rupert, *Morphic Resonance*.

3. Hellinger, Bert, *Love's Hidden Symmetry*.

4. Boring, Francesca Mason, *Connecting to Our Ancestral Past*, p. 17.

5. "Emotion," Dictionary.com.

6. Damasio, Antonio, *The Feeling of What Happens*, p. 42.

7. Thorndike, Edward, "Intelligence and Its Use."

8. Goleman, Daniel, *Emotional Intelligence*.

9. Alcoholics Anonymous: *www.aa.org*.

10. Marcus Aurelius, *Meditations*, Book IV.

11. Klein, Josephine, *Our Need for Others*.

Chapter 4

1. "Ego," AR Online Dictionary.

2. Baltzly, Dirk, "Stoicism."

3. Freud, Sigmund, *The Ego and the Id*.

4. Jung, Carl, *The Portable Jung*.

5. "MBTI Basics."

6. Erikson, Erik H., *Childhood and Society*, p. 36.

7. Maslow, Abraham H., *Toward a Psychology of Being*.

8. Mahler, Pine, and Bergman, *The Psychological Birth of The Human Infant*.

9. Brown, Nina W., *Whose Life is it Anyway?*

10. Winnicott, Donald W., *Boundary and Space*.

11. Bowlby, John, *A Secure Base*.

12. Eden and Feinstein, *Energy Medicine*, p. xix.

13. Wilber, Ken, *The Collected Works of Ken Wilber*.

14. Fossella, Tina, "Human Nature, Buddha Nature."

15. Tolle, Eckhart, *The Power of Now*.

16. *The Journal of Transpersonal Psychology*: *http:// atpweb.org/journal.aspx*.

17. Welwood, John, from his Website, *www.johnwelwood.com/psycholog-yawakening.htm*.

18. Rumi, *The Sufi Path of Love*, p. 162.

19. Johnson, Robert A., *Owning Your Own Shadow*, p. 5.

20. Zweig and Abrams, *Meeting the Shadow*.

21. Johnson, and Ruhl, *Living Your Unlived Life*, p. 4.

22. Chopra, Ford, and Williamson, *The Shadow Effect*, p. 104.

23. St. Teresa of Avila, as quoted in the journal *The Little Lamp* (1981) by Eknath Easwaran. Retrieved from *http://enwikiquote.org/wiki/Teresa_of_Avila*.

24. Tillich, Paul, *Dynamics of Faith*.

25. Cohen, Andrew, *Evolutionary Enlightenment*, p. 11.

26. Washburn, Michael, *The Ego and the Dynamic Ground*, p. 110.

27. Helminski, Kabir, *The Knowing Heart*, p. 49.

28. Kornfield, Jack, *A Path With Heart*, p. 202.

29. Almaas, A.H., *Facets of Unity*, p. 88.

Chapter 5

1. Das, Lama Surya, *Buddha Standard Time*, p. 55.

2. For more information, see Alcoholics Anonymous: *www.aa.org*.

3. Das, Lama Surya, *Buddha Standard Time*, p. 69.

4. Kornfield, Jack, *The Wise Heart*, p. 317.

5. Fields, Taylor, Weyler, and Ingrasci, *Chop Wood, Carry Water*.

6. Thomas Aquinas, *Selected Writings*.

7. Helminski, Kabir, *The Knowing Heart*.

8. Ibid. Helminski quotes the Holy Qur'an (2:115), page 81.

Chapter 6

1. "Hologram," *The American Heritage Science Dictionary*.

2. Weber, Renée, "The Enfolding-Unfolding Universe: A Conversation with David Bohm." In Wilber, Ken, *The Holographic Paradigm*, 44.

3. Pribram, Karl H., *Languages of the Brain*.

4. *Holy Bible* (Deuteronomy 6:4), New King James Version (NKJV).

5. Meister Eckhart, *Selected Writings*.

6. *Holy Bible* (Psalm 46:10), King James Version (KJV).

Chapter 7

1. Iyengar, B.K.S., *Light on the Yoga Sutras of Patanjali*, p. 132.

2. The Victim Triangle was first introduced in the article, "Fairy Tales and Script Drama Analysis," by Stephen B. Karpman, MD, in *Transactional Analysis Bulletin* 7, No. 26, (April 1968).

3. See the Cherokee Nation official Website: *www.cherokee.org*.

4. Pert, Candace B., *Molecules of Emotion*.

5. Lowen, Alexander, *Fear of Life*, p. 49.

6. Lowen, Alexander, *The Voice of the Body*.

7. *Holy Bible* (Isaiah 6:3), King James Version (KJV).

Chapter 8

1. Rohr, Richard, *The Naked Now*, p. 123.

2. Hawkins, Sir David R., *Power vs. Force*.

3. Schucman and Thetford, *A Course in Miracles*.

4. Williamson, Marianne, *A Return to Love*, p. xxii.

5. Rilke, Rainer Maria, *Letters to a Young Poet*, p. 8.

6. Rilke, Rainer Maria, *Rilke on Love and Other Difficulties*, p. 9.

7. James and Friedman, *Grief Recovery Handbook*, p. 3.

8. Kübler-Ross, Elisabeth, *On Death and Dying*.

9. Bradshaw, John, *Healing the Shame that Binds You*.

10. Nathanson, Donald, *Shame and Pride*.

11. Salzberg, Sharon, *Real Happiness*, p. 198.

12. Hanh, Thich Nhat, *Being Peace*.

13. Saint John of the Cross, *The Collected Works*.

14. Easwaran, Eknath, *Classics of Christian Inspiration*, p. 56.

15. Hildegard of Bingen, *The Letters of Hildegard of Bingen*, p. 41.

16. Hildegard of Bingen, *Selected Writings*, p. 120.

17. Fox, Matthew, *The Coming of the Cosmic Christ*, p. 50.

18. "Meister Eckhart," The Catholic Community at Connecticut College.

19. Garvin, Christine, "Stop Spiritually Bypassing Already."

20. Caplan, Mariana, *Eyes Wide Open*, p. xxvii.

21. Shainberg, Diane, *Chasing Elephants*.

Chapter 9

1. Kornfield, Jack, *A Path with Heart*, p. 41.

2. Wilber, Engler, and Brown, *Transformations of Consciousness*.

3. Woodman, Marion, *Holding the Tension of the Opposites*.

4. Miller, Jeffrey C., *The Transcendent Function*, p. 57.

5. Adyashanti, *Emptiness Dancing*, p. 27.

6. Bohm, David, *Wholeness and the Implicate Order*, p. x.

7. Barfield, Owen, *Saving Appearances*.

8. Maharishi Mahesh Yogi, *The Bhagavad-Gita*, p. 470.

9. *Holy Bible* (Matthew 17:20), King James Version (KJV).

10. Sri Ramana Maharshi, *Talks with Ramana Maharshi*, p. 148.

11. Ibid., p. 129.

12. Keating, Thomas, *Open Mind, Open Heart*, p. 114.

13. Rohr, Richard, *The Naked Now*, p. 18.

14. Ibid., p. 19.

15. Namgyal and Lhalungpa, *Mahamudra*, p. 224.

Chapter 10

1. Krishnamurti and Bohm, *The Ending of Time*.

2. Shapiro, Rabbi Rami, *The Divine Feminine in Biblical Wisdom Literature*, p. xvii.

3. *Holy Bible* (Genesis 1:2-3), King James Version (KJV).

4. Keating, Thomas, *Open Mind, Open Heart*, p. 44.

5. Ibid., p. 45.

6. Yogi Bhajan: *www.yogibhajan.com*.

7. Harvey, Andrew, *Teachings of the Christian Mystics*, p. xxx.

8. Schwaller de Lubicz, Isha, *The Opening of the Way*.

9. St. John of the Cross, *Dark Night of the Soul*, p. 47.

10. Louth, Andrew, *The Origins of the Christian Mystical Tradition*.

11. Steinsaltz, Adin, *Opening the Tanya*.

12. Chödrön, Pema, *When Things Fall Apart*, p. 12.

13. Ibid., p. 10.

14. Almaas, A.H., *The Point of Existence*, p. 336.

15. Conze, Edward, *Buddhist Wisdom*, p. 76.

16. Hawking, Stephen W., "Does God Play Dice?"

17. Wilson, et al., "Observation of the Dynamical Casimir Effect."

18. Kaplan, Rabbi Aryeh, *Meditation and Kabbalah*, p. 305.

19. Blakney, Raymond Bernard, *Meister Eckhart*, p. 180.

Chapter 12

1. Watts, Alan, *The Wisdom of Insecurity*.

2. Auden, W.H., *The Age of Anxiety*, p. 105.

3. Rebbe Nachman of Breslov, Bergman, and Mykoff, *Likutey Moharan*.

4. *Holy Bible* (Genesis 2:7), King James Version (KJV).

5. Helminski, Kabir, *The Rumi Collection*, p. 29.

6. Gikatilla, Rabbi Joseph, *Gates of Light*, p. 6.

7. *Holy Bible* (Exodus 3:13–15), King James Version (KJV).

8. His Holiness the Dalai Lama, "Om Mani Padme Hum."

Chapter 13

1. Gikatilla, Rabbi Joseph, *Gates of Light*, p. 60.

2. Secretan, Lance, *The Art and Practice of Conscious Leadership*, p. 83.

3. "Authentic," *Merriam-Webster Online Dictionary*.

4. "Authentic Voice: An Interview with Meredith Monk." *Mountain Record*.

5. Baldwin, J., *Bucky Works*, p. 228.

6. Attwood and Attwood, *The Passion Test*, p. xxv.

7. McCullough, Tsang, and Emmons, "Gratitude in Intermediate Affective Terrain."

8. Shapiro, Rabbi Rami, "Gratitude."

9. Steindl-Rast, Brother David, Gratefulness.org articles.

10. From Thomas Merton's final address, during a conference on East-West monastic dialogue, delivered just two hours before his death (December 10, 1968), quoted in *Religious Education* 73 (1978), p. 292, and in *The Boundless Circle: Caring for Creatures and Creation*, by Michael W. Fox (Quest Books, 1996).

Bibliography

A.C. Bhaktivedanta Swami Prabhupada, and George Harrison. *KRSNA: The Supreme Personality of Godhead (A Summary Study of Srila Vyasadeva's Srimad-Bhagavatam, Tenth Canto, Volume I)*. Alachua, Fl.: The Bhaktivedanta Book Trust, 1970.

Abelson, J. *Jewish Mysticism: An Introduction to the Kabbalah*. Mineola, N.Y.: Dover Publications, 2001.

Adyashanti. *Emptiness Dancing*. Boulder, Colo.: Sounds True, 2006.

Afterman, Allen. *Kabbalah and Consciousness*. Riverdale-on-Hudson, N.Y.: Sheep Meadow Press, 1992.

Ainsworth, Mary D. Salter, Mary C. Blehar, Everett Waters, and Sally Wall. *Patterns of Attachment: A Psychological Study of the Strange Situation*. New York: Psychology Press, 1979.

Alcoholics Anonymous. *www.aa.org*.

Almaas, A.H. *Facets of Unity: The Enneagram of Holy Ideas*. Berkeley, Calif.: Diamond Books, 1998.

———. *The Point of Existence: Transformations of Narcissism in Self-Realization*. Berkeley, Calif.: Diamond Books, 1996.

Ashlag, Rav Yehuda. *Introduction to the Book of Zohar Volume Two: The Spiritual Secret of Kabbalah*. Commentary by Michael Laitman. Toronto: Laitman Kabbalah Publishers, 2005.

Atteshlis, Stylianos. *The Esoteric Teachings: A Christian Approach to Truth*. Translated by Robert and Audrey Browning. Cyprus, Greece: Imprinta Ltd., 1992.

Attwood, Chris, and Janet Bray Attwood. *The Passion Test: The Effortless Path to Discovering Your Life Purpose*. New York: Penguin Group, 2008.

Auden, W.H. *The Age of Anxiety.* Princeton, N.J.: Princeton University Press, 2011.

"Authentic." Merriam-Webster Online Dictionary. *www.merriam-webster.com/dictionary/ authentic.*

"Authentic Voice: An Interview with Meredith Monk." *Mountain Record: The Zen Practitioner's Journal* XXII, No. 4 (Summer 2004). *www.mro.org/mr/archive/22-4/ articles/monk.html.*

Bach, Richard. *The Bridge Across Forever: A True Love Story.* New York: Dell Publishing, 1989.

Baldwin, J. *Bucky Works: Buckminster Fuller's Ideas for Today.* New York: John Wiley and Sons, 1996.

Baltzly, Dirk. "Stoicism." *The Stanford Encyclopedia of Philosophy, Winter 2010 Edition.* Edited by Edward N. Zalta. *http://plato.stanford.edu/archives/win2010/entries/stoicism/.*

Barfield, Owen. *Saving the Appearances: A Study in Idolatry.* Hanover, N.H.: Wesleyan University Press, 1988.

Bartlett, Richard. *The Physics of Miracles: Tapping into the Field of Consciousness Potential.* New York: Atria Books, 2009.

Bentov, Itzhak. *Stalking the Wild Pendulum: On the Mechanics of Consciousness.* Rochester, Vt.: Destiny Books, 1988.

Bhanoo, Sindyan. "How Meditation May Change the Brain." *New York Times* Blog, January 28, 2011. *http://well.blogs.nytimes.com/2011/01/28/ how-meditation-may-change-the-brain.*

Blakney, Raymond Bernard, trans. *Meister Eckhart: A Modern Translation.* New York: Harper and Brothers, 1941.

Boehme, Jacob. *Jacob Boehme: The Way to Christ.* Translated by Peter Erb. New York: Paulist Press, 1978.

Bohm, David. *On Creativity.* Edited by Lee Nichol. New York: Routledge, 2000.

———. *Wholeness and the Implicate Order.* London & New York: Routledge, 2002.

Bollas, Christopher. *Being a Character: Psychoanalysis and Self Experience.* New York: Hill and Wang, 1992.

———. *The Shadow of the Object: Psychoanalysis of the Unthought Known.* New York: Columbia University Press, 1987.

Boring, Francesca Mason. *Connecting to Our Ancestral Past: Healing Through Family Constellations, Ceremony, and Ritual.* Berkeley, Calif.: North Atlantic Books, 2012.

Bowlby, John. *A Secure Base: Parent-Child Attachment and Healthy Human Development.* New York: Basic Books, 1988.

———. *Attachment, 2nd Edition.* Basic Books Classics. New York: Basic Books, 1993.

Bradshaw, John. *Healing the Shame that Binds You.* Deerfield Beach, Fl.: Health Communications, Inc., 2005.

Brennan, Barbara Ann. *Light Emerging: The Journey of Personal Healing.* New York: Bantam Books, 1993.

Brown, Nina W. *Whose Life Is it Anyway?* Oakland, Calif.: New Harbinger Publications, 2002.

Caplan, Mariana. *Eyes Wide Open: Cultivating Discernment on the Spiritual Path.* Boulder, Colo.: Sounds True, 2009.

Chesterton, Gilbert K. *Orthodoxy.* Chicago: Moody Publishers, 2009.

Chödrön, Pema. *When Things Fall Apart: Heart Advice for Difficult Times.* Boston: Shambhala Publications, 2002.

Chopra, Deepak, Debbie Ford, and Marianne Williamson. *The Shadow Effect: Illuminating the Hidden Power of Your True Self.* New York: HarperCollins, 2010.

Choquette, Sonia. *Ask Your Guides: Connecting to Your Divine Support System.* Carlsbad, Calif.: Hay House, 2006.

Cleary, Thomas, trans. *Taoist Meditation: Methods for Cultivating a Healthy Mind and Body.* Boston: Shambhala Publications, 2000.

Cohen, Andrew. *Evolutionary Enlightenment: A New Path to Spiritual Awakening.* New York: Select Books, 2011.

Conze, Edward, trans. *Buddhist Wisdom.* New York: Vintage, 2001.

Damasio, Antonio R. *The Feeling of What Happens: Body and Emotion in the Making of Consciousness.* New York: Harcourt Brace & Company, 1999.

Das, Lama Surya. *Buddha Standard Time: Awakening to the Infinite Possibilities of Now.* New York: HarperOne, 2012.

Das, Subhamoy. "Harrison & Hinduism: Harrison's Idea of God & Reincarnation." About.com. *http://Hinduism.about.com/od/artculture/a/Harrison_2.htm.*

Davis, Madeleine, and David Wallbridge. *Boundary and Space: An Introduction to the Work of D. W. Winnicott.* New York: Brunner/Mazel Publishers, 1981.

Durckheim, Karlfried Graf. *Hara: The Vital Centre of Man.* Translated by Sylvia-Monica von Kospoth and Estelle R. Healey. London: Mandala, 1988.

Dwoskin, Hale. *The Sedona Method: Your Key to Lasting Happiness, Success, Peace and Emotional Well-Being.* Sedona, Ariz.: Sedona Press, 2003.

Easwaran, Eknath. *Classics of Christian Inspiration: Includes Love Never Faileth, Original Goodness, and Seeing with the Eyes of Love.* Tomales, Calif.: Nilgiri Press, 1996.

Eckhart, Meister. *Meister Eckhart: The Essential Sermons, Commentaries, Treatises, and Defense.* Translated by Edmund Colledge and Bernard McGinn. New York: Paulist Press, 1981.

———. *Selected Writings*. London: Penguin Classics, 1995.

Eden, Donna, and David Feinstein. *Energy Medicine: Balancing Your Body's Energies for Optimal Health, Joy, and Vitality*. New York: Jeremy P. Tarcher/Penguin, 2008.

"Ego." AR Online Dictionary. *http://ardictionarycom/Ego.*

"Emotion." Dictionary.com. *http://dictionary.reference.com/browse/emotion.*

Epstein, Mark. *Thoughts Without a Thinker: Psychotherapy From a Buddhist Perspective.* New York: Basic Books, 1996.

Erikson, Erik H. *Childhood and Society*. New York: W.W. Norton & Company, 1993.

Fields, Rick, Peggy Taylor, Rex Weyler, and Rick Ingrasci. *Chop Wood, Carry Water*. New York: Jeremy P. Tarcher/Putnam, 1984.

Finley, Guy. *The Seeker, the Search, the Sacred: Journey to the Greatness Within*. San Francisco: Weiser Books, 2011

Fossella, Tina. "Human Nature, Buddha Nature: On Spiritual Bypassing, Relationship, and the Dharma, an Interview with John Welwood." *Tricycle Magazine*, Spring 2011.

Fowler, James H., and Nicholas A. Christakis. "Dynamic Spread of Happiness in a Large Social Network: Longitudinal Analysis Over 20 Years in the Framingham Heart Study." *British Medical Journal* 337 (2008): a2338.

Fox, Matthew. *Christian Mystics: 365 Readings and Meditations.* Novato, Calif.: New World Library, 2011.

———. *The Coming of the Cosmic Christ: The Healing of Mother Earth and the Birth of a Global Renaissance*. New York: HarperCollins, 1988.

Fox, Michael W. *The Boundless Circle: Caring for Creatures and Creation*. Wheaton, Ill.: Quest Books, 1996.

Frankl, Viktor E. *Man's Search for Meaning*. Boston: Beacon Press, 2006.

Fremantle, Francesca, trans., and Chögyam Trungpa, trans. *The Tibetan Book of the Dead: The Great Liberation Through Hearing in the Bardo*. Boston: Shambhala Publications, 1975.

Freud, Sigmund. *The Ego and the Id*. Edited by James Strachey. New York: W.W. Norton & Company, 1990.

Gambhirananda, Swami, trans. *Eight Upanisads Volume One*. Calcutta, India: Advaita Ashrama, 1957.

———, trans. *Eight Upanisads Volume Two*. Calcutta, India: Advaita Ashram, 1958.

Garvin, Christine. "Stop Spiritually Bypassing Already: An Interview with 'Eyes Wide Open' Author Mariana Caplan." *Living Holistically With a Sense of Humor*, August 25, 2010. *www.holisticwithhumor.com.*

Gemmell, William, trans. *The Diamond Sutra (Chin-Kang-Ching) or Prajna-Paramita*. Berwick, Maine: Ibis Press, 2003.

Gibran, Kahlil. *The Eye of the Prophet*. Berkeley, Calif.: Frog, Ltd., 1995.

Gikatilla, Joseph. *Gates of Light: Sha'are Orah*. Translated by Avi Weinstein. Walnut Creek, Calif.: AltaMira Press, 1998.

Godman, David, ed. *Be As You Are: The Teachings of Sri Ramana Maharshi*. London: Arkana, 1985.

Goenka, S.N. *Satipatthana Sutta Discourses: Talks from a Course in Maha-satipatthana Sutta*. Onalaska, Wash.: Pariyatti Publishing, 1998.

Goleman, Daniel. *Emotional Intelligence: Why It Can Matter More Than IQ*. New York: Bantam, 2006.

Goswami, Amit. *Physics of the Soul: The Quantum Book of Living, Dying, Reincarnation, and Immortality*. Charlottesville, Va.: Hampton Roads, 2001.

Greene, Brian. *The Elegant Universe: Superstrings, Hidden Dimensions, and the Quest for the Ultimate Theory*. New York: Vintage Books, 2000.

Grof, Stanislav, and Hal Zina Bennett. *The Holotropic Mind: The Three Levels of Human Consciousness and How They Shape Our Lives*. San Francisco: HarperSanFrancisco, 1992.

Hanh, Thich Nhat. *Being Peace*. Berkeley, Calif.: Parallax Press, 2005.

Harvey, Andrew. *Love's Fire: Re-Creations of Rumi*. Ithaca, N.Y.: Meeramma Publications, 1988.

———. *Teachings of the Christian Mystics*. Boston: Shambhala Publications, 1998.

Hawking, Stephen W. "Does God Play Dice?" Hawking.org. *www.hawking.org.uk/does-god-play-dice.html*.

Hawkins, David R. *I: Reality and Subjectivity*. Sedona, Ariz.: Veritas Publishing, 2003.

———. *Power vs. Force: The Hidden Determinants of Human Behavior, Revised Edition*. Sedona, Ariz.: Veritas Publishing, 2012.

Hellinger, Bert. *Love's Hidden Symmetry: What Makes Love Work in Relationships*. Phoenix, Ariz.: Zeig, Tucker and Theisen, 1998.

Helminski, Kabir. *The Knowing Heart: A Sufi Path of Transformation*. Boston: Shambhala Publications, 1999.

Helminski, Kabir, ed. *The Rumi Collection*. Boston: Shambhala Publications, 1998.

Hemingway, Mollie Ziegler. "The Parent of All Virtues." Throwing Inkwells, ChristianityToday.com, November 28, 2010. *www.christianitytoday.com/ct/2010/November/28.60.html*.

Hendricks, Gay. *Conscious Living: Finding Joy in the Real World*. New York: HarperCollins, 2000.

Hendrix, Harville. *Getting the Love You Want: A Guide for Couples*. New York: St. Martin's Griffin, 2008.

Hildegard of Bingen. *The Letters of Hildegard of Bingen, Vol. 2.* Translated by Joseph L. Baird and Radd Ehrman. New York: Oxford University Press, 1998.

———. *Selected Writings: Hildegard of Bingen.* Translated by Mark Atherton. London: Penguin Classics, 2001.

Hillman, James, Henry A. Murray, Tom Moore, James Baird, Thomas Cowan, and Randolph Severson. *Puer Papers.* Dallas, Texas: Spring Publications, 1991.

His Holiness the Dalai Lama. "Om Mani Padme Hum." Buddhanet. *www.buddhanet. net/e-learning/buddhistworld/Tibet-txt.htm.*

Hixon, Lex. *Heart of the Koran.* Wheaton, Ill.: Quest/The Theosophical Publishing House, 1988.

Holmes, Ernest. *Love and Law: The Unpublished Teachings.* Edited by Marilyn Leo. New York: Jeremy P. Tarcher/Penguin, 2004.

"Hologram." *The American Heritage Science Dictionary. www.thefreedictionary.com/ hologram.*

Holy Bible. New King James Version (NKJV). Nashville, Tenn.: Thomas Nelson, 1982.

Holy Bible. King James Version (KJV). Public Domain.

Iyengar, B.K.S. *Light on the Yoga Sutras of Patanjali.* London: Thorsons, 1996.

Jacobson, Simon. *Toward a Meaningful Life: The Wisdom of the Rebbe Menachem Mendel Schneerson.* New York: William Morrow, 2004.

Jacoby, Mario. *Individuation and Narcissism: The Psychology of the Self in Jung and Kohut.* New York: Routledge, 1990.

James, John W., and Russell Friedman. *Grief Recovery Handbook: The Action Program for Moving Beyond Death, Divorce, and Other Losses.* New York: HarperCollins, 1998.

Johnson, Robert A. *Owning Your Own Shadow: Understanding the Dark Side of the Psyche.* New York: HarperCollins, 1993.

Johnson, Robert A., and Jerry M. Ruhl. *Living Your Unlived Life: Coping with Unrealized Dreams and Fulfilling Your Purpose in the Second Half of Life.* New York: Jeremy P. Tarcher/Penguin, 2009.

Jung, Carl G. *Memories, Dreams, Reflections.* Edited by Aniela Jaffé. Translated by Richard and Clara Winston. New York: Vintage Books, 1973.

———. *The Portable Jung.* Edited by Joseph Campbell. Translated by R.F.C. Hull. New York: Penguin Books, 1976.

Kabat-Zinn, Jon. *Mindfulness for Beginners: Reclaiming the Present Moment—and Your Life.* Boulder, Colo.: Sounds True, 2011.

Kanamatsu, Kenryo. *Naturalness: A Classic of Shin Buddhism.* Bloomington, Ind.: World Wisdom, 2002.

Kaplan, Rabbi Aryeh. *Meditation and Kabbalah*. Northvale, N.J.: Jason Aronson, Inc., 1995.

———. *Sefer Yetzirah: The Book of Creation*. York Beach, Maine: Samuel Weiser, Inc., 1993.

———. *The Bahir*. York Beach, Maine: Samuel Weiser, 1989.

Karpman, Stephen B., MD. "Fairy Tales and Script Drama Analysis." *Transactional Analysis Bulletin* 7, No. 26 (April 1968).

Katz, Jerry. *One: Essential Writings on Nonduality*. Boulder, Colo.: Sentient Publications, LLC, 2007.

Keating, Thomas. *Intimacy with God: An Introduction to Centering Prayer*. New York: Crossroad Publishing, 2008.

———. *Invitation to Love: The Way of Christian Contemplation*. New York: Continuum, 1994.

———. *Open Mind, Open Heart: The Contemplative Dimension of the Gospel*. Rockport, Mass.: Element Books Limited, 1992.

Kernberg, Otto F. *Love Relations: Normality and Pathology*. New Haven, Conn.: Yale University Press, 1995.

Klein, Josephine. *Our Need for Others and Its Roots in Infancy*. London: Tavistock Publications, 1987.

Knox, Jean. *Self-Agency in Psychotherapy: Attachment, Autonomy, and Intimacy*. New York: W.W. Norton & Company, 2011.

Kohut, Heinz. *The Restoration of the Self*. Madison, Conn.: International Universities Press, 1977.

Kornfield, Jack. *A Path with Heart: A Guide Through the Perils and Promises of Spiritual Life*. New York: Bantam Books, 1993.

———. *The Wise Heart: A Guide to the Universal Teachings of Buddhist Psychology*. New York: Bantam Dell, 2008.

Kornfield, Jack, and David Ian Miller. "Finding My Religion: Buddhist Teacher and Author Jack Kornfield on Mindfulness, Happiness and His Own Spiritual Journey." *SF Gate*, November 28, 2005.

Krishna, Gopi. *Kundalini: The Evolutionary Energy in Man*. Boston, Mass.: Shambhala Publications, 1967.

Krishnamurti, J. *Think on These Things*. Edited by D. Rajagopal. New York: Perennial Library, 1989.

———. *Total Freedom: The Essential Krishnamurti*. San Francisco: HarperSanFrancisco, 1996.

Krishnamurti, J., and David Bohm. *The Ending of Time*. San Francisco: HarperSanFrancisco, 1985.

————. *The Limits of Thought: Discussions.* New York: Routledge, 1999.

Kübler-Ross, Elisabeth, MD. *On Death and Dying.* New York: Scribner, 1997.

Lesser, Elizabeth. *The Seeker's Guide: Making Your Life a Spiritual Adventure.* New York: Villard Books, 1999.

Levine, Stephen. *Healing Into Life and Death.* New York: Anchor Press, 1987.

————. *Turning Toward the Mystery: A Seeker's Journey.* San Francisco: HarperSanFrancisco, 2002.

Lipton, Bruce H., and Steve Bhaerman. *Spontaneous Evolution: Our Positive Future (and a Way to Get There From Here).* Carlsbad, Calif.: Hay House, 2009.

Louth, Andrew. *The Origins of the Christian Mystical Tradition.* New York: Oxford University Press, 2007.

Lowen, Alexander. *The Betrayal of the Body.* New York: Collier Books, 1967.

————. *Fear of Life.* Alachua, Fl.: Bioenergetics Press, 2003.

————. *The Voice of the Body.* Alachua, Fl.: Bioenergetics Press, 2005.

Maharaj, Nisargadatta. *I Am That: Talks with Sri Nisargadatta Maharaj.* Translated by Maurice Frydman. Revised and edited by Sudhakar S. Dikshit. Durham, N.C.: The Acorn Press, 1973.

Maharishi Mahesh Yogi. *The Bhagavad-Gita: A Translation and Commentary, Chapters 1–6.* London: Arkana, 1990.

Mahler, Margaret S., Fred Pine, and Anni Bergman. *The Psychological Birth of the Human Infant: Symbiosis and Individuation.* New York: Basic Books, 2000.

Marcus Aurelius. *Meditations.* Edited by Martin Hammond. New York: Penguin Classics, 2006.

Markides, Kyriacos C. *Fire in the Heart: Healers, Sages and Mystics.* New York: Arkana, 1990.

Mascaro, Juan, trans. *The Dhammapada.* London: Penguin Classics, 1973.

Maslow, Abraham H. *Toward a Psychology of Being, 3rd Edition.* New York: John Wiley & Sons, 1998.

Masterson, James F. *The Emerging Self: A Developmental, Self, and Object Relations Approach to the Treatment of the Closet Narcissistic Disorder of the Self.* New York: Brunner/Mazel Publishers, 1993.

————. *The Search for the Real Self: Unmasking the Personality Disorders of Our Age.* New York: The Free Press, 1988.

Matt, Daniel C. *The Zohar: Volume One (Pritzker Edition).* Stanford, Calif.: Stanford University Press, 2004.

———. *The Zohar: Volume Two (Pritzker Edition)*. Stanford, Calif.: Stanford University Press, 2004.

"MBTI Basics." The Myers & Briggs Foundation. *www.myersbriggs.org/my-mbti-personality-type/mbti-basics*.

McColman, Carl. *The Big Book of Christian Mysticism: The Essential Guide to Contemplative Spirituality*. Charlottesville, Va.: Hampton Roads, 2010.

McCown, Karen Stone, Joshua M. Freedman, Anabel L. Jensen, and Marsha C. Rideout. *Self-Science: The Emotional Intelligence Curriculum, 2nd Revised Edition*. Hillsborough, Calif.: Six Seconds, 1998.

McCullough, M.E., J. Tsang, and R.A. Emmons. "Gratitude in Intermediate Affective Terrain: Links of Grateful Moods with Individual Differences and Daily Emotional Experience." *Journal of Personality and Social Psychology* 86, No. 2 (2004): 95–309.

McGinn, Bernard, and Patricia Ferris McGinn. *Early Christian Mystics: The Divine Vision of the Spiritual Masters*. New York: Crossroad Publishing, 2003.

McGinn, Bernard. *The Foundations of Mysticism—Vol. I of The Presence of God: A History of Western Christian Mysticism*. New York: Crossroad Publishing, 2002.

———. *The Growth of Mysticism—Vol. II of The Presence of God: A History of Western Christian Mysticism*. New York: Crossroad Publishing, 2004.

"Meister Eckhart." The Catholic Community at Connecticut College, January 31, 2009. *www.conncoll.edu/ChapelDocs/MeisterEckhart.pdf*.

Merriam-Webster's Collegiate Dictionary, 11th Edition. Springfield, Mass.: Merriam-Webster, Inc., 2004.

Merton, Thomas. *The Hidden Ground of Love*. Edited by William H. Shannon. New York: Harcourt Brace Jovanovich, 1993.

Michaels, Pamela Samantha, MA. "Cultivating Joy." MindfulRecovery.net. *www.mindful-recovery.net/mindbodyspirit.html*.

Miller, Jeffrey C. *The Transcendent Function: Jung's Model of Psychological Growth through Dialogue with the Unconscious*. Albany, N.Y.: State University of New York Press, 2004.

Mooney, Carol Garhart. *Theories of Attachment: An Introduction to Bowlby, Ainsworth, Gerber, Brazelton, Kennell, and Klaus*. St. Paul, Minn.: Redleaf Press, 2009.

Moore, Thomas. *Dark Nights of the Soul: A Guide to Finding Your Way Through Life's Ordeals*. New York: Gotham Books, 2004.

Myss, Caroline. Daily Message Archive on Myss.com. *www.myss.com/library/dailymessage*.

———. *Entering the Castle: An Inner Path to God and Your Soul*. New York: Free Press, 2007.

Nachman of Breslov, Ozer Bergman, and Moshe Mykoff, eds. *Likutey Moharan, Bilingual Edition.* Jerusalem: Breslov Research Institute, 1995.

Namgyal, Dakpo Tashi. *Mahamudra: The Moonlight—Quintessence of Mind and Meditation.* Translated by Lobsang P. Lhalungpa. Boston: Wisdom Publications, 2006.

Nathanson, Donald. *Shame and Pride: Affect, Sex, and the Birth of the Self.* New York: W.W. Norton & Company, 1994.

Nin, Anaïs. *The Diary of Anais Nin, Vol. 4: 1944–1947.* Edited by Gunther Stuhlmann. New York: Harcourt Brace Jovanovich, 1971.

"Oprah Winfrey Quotes." Power-of-Giving.com. *www.power-of-giving.com/orpah-win-frey-quotes.html.*

Panko, Stephen M. *Martin Buber.* Edited by Bob E. Patterson. Waco, Texas: Word Books Publisher, 1978.

Pearce, Joseph Chilton. *The Biology of Transcendence: A Blueprint of the Human Spirit.* Rochester, Vt.: Park Street Press, 2002.

———. *The Death of Religion and the Rebirth of Spirit: A Return to the Intelligence of the Heart.* Rochester, Vt.: Park Street Press, 2007.

Pert, Candace B. *Molecules of Emotion: The Science Behind Mind-Body Medicine.* New York: Touchstone, 1999.

Pink, Daniel H. *A Whole New Mind: Why Right-Brainers Will Rule the Future.* New York: Riverhead Books, 2006.

Pinson, DovBer. *Meditation and Judaism: Exploring the Jewish Meditative Paths.* Lanham, Md.: Rowman & Littlefield Publishers, 2004.

Pourafzal, Haleh, and Roger Montgomery. *The Spiritual Wisdom of Hafez: Teachings of the Philosopher of Love.* Rochester, Vt.: Inner Traditions, 1998.

Prendergast, John J., and G. Kenneth Bradford, eds. *Listening From the Heart of Silence: Nondual Wisdom & Psychotherapy, Volume 2.* St. Paul, Minn.: Paragon House, 2007.

Pribram, Karl H. *Languages of the Brain: Experimental Paradoxes and Principles in Neuropsychology.* Upper Saddle River, NJ: Prentice-Hall, 1971.

"Programming." *Merriam-Webster's Collegiate Dictionary, 11th Edition.* Springfield, Mass.: Merriam-Webster, Inc., 2004.

Ramana Maharshi. *The Spiritual Teachings of Ramana Maharshi.* Foreword by C.G. Jung. Boston: Shambhala Publications, 1988.

———. *Talks with Ramana Maharshi.* Carlsbad, Calif.: Inner Directions Publishing, 2000.

The Rig Veda. Penguin Classics. Edited and translated by Wendy Doniger. New York: Penguin, 2005.

Rilke, Rainer Maria. *Letters to a Young Poet.* Translated by Stephen Mitchell. New York: First Vintage Books, 1986.

————. *Rilke on Love and Other Difficulties.* Translated by John J.L. Mood. New York: W.W. Norton & Company, 2004.

Roberts, Bernadette. *The Experience of No-Self: A Contemplative Journey.* Albany, N.Y.: State University of New York Press, 1993.

Rohr, Richard. *The Naked Now: Learning to See as the Mystics See.* New York: Crossroad Publishing, 2009.

Rossi, Ernest L., and David B. Cheek. *Mind-Body Therapy: Ideodynamic Healing in Hypnosis.* New York: W.W. Norton & Company, Inc., 1988.

Roth, Gabrielle. *Connections: The 5 Threads of Intuitive Wisdom.* New York: Jeremy P. Tarcher/Penguin, 2004.

Rumi. *The Sufi Path of Love: The Spiritual Teachings of Rumi.* Translated by William C. Chittick. New York: State University of New York Press, 1984.

Rumi, Maulana Jalalu-'d-din Muhammad I. *The Mathnawi: The Spiritual Couplets of Maulana Jalalu-'d-din Muhammad I Rumi.* Translated by E.H. Whinfield. London: Watkins Publishing, 2002.

Saint John of the Cross. *The Collected Works of St. John of the Cross.* Translated by Kieran Kavanaugh and Otilio Rodriguez. Washington, DC: ICS Publications, 1991.

————. *Dark Night of the Soul.* Translated and edited by E. Allison Peers, from the critical edition of P. Silverio De Santa Teresa, CD. New York: Image Books/Doubleday, 1990.

————. *Dark Night of the Soul.* Edited by T.N.R. Rogers and Paul Negri. New York: Dover Publications, 2003.

Salzberg, Sharon. *Lovingkindness: The Revolutionary Art of Happiness.* Boston, Mass.: Shambhala Publications, 2002.

————. *Real Happiness: The Power of Meditation—A 28-Day Program.* New York: Workman Publishing Co., 2011.

Schaef, Anne Wilson. *Living in Process: Basic Truths for Living the Path of the Soul.* New York: Wellspring/Ballantine, 1999.

Schäfer, Peter. *The Hidden and Manifest God: Some Major Themes in Early Jewish Mysticism.* Albany, N.Y.: State University of New York Press, 1992.

Scholem, Gershom. *On the Mystical Shape of the Godhead: Basic Concepts in the Kabbalah.* New York: Schocken Books, 1991.

————. *Origins of the Kabbalah.* Translated by Allan Arkush, Edited by R.J. Zwi Werblowsky. Princeton, N.J.: Princeton University Press, 1990.

Schopenhauer, Arthur. *Parerga and Paralipomena: A Collection of Philosophical Essays.* Translated by T. Bailey Saunders. New York: Cosimo, 2007.

Schucman, Helen, and William Thetford. *A Course in Miracles*. Mill Valley, Calif.: Foundation for Inner Peace, 2008.

Schwaller de Lubicz, Isha. *Her-Bak: Egyptian Initiate*. Rochester, Vt.: Inner Traditions, 1978.

———. *The Opening of the Way: A Practical Guide to the Wisdom Teachings of Ancient Egypt*. Rochester, Vt.: Inner Traditions, 1995.

Schwaller de Lubicz, R.A. *Nature Word: Verbe Nature*. Rochester, Vt.: Inner Traditions, 1990.

Secretan, Lance. *The Art and Practice of Conscious Leadership*. Caledon, Calif.: The Secretan Center, Inc., 2006.

Shainberg, Diane. *Chasing Elephants: Healing Psychologically with Buddhist Wisdom*. New York: Asti-Rahman Books, 2000.

———. *Healing in Psychotherapy: The Process of Holistic Change*. Philadelphia, Pa.: Gordon and Breach Science Publishers, 1983.

Shapiro, Rabbi Rami. *The Divine Feminine in Biblical Wisdom Literature*. Woodstock, Vt.: SkyLight Paths Publishing, 2005.

———"Gratitude." Spirituality&Health.com. *www.spiritualityhealth.com/soul-body/practice/gratitude-rabbi-rami-shapiro*.

———. *Open Secrets: The Letters of Reb Yerachmiel ben Yisrael*. Rhinebeck, N.Y.: Monkfish Book Publishing, 2004.

Sheldrake, Rupert. *Morphic Resonance: The Nature of Formative Causation*. Rochester, Vt.: Park Street Press, 2009.

———. *The Sense of Being Stared at and Other Aspects of the Extended Mind*. New York: Crown Publishers, 2003.

Shimoff, Marci, and Carol Kline. *Happy for No Reason: 7 Steps to Being Happy from the Inside Out*. New York: Free Press, 2009.

Shulman, Jason, *Kabbalistic Healing: A Path to an Awakened Soul*. Rochester, Vt.: Inner Traditions, 2004.

Simon, Maurice, and Paul P. Levertoff. *The Zohar: Volume IV*. London: The Soncino Press Ltd., 1984.

Smith, Jean, ed. *Radiant Mind: Essential Buddhist Teachings and Texts*. New York: Riverhead Books, 1999.

Sperling, Harry, and Maurice Simon. *The Zohar: Volume I*. London: The Soncino Press Ltd., 1984.

Steindl-Rast, Brother David. Gratefulness.org. "A New Reason for Gratitude" (*www.gratefulness.org/readings/dsr_reason.htm*) and "Giving Thanks for All the Little (and Big) Things in Life" (*www.gratefulness.org/readings/dsr_GivingThanksforAll.htm*).

Steinsaltz, Adin. *Opening the Tanya: Discovering the Moral and Mystical Teaching of a Classic Work of Kabbalah*. San Francisco: Jossey-Bass, 2003.

———. *The Thirteen Petalled Rose: A Discourse on the Essence of Jewish Existence and Belief*. New York: Basic Books, 1980.

Sumedho, Ajahn. *The Sound of Silence: The Selected Teachings of Ajahn Sumedho*. Preface and introduction by Ajahn Amaro. Boston: Wisdom Publications, 2007.

Talbot, Michael. *The Holographic Universe*. New York: HarperPerennial, 1992.

Tarrant, John. *The Light Inside the Dark: Zen, Soul, and the Spiritual Life*. New York: HarperPerennial, 1999.

Thomas Aquinas. *Thomas Aquinas: Selected Writings*. Edited by Ralph McInerny. London: Penguin Classics, 1999.

Thompson, Keith, ed. *To Be A Man: In Search of the Deep Masculine*. Los Angeles: Jeremy P. Tarcher, Inc., 1991.

Thoreau, Henry David. *Excursions, Poems and Familiar Letters V1*. Whitefish, Mont.: Kessinger Publishing, LLC, 2007.

Thorndike, Edward. "Intelligence and Its Use." *Harper's Magazine* 140 (1920): 227–235.

Tillich, Paul. *Dynamics of Faith*. New York: Perennial Classics, 2001.

Tishby, Isaiah. *The Wisdom of the Zohar: An Anthology of Texts, Volume I*. Rendered into Hebrew by Fischel Lachower and Isaiah Tishby. English translation by David Goldstein. Portland, Ore.: The Littman Library of Jewish Civilization, 2002.

———. *The Wisdom of the Zohar: An Anthology of Texts, Volume II*. Rendered into Hebrew by Fischel Lachower and Isaiah Tishby. English translation by David Goldstein. Portland, Ore.: The Littman Library of Jewish Civilization, 2002.

———. *The Wisdom of the Zohar: An Anthology of Texts, Volume III*. Rendered into Hebrew by Fischel Lachower and Isaiah Tishby. English translation by David Goldstein. Portland, Ore.: The Littman Library of Jewish Civilization, 2002.

Tolle, Eckhart. *A New Earth: Awakening to Your Life's Purpose*. New York: Penguin, 2008.

———. *The Power of Now: A Guide to Spiritual Enlightenment*. Novato, Calif.: New World Library, 2004, and Vancouver: Namaste Publishing, 1999.

Trapnell, Judson B. *Bede Griffiths: A Life in Dialogue*. Albany, N.Y.: State University of New York Press, 2001.

University of Manchester. "Meditation Reduces the Emotional Impact of Pain, Study Finds." ScienceDaily.com, June 2, 2010. *www.sciencedaily.com/releases/2010/06/100602091315.htm*.

Unno, Taitetsu. *River of Fire, River of Water: An Introduction to the Pure Land Tradition of Shin Buddhism*. New York: Doubleday, 1998.

Vaughn, Frances. *Inward Arc: Healing in Psychotherapy and Spirituality*. An Authors Guild Back In Print Edition. Bloomington, Ind.: IUniverse, 2001. Originally published by Shambhala.

Waite, Dennis. *Back to The Truth: 5000 Years of Advaita*. Winchester, UK: O Books, 2007.

Washburn, Michael. *The Ego and the Dynamic Ground: A Transpersonal Theory of Human Development*. Albany, N.Y.: State University of New York Press, 1988.

———. *Embodied Spirituality in a Sacred World*. Albany, N.Y.: State University of New York Press, 2003.

———. *Transpersonal Psychology in Psychoanalytic Perspective*. Albany, N.Y.: State University of New York Press, 1994.

Watts, Alan. *The Wisdom of Insecurity: A Message for an Age of Anxiety*. New York: Pantheon Books, 1951.

Whitman, Walt. *The Complete Poems*. London: Penguin Classics, 2005.

Wilber, Ken. *The Collected Works of Ken Wilber*. Boston: Shambhala, 1999.

———. *The Spectrum of consciousness*. Wheaton, Ill.: Quest Books, 1993.

Wilber, Ken, ed. *The Holographic Paradigm and Other Paradoxes: Exploring the Leading Edge of Science*. Boston: New Science Library, 1985.

Wilber, Ken, Jack Engler, and Daniel P. Brown. *Transformations of Consciousness: Conventional and Contemplative Perspectives on Development*. Boston: New Science Library, 1986.

Williamson, Marianne. *A Return to Love: Reflections on the Principles of "A Course in Miracles."* New York: HarperCollins, 1996.

Wilson, C.M., G. Johansson, A. Pourkabirian, M. Simoen, J.R. Johansson, T. Duty, F. Nori, and P. Delsing. "Observation of the Dynamical Casimir Effect in a Superconducting Circuit." *Nature* 479 (17 November 2011): 376–379.

Winnicott, Donald W. *Boundary and Space*. New York: Brunner-Routledge, 1987.

Woodman, Marion. *Holding the Tension of the Opposites*. Boulder, Colo.: Sounds True Audio, 2007.

———. *The Owl Was a Baker's Daughter: Obesity, Anorexia Nervosa and the Repressed Feminine*. Toronto: Inner City Books, 1980.

Yogananda, Paramahansa. *Journey to Self-Realization: Discovering the Gifts of the Soul*. Los Angeles: Self-Realization Fellowship, 1997.

Young-Eisendrath, Polly, and Melvin E. Miller, eds. *The Psychology of Mature Spirituality: Integrity, Wisdom, Transcendence*. New York: Routledge, 2005.

Zona, Guy. *The Soul Would Have No Rainbow if the Eyes Had No Tears and Other Native American Proverbs*. New York: Touchstone, 1994.

Zweig, Connie, and Jeremiah Abrams. *Meeting the Shadow: The Hidden Power of the Dark Side of Human Nature*. New York: Jeremy P. Tarcher/Putnam, 1991.

Index

About the Author

Jennifer Howard, PhD, is passionately dedicated to helping people experience deep and lasting transformation for greater ease, freedom, and joy. A recognized thought leader on psychology and spirituality, she's an internationally known licensed psychotherapist, business and life coach, Nondual Kabbalistic Healer®, professional speaker, and radio talk show host. Dr. Howard combines over 20 years of experience with extensive training and expertise in mind-body psychology, meditation, and the healing arts. A Huffington Post blogger, she's a featured expert in the national wellness campaign, Walk with Walgreens, and has appeared as an expert on numerous national network television shows, including: *The Maury Povich Show, Rolanda, America's Talking, Turning Point, Charles Perez, & News Talk TV*. On her weekly radio talk show, *A Conscious Life*, she has inspiring, informative, and fun conversations with such distinguished guests as Sharon Salzberg, Gay Hendricks, Hale Dwoskin, Marci Shimoff, Andrew Harvey, Dr. Bruce Lipton, PhD, Sonia Choquette, Mathew Fox, Bernie Siegel, MD, Lama Surya Das, Rabbi Rami Shapiro, among others. Dr. Howard maintains a private practice with offices in New York City and Long Island, and has an extensive phone practice.

Dr. Jennifer Howard teaches the art of conscious living—being more awake, aware, and alive in every moment. She's equally at home sharing ancient spiritual wisdom, the latest scientific understanding, and the proven and practical life-changing techniques she's developed in her work as a psychotherapist, energy healer, and spiritual teacher. As an author and professional speaker, Dr. Howard's energetic style, along with her sense of humor, helps her audiences—beginner and advanced alike—assimilate what is being taught, even when the material appears to be complex. She's a former faculty member of the graduate studies program,

A Society of Souls: The School for Nondual Healing and Awakening, and taught meditation classes for many years at Marble Collegiate Church, in New York City.

Dr. Jennifer, as she's known in social media, was named one of the TOP 25 Celebrity Doctors on Twitter, as well as being dubbed, "The Funniest Shrink on Twitter." She's also gained a reputation on Facebook for her compassion, as well as her wit.

She's the creator of the audio series, *The Keys to Healthy Relationships*, and the CD, *Paths of Healing: Meditations for Relaxation and Healing*. To find out about Dr. Howard's upcoming classes, seminars, and workshops, as well as the products she has available, visit her Website: *www.DrJenniferHoward.com*.

twitter: @DrJennifer

facebook: www.facebook.com/DrJenniferFanPage

Her media site: *www.DrJenniferHoward.tv*

You can also go to: *www.YourUltimateLifePlan.com* to download free meditations, exercises, journaling prompts and worksheets from Your Ultimate Life Plan.